COMPETITION LAW CHALLENGES IN THE NEXT DECADE

P.I.E. Peter Lang

Bruxelles · Bern · Berlin · Frankfurt am Main · New York · Oxford · Wien

EUROCLIO is a scientific and editorial project, a network of research institutions and researchers, and an ideas forum. EUROCLIO as an editorial project consists of two aspects: the first concerns studies and documents, the second concerns tools. Both are aimed at making the results of research more accessible, and also at opening up paths through the history of European construction/integration/unification.

The EUROCLIO series meets a dual objective:

- to provide reference tools for research,
- to provide a platform for this research in terms of the publication of results.

The series thus consists of two sub-series that satisfy these requirements: the Studies and Documents series and the References series. These two series are aimed at general libraries and/or university history departments, teachers and researchers, and in certain cases, specific professional circles.

The Studies and Documents series consists of monographs, collections of articles, conference proceedings, and collections of texts with notes for teaching purposes.

The References series consists of bibliographies, guides and other tools. It thus contributes to the creation of a database making up a "Permanent catalogue of sources and bibliographies on European construction".

Edited by
Éric Bussière, Université de Paris-Sorbonne (France),
Michel Dumoulin, Louvain-la-Neuve (Belgique),
& Antonio Varsori, Universitá degli Studi di Padova (Italia)

COMPETITION LAW CHALLENGES IN THE NEXT DECADE

Sofia OLIVEIRA PAIS (ed.)

Euroclio
Vol. 94

This publication has been produced with the financial support of the Training of National Judges Programme of the European Union.

This publication has been peer-reviewed.

Éditions scientifiques internationales
Brussels, 2016
1 avenue Maurice, B-1050 Brussels, Belgium
pie@peterlang.com ; www.peterlang.com

ISSN 0944-2294
ISBN 978-2-87574-328-2
eISBN 978-3-0352-6602-3
D/2016/5678/24

Printed in Germany

CIP available from the British Library, UK and from the Library of Congress, USA.

"Die Deutsche National Bibliothek" lists this publication in the "Deutsche Nationalbibliografie"; detailed bibliographic data is available on the Internet at <http://dnb.de>.

CONTENTS

Preface

Competition Law has come a long way in the European Union since the Treaty of Rome came into force in 1958. It has expanded and matured becoming highly successful, benefiting from the match of old and new political-economic wisdom and from the decentralisation process of competition law, which spilled from the hands of the European Commission to national courts and EU Member States' national competition authorities. The fundamental role of EU competition law – to promote consumer welfare, economic progress and the public interest in general – justifies the need to examine critically some of its challenges in the next decade.

The core issues of this book are, therefore, to analyse and discuss some open questions concerning three particular topics of competition law that are becoming highly relevant in the European and national *praxis* – antitrust private enforcement, exclusionary abuses and state aid.

The first part of the book gathers the contributions of António Ferreira Gomes, Sofia Oliveira Pais, Petri Kuoppamaki, Anna Piszcz, Henrique Sousa Antunes and Agostinho Guedes and focuses on the Damages Directive, asking the fundamental question: is the Directive able to meet the need for a coherent European approach to antitrust private enforcement? Taking into account the Finish, Polish and Portuguese experiences, this part of the book reflects upon the real achievements of the Directive.

The second part, with chapters by Paul Nihoul, Alison Jones, Rosa Greaves, Svetlana Nasibyan and Rita Leandro Vasconcelos, considers specific types of abuses and remedies, such as exclusionary abuses dealing with low cost pricing, refusal to license intellectual property rights, abuses on aftermarkets and the scarce remedial experience at European level. It analyses the evolution of these practices in the ECJ case law and Commission's decisions, explores what changes can be anticipated in the near future and reflects upon the need to find coherence and certainty in the application of EU competition law.

The third part, with contributions from Manuel Fontaine Campos, Mariana Tavares, Isabel Fernández-Torres and Nuno Castro Marques, deals with particular new trends in state aid. After addressing the evolution of the 'effects on trade' and 'distortion of competition' under the EU state aid regime, this part of the book focuses on particular issues in the

Iberian context, namely the problem with public financing of airports and airlines that took place in Spain and the Portuguese experience concerning the complementary role that Member States can fulfil in the state aid context, either using soft law to limit the negative effects of an aid in competition or encouraging the better use of public resources through the creation of a national development bank.

This publication is based on two seminars and international conferences that took place at Porto Law School – Catholic University of Portugal in March 2014 and March 2015, with the support of the European Commission, in order to contribute to a productive debate about the challenges of European Competition law in the next decade.

Part I

Antitrust private enforcement: National perspectives on the Damages Directive

Competition law: achievements and challenges

António Ferreira GOMES[1]

I would first like to thank Católica Porto Law School for the kind invitation to participate in the opening session of this Conference and to congratulate its organizers for the excellent program.

This Conference is a testament to the growing awareness regarding the importance of competition among the legal community. Competition generates benefits for everyone – consumers, businesses, government and the overall economy – and should be seen as an engine of economic growth. Competition is vital to ensure a dynamic, competitive and robust economy by promoting and rewarding merit.

When competition is eliminated or restricted, companies lose incentives to innovate and to reduce costs, becoming less efficient. This is harmful to consumers, but also to the companies themselves, as they become less prepared to face new challenges.

In a context of crisis, when citizens and taxpayers are already in a vulnerable situation, a prohibited practice, such as a cartel, is particularly detrimental to consumers, as it forces them to pay higher prices for products or services. The same applies to companies which need inputs from other companies themselves, and to the State as a buyer of goods and services.

It is therefore important to be aware of the benefits of competition, but also of the detrimental effects of violations to competition law. The Portuguese Competition Authority is committed to combine both dimensions, acting as a proactive advocate for competition and a vigorous enforcer of competition law in Portugal.

The growing awareness of the benefits of competition and of the consequences of infringing competition law is leading to an increasing importance of private enforcement of competition law.

More and more, we see parties in civil actions grounding their claims on competition law, which poses an additional challenge for national Courts in general to deal with this area of law.

---

1 President of the Portuguese Competition Authority.

This expansion in the application of competition law, beyond public enforcement, has recently been reinforced in Europe with the approval of the Directive on "private enforcement" in December 2014. The Directive aims at ensuring that any citizen or business has a *right to full and effective compensation* for the harm caused by an infringement of the competition rules. The Directive will be implemented in each Member State until December 2016, and the Portuguese Competition Authority is actively participating in that process at national level.

Private enforcement in Portugal will most certainly primarily develop in the form of civil actions following PCA's decisions – the so-called "follow-on actions". Recent developments in Portugal confirm this, as civil actions are being brought in national Courts following the PCA's decision against an abuse of a dominant position by Sport TV, a premium sports channel provider. These are important developments that illustrate the advantages for private enforcement deriving from vigorous and solid public enforcement by the PCA.

When applying competition law, national Courts may benefit from cooperation between Courts and also from cooperation with competition authorities.

First, national Courts may submit a reference for a preliminary ruling to the Court of Justice to assist them in the interpretation of EU law. In Portugal, there is a recent example of a preliminary ruling submitted by the Lisbon Court of Appeal to the Court of Justice regarding an appeal against a decision taken by the Portuguese Competition Authority. The case concerned the Association of chartered accountants and rules relating to a system of compulsory training for chartered accountants. In February 2013, the Court of Justice confirmed that those rules could amount to a restriction on competition prohibited by Article 101 TFEU. This clarification of the scope of application of EU law then led to the confirmation, by national Courts, of the PCA's sanctioning decision.

In addition, under Regulation (EC) No. 1/2003, national Courts may ask the European Commission to give its opinion on questions regarding the application of the EU competition rules. Moreover, both the Commission and national competition authorities may intervene in the Court's procedures as *amicus curiae* by submitting observations to the Court.

The cooperation mechanisms between Courts, as well as between Courts and Competition Authorities, are crucial to ensure a consistent and effective enforcement of competition law. I would like to stress that the PCA is committed in the development of a close and constructive institutional dialogue with national Courts.

The fact that competition law is more widely applicable in Courts today makes it more important that the legal community is aware of some specific characteristics of this area of law.

Two important and challenging characteristics may be highlighted: the fundamental link with European Union law and the interplay with economics.

The connection between national law and EU law in the field of competition is particularly strong. The provisions on competition of the EU Treaties are directly applicable at national level and are enforceable by the Competition Authorities and by National Courts in parallel with national law. This means that the case-law developed by the Court of Justice of the European Union is also applicable in all Member States.

Moreover, the large degree of convergence between national and EU competition law strengthens the relevance of EU case-law even in a purely national case in order the ensure consistency in the interpretation of law.

As recently pointed out in a Judgement by the Portuguese Competition, Regulation and Supervision Court, "given the profound convergence between national and EU competition law, the joint application of both does not cause difficulties in the majority of the cases".[2] However, this implies an additional effort in the interpretation of competition law, and a need for constant updating on the most recent decisions of the EU Court of Justice.

Regarding the interplay with economics, it is important that competition law practitioners and enforcers understand the economics underlying the various types of infringements to competition law. The complexity of economic analysis in competition cases has increased over the years, as we have moved into less formal approaches to competition law enforcement. This is particularly true for cases of abuse of dominance, which will be the focus of this morning's first panel.

The interplay between law and economics poses a challenge to competition authorities, in particular in the way they present complex economic analysis, not only in their decisions but also before the Courts.

I would like to mention a recent good example where discussion on complex economic issues took place before the Courts in Portugal: the recent appeal before the Portuguese Competition Court of the PCA's decision imposing a fine on Sport TV for an abuse of its dominant position.

The case was heavily supported in economic evidence and the Competition Court took a novel approach during the hearings by using

---

2 Judgement of 04.06.2014, case 204/13.6YUSTR.

economic experts as advisers. The appealing party and the PCA also had their own economic advisers.

This was a pragmatic solution, used for the first time in appeals of the PCA's decisions, which ensured that the Court was well-advised by experts and could ultimately reach a solid decision in terms of economics. I am pleased to say that the Competition Court upheld the PCA's decision and its economic reasoning. This was the first ever judicial confirmation of a PCA's decision concerning an abuse of a dominant position, thus representing a major step in competition enforcement in Portugal.

Therefore, the link between law and economics in the area of competition challenges enforcers to ground their decisions in economic reasoning, seeking the necessary expertise to ensure sound decisions but also to explain economic reasoning in a clear way.

There are two topical issues, which fully illustrate the points that I have just raised: Exclusionary Abuses and State Aid Rules. In both these areas, the Portuguese Competition Authority has a particular role to play. And so do the Courts.

Regarding abuses of dominance, the PCA's experience has had positive developments recently. The Sport TV case that I have just mentioned was confirmed just this week by the Lisbon Court of Appeal, a decision which we naturally welcome. This is the first time that a decision on abuse of dominance was confirmed by Portuguese Courts on 1st and 2nd instances.

One of the reasons for the lack of confirmation by Courts of previous decisions by the PCA was the statute of limitation. Abuse of dominance cases are usually lengthy, as they typically involve large volumes of evidence and complex economic analysis, which makes them more prone to becoming time-barred.

This was acknowledged in the recent legislative reform of the Portuguese Competition Act in 2012, which now foresees that the limitation period is suspended up to three years during the judicial appeals. This legal amendment will hopefully allow Courts more time to assess these complex cases. In any case, the PCA will continuously seek to shorten the time of its investigations on restrictive practices to avoid that violations of competition law may end up unpunished due to the statute of limitation.

Turning now to the topic of State Aid, I would like to highlight that, in this area, the PCA has the power to issue recommendations regarding public aid aimed at eliminating any negative impact on competition and to monitor the implementation of its recommendations by the public bodies. However, these recommendations are not binding.

The PCA has recently used this advocacy power with regards to State aid in the energy sector. In November 2013, the PCA issued a Recommendation to the Government regarding compensations to power generators in order to avoid overcompensation.

In April 2014, the Government published a set of corrective measures in order to address the PCA's recommendation, which include an Audit to calculate the amount of past overcompensations to be returned to consumers. This is a successful example of advocacy in the field of State aid.

National Courts play a relevant role in the field of State aid. National Courts may apply the EU Treaty provisions on State aid law, namely in actions by parties seeking compensation, or the imposition of injunctive or interim measures in cases of implementation of unlawful State aid, namely in breach of the "standstill obligation". To this end, national Courts are entitled to interpret the notion of State aid even if they do not have the power to declare a State aid measure compatible with the Treaty. The enforcement powers of the Courts in this area are thus key in ensuring a level playing field for all market players.

I would like to conclude by wishing all participants a productive Conference. I am confident that this initiative will strengthen the awareness on the importance of protecting and promoting competition to reinforce competitiveness and economic growth.

Antitrust private enforcement and collective redress in Portugal[1]

Sofia Oliveira Pais[2]

1. Introduction

In Portugal there are no specific rules for antitrust infringements. General substantive and procedural rules, provided in the Portuguese Civil Code, Code of Civil Procedure and Portuguese Competition Law (Law 19/2012, 8 May), apply.[3] The majority of cases are public enforcement cases; the Portuguese Competition Authority investigates the antitrust infringements on its own initiative or following complaints (and its decision can be reviewed by the Competition, Regulation and Supervision Court, and then by the Lisbon Court of Appeal). The Portuguese Competition Authority can impose sanctions, but cannot award damages.[4] In few cases, the plaintiff

---

1 This paper was discussed in the Católica Seminar "Training judges in competition law – 2014" and its first part draws on the text "Practical Private Enforcement: Enforcing EU Law through national action – Portugal", presented in the conference organized, in 2014, by the Faculty of Law – University of Uppsala and the Swedish Network for European Legal Studies.

2 Associate Professor, Católica Porto Law School, Catholic University of Portugal; Jean Monnet Chair, Researcher/Coordinator at Católica Research Centre for the Future of Law (Porto).

3 On the topic of antitrust private enforcement see Rodger, B. (ed.), *Competition Law Comparative Private Enforcement and Collective Redress across the EU*. New York: Wolters Kluwer Law & Business, 2014, and Foer, A.; Cuneo, J. (eds.), *The International Handbook on Private Enforcement of Competition Law*. Oxford: Edward Elgar Publishing, 2012. See also Wils, W., "Should private antitrust enforcement be encouraged in Europe?", *World Competition* (WC) 26 (3) (2003), p. 473; Killeen, D., "Following in 'Uncle Sam's' footsteps? The evolution of private antitrust enforcement in the European Union", *European Competition Law Review (ECLR)*, 39 (4) (2013), p. 480; Stephen, A., "Cartels", in Lianos, I.; Geradin, D. (eds.), *Handbook on European Competition Law Substantive Aspects*. Oxford: Edward Elgar, 2013.

4 Should Competition Authorities inform potential victims of antitrust decisions and mention the possibility of claiming damages? Rossi and Ferro have already suggested that the Portuguese legislator should create, for the antitrust procedures conducted by the Portuguese Competition Authority, a rule similar to Article 75 (1) of the Portuguese Criminal Code of Procedure. This article states that, when the investigating authorities become aware of possible injured persons, they are obliged to inform them of the

complained to a civil court and asked for compensation. Antitrust private enforcement in Portugal is, therefore, taking the first steps. This article will introduce two major Portuguese cases, presenting some preliminary thoughts concerning the future of private enforcement in Portugal, taking into account the solutions established in the new Directive 2014/104/EU.[5]

2. Main features of the national system

2.1 Private enforcement

Victims of antitrust violations can complain to a civil court and seek for compensation of damages (covering actual loss and loss of profits – Articles 562 and 564 of the Civil Code) and/or challenge the validity of an agreement (Article 9 (2) of the Portuguese Competition Law and Articles 280 and 294 of the Civil Code) through common declaratory actions or through collective actions (mainly popular actions, which is an opt-out collective redress model).[6] Therefore, any individual or undertaking that has suffered injury as a consequence of an anti-competitive conduct may sue for damages. The claimant will have, nevertheless, to prove the defendant's fault or negligence in the unlawful conduct, the extent of the damages and the causal link between the two (Articles 483, 487 and 563 of the Civil Code). The burden of proof lies on the claimant, who invokes the facts (Article 342 Civil Code); the burden of proof can only be reversed in special cases (for instance, in contractual liability, there is a rebuttable presumption of fault of the debtor – see Article 799 of the Civil Code). The action (non-contractual liability) shall be filed within three years from the moment the plaintiff becomes aware of the alleged right to claim damages. The decision of a civil court can be reviewed by the Court of Appeal and, if legally possible, by the Supreme Court. The parties bear the legal costs, but in the end the winning party is entitled to collect them from the losing party.

---

possibility to ask for compensation within the criminal procedure and of the formalities that should be observed. Cf. Rossi, L.; Ferro, M., "Private enforcement of competition law in Portugal (Ii): actio popularis – facts, fictions and dreams", *Revista de Concorrência e Regulação*, Ano 4, 13 (2013), p. 80.

5 Directive 2014/104/EU of the European Parliament and of the Council of 26 November 2014 on certain rules governing actions for damages under national law for infringements of the competition law provisions of the Member States and of the European Union, 2014, OJ L 349/1 (hereinafter Directive on antitrust damages actions or Directive).

6 Cf. Pais, S. O.; Piszcz, A., "Package on actions for damages based on breaches of EU competition rules: can one size fit all?", *Yearbook of Antitrust and Regulatory Studies*, 7 (10) (2014), p. 214.

2.2 Collective redress

Portugal has an opt-out system[7] called Popular Action (*Ação Popular*), which has been applied, namely, by consumer associations.[8] The Popular Action is mentioned in Article 52(2) of the Portuguese Constitution and was implemented by the Popular Action Act (Law 83/95, 31 August). The list of interests mentioned in Article 1 of the Popular Action Act is merely exemplary, so damages from antitrust infringements can be compensated through the Popular Action (and the Portuguese Supreme Court, apparently, accepted this solution in its judgement of 7 October 2003).[9] Under Articles 2, 3 and 16 of the Popular Action Act, standing to initiate a Popular Action is granted to any citizen, any legal association or foundation (a legal entity whose powers must include the interests covered by the Popular Action, which is not involved in any kind of professional business competing with undertakings or liberal professionals), to local authorities (in relation with the interests of all those who are located in the respective area) and to the public prosecutor's office, which may replace the claimants if the contested behaviour endangers the interests involved (Article 16 (3) of the Popular Action Act). The Popular Action Act establishes certain special procedural rules, for instance: "it is up to the judge's own initiative to collect evidence and [the judge] is not bound by the initiatives of the parties" (Article 17 of the Popular Action Act), and even

---

7 In the opt-out model, the court decision is binding on everyone that did not opt-out. This solution can increase the effectiveness of this mechanism as it overcomes the passive nature of victims of antitrust infringements (antitrust claims are not very relevant, which discourages access to courts). In the opt-in model (which the European Commission prefers) the judgement is only binding for those who opted-in. This solution, according to the Commission, is compatible with the legal traditions of EU Member States, avoids litigation abuses and respects the freedom of potential claimants. On this topic see, Lein, E.; Fairgrieve, D.; Crespo, M. O.; Smith, V. (eds.), *Collective redress in Europe – why and how?* UK: British Institute of International and Comparative Law, 2015 and Panagiotis, D.; Tzakas, L., "Effective collective redress in antitrust and consumer protection matters: a panacea or a chimera?", *Common Market Law Review*, 48 (2011), p. 1125.

8 In Portugal, DECO (Portuguese Consumer Protection Association) has effectively used the mechanism of the Popular Action once – see *DECO (Portuguese Consumer Protection Association) v Portugal Telecom* (*Supremo Tribunal de Justiça* [Supreme Court of Justice], 07.10.2003, proc. No. 03A1243). Although competition law was invoked (the Consumer Association DECO argued that it was an abuse of dominant position), the case was decided on other grounds. In this case, Portugal Telecom forced an unlawful "activation charge" on all clients regarding all phone calls and was condemned by the Court. Following the judgement, DECO and Portugal Telecom agreed on a compensation of an amount around €120 million, which was translated into free national calls for all Portugal Telecom's clients on several consecutive Sundays.

9 *DECO (Portuguese Consumer Protection Association) v Portugal Telecom*, cit.

"if a particular appeal has no suspensive effect, in general terms, the judge may, in a class action, give that effect, to prevent damage irreparable or difficult to repair" (Article 18 of the Popular Action Act). Regarding costs expenses, the Popular Action Act states that the claimant is exempt from the payment of costs if the application is partially granted (Article 20 (2) of the Popular Action Act). However, if the claim is totally unsuccessful, the claimant will have to pay an amount fixed by the judge ranging between 10% and 50% of the costs that would be normally payable, taking into account the claimant's financial situation and the formal or substantive reason for the dismissal (Article 20 (3) of the Popular Action Act). Concerning compensation, the court is obliged to determine a compensation for the infringement of the interests of those not individually identified (Article 22 (2) of the Popular Action Act). The right to damages shall be extinguished within three years from the final judgement that has recognized the damage and the unclaimed funds shall be delivered to the Ministry of Justice (Article 22 (4 and 5) of the Popular Action Act). The Ministry will create a special account and allocate the payment to attorney fees and to support access to the courts (Article 22 (5) of the Popular Action Act).[10]

3. Portuguese Case Law

3.1 Stand-alone actions – The Toyota Case

Stand-alone actions are legally possible in Portugal under the general procedural and substantive rules established in the Portuguese Code of Civil Procedure and in the Portuguese Civil Code, coupled with those provided by the Portuguese Competition Law (Law 19/2012, 8 May) and by the Treaty on the Functioning of the European Union (TFEU).[11]

In a recent survey concerning competition law cases in Portuguese Courts,[12] it was possible to identify more than thirty decisions, in which competition issues were raised notably as a means of defence, regarding the validity of agreements or contractual clauses, and dealt mainly with vertical relations between a manufacturer and its distributors. Nevertheless, only once did the Court award damages to a

10 Pais, S. O.; Piszcz, A., "Package on actions for damages based on breaches of EU competition rules: can one size fit all?", cit., p. 218.

11 DAF/COMP/WP3/WD(2015)15, Working Party No. 3 on Co-operation and Enforcement, Relationship Between Public and Private Antitrust Enforcement – Portugal, Organisation for Economic Co-operation and Development, Directorate for Financial and Enterprise Affairs, Competition Committee, 10 Jun. 2015, p. 3.

12 Cf. Rossi, L.; Ferro, M., "Private enforcement of competition law in Portugal (I): an overview of case law", *Revista de Concorrência e Regulação*, Ano 3, 10 (2012), p. 91.

private party on the basis of an infringement of competition law.[13] In fact, the Portuguese Supreme Court recently decided the Toyota case,[14] concerning a stand-alone action related to a situation of an "abuse of economic dependency."[15] In this case, Toyota SC Comércio (Toyota) is the only importer of Toyota's vehicles in Portugal. In 2002, Toyota notified the termination, in 2004, of an exclusive dealership agreement with Auto-AA, an authorized distributor in the north of Portugal. In addition, in 2003, Toyota introduced a selective distribution system for its vehicle sales and did not accept, in 2004, Auto-AA as an authorized dealer (in fact, Toyota intended to replace Auto-AA with another company, which was controlled by Toyota). The Court of First Instance and the Court of Appeal of Oporto considered that this situation – excluding a company with weak bargaining power, unable to find an equivalent alternative with other commercial partners in a reasonable period of time – should be considered an abuse. The two Courts awarded compensation. The Supreme Court of Justice upheld the previous national court decisions, confirmed the existence of an abuse of economic dependency and awarded compensation to Auto-AA. The Toyota case is the first case in Portugal in which the Supreme Court of Justice awarded compensation for antitrust infringement, strengthening the enforcement of competition law. Nevertheless, this decision has been criticized as being "simplistic",[16] as the Courts did not justify the economic dependence, relying only on the obligation of exclusivity and on the integration of the undertaking in the distribution network.

---

13 See Case *Carrefour v Orex Dois* (Tribunal da Relação de Lisboa [Lisbon Court of Appeal], 24.11.2005, proc. No. 6882/2005-8). On this case, the Lisbon Court of Appeal declared the contracts null and void on the basis of an infringement of the national equivalent to Article 101 (1). The declaration has retroactive effect, so Carrefour was ordered to return the payments in the amount of €49,000, made by the Orex Dois under those contracts. See also Case *Toyota v Auto-AA* (Supremo Tribunal de Justiça [Supreme Court of Justice], 20.06.2013, proc. No. 178/07.2TVPRT.P1.S1). It concerned an abuse of economic dependency, which consisted in the abusive exploration by one or more undertakings of a state of economic dependence in which suppliers and customers have no alternative, affecting the functioning of the market or the structure of the competition [Article 12 of the Competition Law].

14 Supremo Tribunal de Justiça (Supreme Court of Justice), Toyota, 20.06.2013, proc. No. 178/07.2TVPRT.P1.S1.

15 Article 12, Law 19/2012, prohibits the abuse of economic dependency consisting of the abusive exploration by one, or more undertakings, of a state of economic dependence in which suppliers and customers have no alternative, affecting the functioning of the market or the structure of the competition.

16 See Rossi. L.; Ferro, M., *op. cit.*, loc. cit.

3.2 Follow-on actions – The Sport TV Case

3.2.1 The facts

There are no specific rules for antitrust damages actions concerning follow-on actions in the Portuguese context. To the best of our knowledge, there is only one follow-on action – the Sport TV Case – still pending in the Lisbon Court.[17-18]

In June 2013, following up on a complaint, the Portuguese Competition Authority found that Sport TV,[19] between 2005 and 2011, abused its dominant position by having imposed discriminatory conditions on operators, limiting, therefore, the development and investment in the market of pay-TV.

Sport TV had a dominant position in the Portuguese market, as, at the time of the proceedings, it was the only pay-TV premium sports channel in Portugal which broadcasted major sport events. At the time, Sport TV was owned by ZON Multimédia – Serviços de Telecomunicações e Multimédia, SGPS, S.A. (hereinafter, ZON) and Sportinveste, SGPS, S.A., and each shareholder had 50% of the share capital. Between 2005 and 2011, Sport TV had demanded mandatory compensation fees on its distribution agreements for the supply of its channels, conferring, however, commercial advantages to Zon Multimédia on the pay-TV retail market. In other words, Sport TV imposed discriminatory prices and unequal commercial conditions to the various pay-TV operators, which provided equivalent services.

---

17 Tribunal da Relação de Lisboa [Lisbon Court of Appeal], Judgement of March 11, 2015, Proc. No. 204/13.6YUSTR.L1. Cf. Rossi, L.; Ferro, M., "Private enforcement of competition law in Portugal (I): an overview of case law", cit., p. 91 ff.; DAF/COMP/WP3/WD(2015)15, Working Party No. 3 on Co-operation and Enforcement, Relationship Between Public and Private Antitrust Enforcement – Portugal, Organisation for Economic Co-operation and Development, Directorate for Financial and Enterprise Affairs, Competition Committee, 10 Jun. 2015, p. 2.

18 Press Package, "Portuguese Competition Observatory Initiates Collective Enforcement Action Against Sport TV to Compensate Consumers for Damages Caused by Infringements of Competition Law", Portuguese Competition Observatory, 12 March 2015; DAF/COMP/WP3/WD(2015)15, Working Party No. 3 on Co-operation and Enforcement, Relationship Between Public and Private Antitrust Enforcement – Portugal, Organisation for Economic Co-operation and Development, Directorate for Financial and Enterprise Affairs, Competition Committee, 10 Jun. 2015, p. 2.

19 Sport TV had a dominant position in two relevant products/services markets: the wholesale domestic market of conditional access channels with premium sports content (upstream), and in the retail market of subscription television (downstream).

3.2.2 The PCA decision and the judgement of the Court of Competition Regulation and Supervision

Sport TV was condemned by the Portuguese Competition Authority for abuse of dominant position, according to Articles 6, 4, No. 1, paragraphs c) and e), 42, 43, No. 1, paragraph a), 44 and 45, all of Law No. 18/2003, June 11, and also according to Article 102 TFEU. Therefore, the Portuguese Competition Authority condemned Sport TV to a fine of €3.7 million and to the publication of the decision in the Portuguese official journal as an ancillary sanction.[20]

Sport TV appealed from the Portuguese Competition Authority's decision to the Court of Competition, Regulation and Supervision. The latter, by judgement of June 4, 2014, partially upheld the PCA decision and condemned Sport TV to a fine, which was reduced to the amount of €2.7 million.[21]

Sport TV appealed from the judgement of the Court of Competition, Regulation and Supervision to the Court of Appeal of Lisbon. While the proceedings were pending in the Court of Appeal of Lisbon, the reporting judge ordered that the confidential version of the judgement of the Court of Competition, Regulation and Supervision should be made public and the access to it should follow the Code of Criminal Procedure. The reporting judge also ordered the maintenance of the confidentiality status of the confidential documents of the proceedings, notwithstanding further consideration and an eventual case-by-case basis decisions.[22] Sport TV also appealed from the referred order of the reporting judge to the Lisbon Court of Appeal.

3.2.3 Judgement of the Lisbon Court of Appeal

The Lisbon Court of Appeal dismissed both appeals, upholding the order issued by the reporting judge and the judgement of the Court of Competition, Regulation and Supervision.[23]

The Lisbon Court of Appeal started by acknowledging that the underlying principle safeguarded by the competition rules is the effective

---

20 Case number 204/13.6YUSTR.L1, Lisbon Court of Appeal, part I, paragraph 1, pp. 1-2.

21 Case number 204/13.6YUSTR.L1, Lisbon Court of Appeal, part I, paragraph 1, pp. 1-2. Tribunal da Relação de Lisboa [Lisbon Court of Appeal], 11.03.2015, proc. No. 204/13.6YUSTR.L1.

22 Case number 204/13.6YUSTR.L1, cit., pp. 178 and 180.

23 Case number 204/13.6YUSTR.L1, cit., p. 216.

competition based on economic efficiency as an essential element of the economic democracy, which is an ingredient of the political democracy.

In casu, the Lisbon Court of Appeal ruled that Articles 6, No. 3, paragraph a), and 4, No. 1, paragraph e) of the Portuguese Competition Law were infringed. The Sport TV was an undertaking in a dominant position that applied discriminatory prices and unequal commercial conditions to equivalent transactions.

Although Sport TV recognized that it had applied different contractual conditions to several pay-TV operators, it argued that those conditions were not discriminatory, since the situations were not similar and the policy of rebates intended to stimulate the subscriptions of Sport TV's channels. In addition, Sport TV argued that there was no vertical integration between Sport TV and ZON, because Sport TV did not integrate the ZON group; so, it would be difficult to find a situation of discrimination. In addition, exploitative abuses are not the priority of the European Commission. Furthermore, Sport TV argued that its price policies were completely justified by economic reasons, because they promoted the increasing of subscribers and, therefore, contributed for a decrease in fixed costs of the business.[24]

The Lisbon Court of Appeal did not follow those arguments and ruled that there was a special link between Sport TV and ZON, as ZON had the possibility to exercise a negative exclusive control, since it had 50% of Sport TV's share capital. The Court explained, furthermore, that exploitive abuses are also prohibited by Article 82 [now 102 TFUE] and noticed that the acceptance of an economic justification is dependent on the necessity, proportionality or reasonableness of the measures adopted. According to the Court those measures were neither proportional, nor reasonable; the applicability of a system of quantity rebates would be perfectly capable to achieve the suggested purposes and it would not impose on pay-TV operators the obligation to pay for non-existent subscribers.[25]

To define the concrete amount of the fine, the Lisbon Court of Appeal stressed that, according to article 44 of Law No. 18/2003, it should take into account several elements, such as the nature and severity of the infringement for the maintenance of effective competition in the national market, the advantages obtained by the infringers and if the infringer cooperated, or not, with the Competition Authority. *In casu*, taking into account the degree of discrimination between pay-TV operators, the

---

[24] Case number 204/13.6YUSTR.L1, cit., pp. 142-143.

[25] Case number 204/13.6YUSTR.L1, cit., p. 208.

damages caused to pay-TV operators and to consumers, the profits earned by Sport TV and the systematic nature of its conduct, the Lisbon Court of Appeal found the infringement severe. On the other hand, the Court recognized that Sport TV had no record of administrative infringements, had collaborated with the Competition Authority, giving information and providing the documents requested, and had changed the contract terms (which were also justified by market developments). Therefore, the Court upheld the previous decision and concluded that a fine of €2 million was adequate.

3.2.4 The Popular Action

On 12 March 2015, the Portuguese Competition Observatory, a non-profit association of academics from several Portuguese universities, after the Lisbon Court of Appeal decision was issued, filed a mass damages claim against Sport TV through a popular action. The action seeks "to compensate over 600,000 clients for damages allegedly resulting from a number of anticompetitive practices, but also to compensate those who were excluded from the benefit of these channels due to the inflation of prices and all Portuguese pay-TV subscribers, between 2005 and June 2013 (over 3 million at the end of the period), who suffered from a reduction of competition on this market."[26] It is the first follow-on action in the Portuguese context and the development of the procedure is closely followed by antitrust experts. In fact, high expectation concerning a more effective antitrust private enforcement, in the Portuguese context, arises not only with this new action but also with the entry into force of the Directive, which will require, as we will see, some changes in our national system.

4. New opportunities with the Directive 2014/104/EU

The Directive of 26 November 2014, that has to be implemented in the period of two years, intends to strengthen the enforcement of European antitrust rules by giving victims easier access to the courts (as well as more time to make their claims), preserving, at the same time, the attractiveness of leniency and settlement programmes. It clarifies certain issues, such as the role of passing-on defence or the exclusion of punitive damages, or the presumption of harm by cartels, which might imply changes in some Member States. In Portugal, those issues are not, at first sight,

[26] Ferro, M. S., "Collective redress: will Portugal show the way?", *Journal of European Competition Law & Practice Advance Access* published April 7, 2015, pp. 1-2.

problematic, as punitive damages are not available;[27] passing-on defence seems admissible under the general rules of unjustified enrichment,[28] and the rebuttable presumption that cartels cause harms is supported by several studies.[29] Nevertheless, other solutions provided by the directive will imply changes in the Portuguese law. We will refer some of the difficulties raised by the Directive in the Portuguese context which can become an opportunity to increase the effectiveness of private enforcement at national level.

4.1 Effect of national antitrust decisions

Article 9 of the Directive provides that final decisions made in another Member State by national competition authorities or reviews by national courts are merely *prima facie* evidence that an infringement of competition law has been established. However, the National Court is bound by the previous antitrust national decision, if the cartel decision and the claim for damages occur within one and the same Member State. The previous proposal, considering cartel decisions of national courts and national competition authorities binding for judges of other Member States was, therefore, set aside, allegedly to protect the independence of the judges (and the Member States).[30] In the Portuguese system, however, courts are not bound by Portuguese Competition Authority decisions. So, Article 9 of the Directive will require some changes in the Portuguese law, contributing to increase the effectiveness of private enforcement.

27 Nonetheless, there are some doubts concerning the law on intellectual property, namely, Directive No. 2004/48/CE, 24th April; there are doubts whether with its implementation, in the Portuguese context, punitive damages were introduced. Sustaining an affirmative answer, see Antunes, H. S., *Da inclusão do lucro ilícito e de efeitos punitivos entre as consequências da responsabilidade civil extracontratual: a sua legitimidade pelo dano.* Coimbra: Coimbra Editora, 2011, p. 432.

28 "The claimant is only entitled to recover damages which were actually suffered. Damages are purely compensatory, covering actual loss and loss of profits" (Article 564 of the Civil Code). Therefore, if some of the damages were passed-on to a third person, the claimant is not entitled to them. A different solution would constitute an unjustified enrichment of the claimant, under the Portuguese law.

29 See Connor, John M.; Robert H. Lande, "Cartel Overcharges and Optimal Cartel fines", *Issues in Competition Law and Policy*, S.W. Waller (ed.), Vol. 3, AMA Section of Antitrust Law, Chapter 88, (2008), pp. 2203-2218; and Boyer M.; Kotchoni. R., "How Much Do Cartels Overcharge?", *Working Paper No. Toulouse School of economics (TSE) – 462*, January 2014, p. 1. http://www.tse-fr.eu/sites/default/files/medias/doc/wp/etrie/wp_tse_462_v2.pdf (last visited 1.6.2015).

30 For a critical view of this solution, see Weidt, C. F., "The Directive on actions for antitrust damages after passing the European Parliament", *European Competition Law Review* [E.C.L.R.] 35 (9) (2014), pp. 438-444.

4.2 Limitation period rules

Article 10 of the Damages Directive provides that the limitation period shall be at least five years and shall not begin until the infringement of competition law has ceased and the injured party knows or can be expected to know "(a) of the behaviour and the fact that it constitutes an infringement of competition law; (b) of the fact that the infringement of competition law caused harm to it; and (c) the identity of the infringer". In addition, the limitation period is suspended during investigations or proceedings of competition authorities. In Portuguese law, however, victims in non-contractual liability have three years, from the moment they become aware of their right (even if they don't know the identity of the infringer), to submit an action for damages (Article 498 of the Civil Code).[31] The limitation period for the Portuguese Competition Authority to initiate proceedings for antitrust infringements, under Article 74 (1), paragraph a), of the Portuguese Competition Law, is, however, five years. The new solution established in the Damages Directive should, therefore, be particularly welcome in the Portuguese context as it will allow the harmonization of limitation periods in judicial and administrative proceedings.[32]

4.3 Disclosure of evidence

One of the main concerns of the Damages Directive is that victims (namely, consumers and small and medium enterprises) can obtain information about competition infringements and take the necessary legal actions. Article 5 of the Damages Directive enables the parties to seek disclosure of relevant evidence subject to certain conditions. For instance, the national court cannot, for the purpose of an action for damages, order a party or third party to disclose leniency statements or settlement submissions. In addition, disclosure of investigation documents such as statements of objections is deferred until the competition authority has closed its investigation (Article 7). The solutions provided in the Damages Directive modify, therefore, the test developed by the Court of Justice in Pfleiderer, which assigned the national courts the role to balance the

---

31 There is a twenty-year absolute limitation period, see Article 309 of the Civil Code.

32 Kersting, C., "Removing the tension between public and private enforcement: disclosure and privileges for successful leniency applicants", *Journal of European Competition Law and Practice* 5 (1) (2014), pp. 2-3. See also Lang, J. T., "The implications of the Commission's leniency policy for national competition", *European law Review* 28 (3) (2003), p. 435.

arguments in favour and against disclosure of relevant documents requested by the claimants.[33]

The general rule in Portuguese Competition Law provides that any person presenting a legitimate interest may request access to non-confidential documents (Article 33 (3)). Proceedings of the Portuguese Competition Authority are public, except if that Authority asked for its confidentiality ("secret of justice") until the end of the procedure (Article 32). In addition, under Article 90 of that Law, the Portuguese Competition Authority has the duty to publish in its site the non-confidential version of the decisions, referring whether these are still pending or not. Moreover, the non-confidential version of the rulings of the Portuguese Civil and Administrative Court of Appeals and Supreme Courts are published online in a specific database.[34]

In judicial proceedings, the parties can ask the court to order the delivery of documents that are in possession of the other party or third party (Articles 429 and 432 of the Civil Code of Procedure). There are no specific rules concerning confidential information in antitrust actions other than those regarding leniency applications and settlements or the general principles of protection of business secrets. It is, therefore, up to the court to determine what information is confidential and whether to order its disclosure or not (the law provides that the breach of confidential information might be considered criminal offence under Article 371 of the Portuguese Criminal Code).

Regarding leniency programs, Article 81 (1) of the Portuguese Competition Law states that the leniency applications, along with all supporting documents and information, are confidential. The access by third parties is only possible if authorized by the applicant (Article 81 (3)). A similar solution is provided for settlements: the Competition Authority does not grant third party access to settlements, unless authorized by the author (Article 22 (15)).

The prohibition of disclosure without consent also finds some support in the Court of Justice case law. In fact, in Pilkington, the Court of Justice[35] upheld the General Court decision of restraining the Commission from publishing a non-confidential version of a cartel decision, as the

---

33 Case C-360/09, *Pfleiderer AG v Bundeskartellamt* [2011] ECR I-5161. See Pais, S. O., "Entre clemência e responsabilidade – uma história de sucesso? Acórdão do Tribunal de Justiça (Grande Secção) de 14.6.2011, Proc. C-360/09", *Cadernos de Direito Privado* 37 (2012), pp. 1-9.

34 Cf. www.dgsi.pt.

35 Order of the Vice-President of the Court, 10 September 2013, Case C-278/13 P(R), *European Commission v Pilkington Group Ltd*, not yet published.

publication of that material could cause irreparable harm to the applicant. Nevertheless, in Akzo[36] the General Court held that the Commission could publish certain information of leniency materials in order to disclose an extended version of the non-confidential decision. Therefore, the Court rejected Akzo Nobel NV's request to prohibit the European Commission from releasing a fuller version of its 2006 cartel decision. In this case, the Court decided that the company was not entitled to special protection from antitrust infringements claims.

In spite of certain "inconsistencies" in the case law,[37] there are now specific prohibitions in the Damages Directive, namely those preventing the disclosure of leniency and settlement documents; therefore, Portuguese Law might need to be adapted to ensure full compliance with European law. Although the achievement of the right balance between the interests of Competition Authorities, in the protection of leniency and settlement declarations (considered crucials to reveal secret cartels), and the interests of the victims of antitrust violations, to access those declarations (in order to obtain a compensation for damages), is not easy, the solutions provided by the Damages Directive seem to be (generally) appropriate.

4.4 Joint and several liability

Article 11 of the Directive provides that Member States shall ensure that "undertakings which have infringed competition law through joint behaviour [such as cartels] are jointly and severally liable for the harm caused by the infringement of competition law"; therefore, the injured party has the right to require "full compensation from any of them until he has been fully compensated". The infringer can later (if possible) recover from the co-infringer. Specific rules apply if the infringer is a small or medium-sized enterprise (SME), as defined in the Commission Recommendation 2003/361/EC, and to immunity recipients (in principle, relieved from that liability). In addition, the immunity recipient, in principle, will only be liable for the harm caused to its own direct or indirect purchasers or providers.

In the Portuguese Civil Code, according to the general law on civil liability, joint and several liability is the exception and not the rule

---

36 Case T-345/12, Judgment of the General Court (Third Chamber) of 28 January 2015, *Akzo Nobel NV and Others v European Commission*, not yet published.

37 The lack of harmony also extends to the European Commission, as Annelli Howard noticed, referring namely the Air Cargo and Mastercard decisions, see Howard, A., "Disclosure of infringement decision in competition damages proceedings: how the UK Courts are leading the way ahead of the damages directive", *Journal of Competition Law and Practice*, 6 (4) (2015), p. 259.

(Article 513). In other words, joint and several liability is only applicable where there is a contractual clause establishing specifically joint and several liability, or a legal disposition providing that solution, such as Article 497 of the Civil Code, which concerns tort liability and establishes joint and several liability (the right to recover depends on the guilt of each infringer, and is presumed equal). As there is no specific rule concerning damages by the infringement of competition rules, Portuguese law should be adapted to consider the solutions provided by the directive, namely the specific solutions concerning the immunity recipient.

5. Conclusion

Private enforcement in Portugal is still quite modest, although the praxis of the Portuguese courts is changing, as the Toyota and Sport TV cases clearly show. The new Directive 2014/104/EU intends to strengthen the private enforcement of antitrust rules by giving victims easier access to the courts and should, therefore, be seen as an opportunity by the Member States to change their laws in order to achieve better solutions, increasing legal security. In the Portuguese context, rules concerning, namely, the effects of national antitrust decisions, limitation period, disclosure of evidence and joint and several liability will have to be adapted in order to comply with the new Damages Directive, which has reached a certain equilibrium between the different interests involved.

Bibliography

Boyer M.; Kotchoni R., "How Much Do Cartels Overcharge?", *Working Paper No. Toulouse School of economics (TSE) – 462*, January 2014.

Connor, John M.; Robert H. Lande, "Cartel Overcharges and Optimal Cartel fines", *Issues in Competition Law and Policy*, S.W. Waller (ed.), Vol. 3, AMA Section of Antitrust Law, Chapter 88, (2008).

Ferro, M. S., "Collective redress: will Portugal show the way?", *Journal of European Competition Law & Practice, Advance Access,* April 7, 2015.

Foer, A.; Cuneo, J. (eds.), *The international handbook on private enforcement of competition law*. Oxford: Edward Elgar Publishing, 2012.

Howard, A., "Disclosure of infringement decision in competition damages proceedings: how the UK Courts are leading the way ahead of the damages directive", *Journal of Competition Law and Practice*, 6 (4) (2015).

Kersting, C., "Removing the tension between public and private enforcement: disclosure and privileges for successful leniency applicants", *Journal of European Competition Law and Practice,* 5 (1) (2014).

Killeen, D., "Following in 'Uncle Sam's' footsteps? The evolution of private antitrust enforcement in the European Union", *European Competition Law Review (ECLR)*, 39 (4) (2013).

Lang, J. T., "The implications of the Commission's leniency policy for national competition", *European law Review,* 28 (3) (2003).

Lein, E.; Fairgrieve, D.; Crespo, M. O.; Smith, V. (eds.), *Collective redress in Europe – why and how?* UK: British Institute of International and Comparative Law, 2015.

Pais, S. O., "Entre clemência e responsabilidade – uma história de sucesso? Acórdão do Tribunal de Justiça (Grande Secção) de 14.6.2011, Proc. C-360/09", *Cadernos de Direito Privado,* 37 (2012).

Pais, S. O.; Piszcz, A., "Package on actions for damages based on breaches of EU competition rules: can one size fit all?", *Yearbook of Antitrust and Regulatory Studies*, 7 (10) (2014).

Panagiotis, D.; Tzakas, L., "Effective collective redress in antitrust and consumer protection matters: a panacea or a chimera?", *Common Market Law Review*, 48 (2011).

Rodger, B. (ed.), *Competition law, comparative private enforcement and collective redress across the EU.* New York: Wolters Kluwer Law & Business, 2014.

Rossi, L.; Ferro, M., "Private enforcement of competition law in Portugal (II): Actio Popularis – facts, fictions and dreams", *Revista de Concorrência e Regulação*, Ano 4, 13 (2013).

Rossi, L.; Ferro, M., "Private enforcement of competition law in Portugal (I): an overview of case law", *Revista de Concorrência e Regulação*, Ano 3, 10 (2012).

Stephen, A., "Cartels", in Lianos, I.; Geradin, D. (eds.), *Handbook on European competition law substantive aspects*. Oxford: Edward Elgar, 2013.

Wils, W., "Should private antitrust enforcement be encouraged in Europe", *World Competition* (WC) 26 (3) (2003).

Reflections on damage actions – the Asphalt case

Petri KUOPPAMÄKI[1]

1. Introduction

Private enforcement is rapidly becoming an important element of the Finnish competition law system. The same trend is currently seen in many EU countries as well. Earlier in Finland, damages resulting from competition law infringements were mainly settled out of court. In many cases, damages were dealt with by arbitration. However, in recent times, private enforcement has taken up in the Finnish court system. For instance, the asphalt cartel not only resulted in major fines imposed by the Supreme Administrative Court[2] but also led to significant damage claims being filed by the cartel victims in civil courts.

In Finland there have been four significant private follow-on cartel damage cases so far. Three are still pending in the court system and one has been settled with a damage award. The total amount of damage claims exceeds 500 million euros.

So far the claims for antitrust damages made in the courts of general jurisdiction have been *follow on claims* that have been filed after a decision given by the Finnish Competition Authority (FCCA), the Market Court or the Supreme Administrative Court, finding that a competition law infringement has taken place.[3]

---

1 Professor of Law, Business Law at Aalto University School of Business.

2 Supreme Administrative Court's decision, 29 Sep. 2009, KHO:2009:83, Dnro 188/3/0 8, 189/3/08, 190/3/08, 191/3/08, 196/3/08, 197/3/08 and 199/3/08, file copy 2389.

3 There is, however, one direct claim under the national equivalent of nullity provision similar to Article 101 (2) TFEU. The case concerned abuse of dominant position by a copyright collecting society. A significant price increase was deemed to be abusive and was declared null and void by the Helsinki Court of Appeals. Decision of the Helsinki Court of Appeals, 30.6.2011 Säveltäjäin Tekijänoikeustoimisto Teosto ry v. Imatran Kylpylä Oy, Lomaliitto ry:n konkurssipesä, Savonlinnan Kylpylaitos Oy:n konkurssipesä, Ylläs Saaga Oy, Levin Matkailukeskus Oy, Lomakeskus Revontuli Oy, Night People Oy, Nisu-Aitta Oyand Suomen Onnelat Oy; No 2215; Diary number S 08/2682.

This article will discuss the most interesting aspects of the Asphalt case that will continue in Court of Appeal. Also other major cases are covered. Towards the end of the article it is discussed what can be said so far on the basis of the developing Finnish case law.

2. Competition Law Infringements and Tort Law in Finland

Under Finnish law, those affected by violations of competition law may seek damages before the civil courts. The Competition Act (948/2011) includes in its section 20 a specific provision regarding damages payable for competition restrictions. According to section 20, any undertaking or association of undertakings that intentionally or negligently violates one of the prohibitions in sections 5 or 7 or Articles 101 or 102 TFEU is liable to compensate those who have suffered damages. Damages can include compensation for costs, price differences, lost profits and other direct and indirect damages caused by the competition restriction.[4]

Under section 20, damages awarded for a competition law infringement will cover compensation for both direct and indirect financial damage caused by the competition law infringement; for example, the award may include a compensation for costs, difference in price and lost profits.[5] Naturally, as a general principle damage law, there must be a causal connection between the competition restriction and the damages. Therefore, it must be shown that the damages have been caused by the competition restriction. For example, it must be shown that an alleged overprice has been caused by a competition restriction and not for instance by the market situation. Compensated damages must be based on the foreseeable effects of competition restrictions. If the competition restriction leads to very surprising effects or the effects are very distant from the original cause, the claim for damages cannot be successful.[6]

The cases that have been decided so far have been decided on the basis of the former Act on competition restrictions from the year 1992, to which a provision on compensation of damages was added in 1998. The old damage provision, Section 18 a) of the Act on Competition Restrictions, was for most parts similar to the current Section 20 of the Competition Act. However, there were some important differences.On the basis of the

---

4 It should be noted that any contract clauses under which a party waives his right to damages prior to the occurrence of the damage are considered to be null and void. Such agreements may, however, be made after the damage has actually occurred and the parties are in a position to estimate the actual scope of the damage.

5 Government proposal (88/2010), p. 66.

6 Government proposal (88/2010), p. 66.

old law, damages could be awarded only to other "undertakings". This limitation was removed from Section 20 of the new Competition Act.[7] The amendment was considered necessary because parties other than undertakings, such as *consumers* or *public bodies*, may also be subject to the negative effects of competition law violations.[8] It can be claimed that the old Act was, in this regard, not in harmony with the EU Courts decision in *Manfredi* that discusses and also requires the possibility the award of damages to consumers. As stated in *Courage*, under EU law "every individual" must have the possibility to claim damages for the harm caused by a competition law infringement. As a result of the reform, persons and bodies other than undertakings can now also qualify for damages when they have been harmed by a competition restriction. Indeed, the case law of the CJEU prescribes that all parties that have suffered damage due to a competition law infringement should be entitled to compensation.[9]

Furthermore, the time limit for claiming damages was extended in the new Competition Act. In the former Act on Competition Restrictions, the right to compensation for damages would expire if the claim had not been made within five years from the day that an undertaking found out or should have found out that damage had occurred.[10] Under the current Competition Act, the right to damages will expire if the claim for damages has not been made within *ten years* from the day that the *violation* took place, or in the case of a continuous violation, within ten years from the day that the violation ended. However, if the damage claim is based on a decision of the FCCA finding a violation of the Competition Act or proposing a fine to be set by the Market Court, then the right to damages will expire if the claim has not been made within *one year* from the day that the decision became final and is no longer subject to appeal.

The calculation of the limitation periods has been one key issue in the litigation. The additional one-year period of the new Competition

7 The former Act on Competition Restrictions (480/1992) also included a special provision on the adjustment of damages. Section 18 a(2) of the Act on Competition Restrictions. The compensation could be adjusted if full compensation was unreasonable when considering the nature of the violation, the scope of the damage, the position of the parties and certain other issues. In the current Act, the specific provision concerning the adjustment of damages was replaced by a reference to the provisions concerning adjustment in the Tort Liability Act. This was more a technical change.

8 Government proposal (88/2010), p. 66. As for the case law of the Court of Justice of the European Union, the Government proposal expressly refers to the cases C-453/99, *Courage*, Judgement of the Court of 20 Sep. 2001, ECR 2001, p. I-06297 and joined cases C-295/04 to C-298/04, *Manfredi*, Judgement of the Court of 13 Jul. 2006, ECR 2006, p. I-06619.

9 Government proposal (88/2010), p. 67.

10 Section 18 a(3) of Act on Competition Restrictions.

Act removed legal uncertainty. On the other hand it may significantly extend the limitation period. The fact that the former Act on Competition Restrictions only covered damages caused to another business undertaking and not, for example, damages suffered by consumers or public authorities was also removed.

It must, however, be noted that the Finnish law is quite flexible as regards alternative legal grounds for a damage suit based on a competition law infringement.

It is important to note that there are alternative grounds upon which damages may be sought, including but not limited to:

a) the Tort Liability Act (where there are especially weighty reasons, damages shall constitute compensation for economic loss that is not connected to personal injury or damage to property in accordance with the Tort Liability Act 5:1.);[11]
b) refund of benefit by unjust enrichment (overpricing may be considered as constituting unjust enrichment);
c) contractual liability for damages;
d) invalidity of a contract or a clause of it on the basis of section 10 of the Competition Act (or the preceding section 18 of the Act on Competition Restrictions);
e) adjustment of an unreasonable contract condition on the basis of section 36 of the Contracts Act;[12]
f) invalidity of a contract based on the Contracts Acts.

According to Finnish legal literature[13] these claims can be brought cumulatively. In practice plaintiffs have utilized the flexibility of the law by making alternative claims. A practical reason for this approach has been that the rules on liability, burden of proof and the limitation periods differ somewhat for these alternative causes of action. Due to the limitation periods, in cases brought under the old Act of Competition Restriction cases were filed already while the public enforcement case was still ongoing.

It should be noted that also the *efficiency principle*, as stated in the decisions of the EU court, has affected the Finnish case law. In its landmark

[11] Tort Liability Act (412/1974). An unofficial translation in English is available in Finlex database at: http://www.finlex.fi/fi/laki/kaannokset/1974/en19740412.pdf.

[12] Contracts Act (228/1929). An unofficial translation in English is available in Finlex database at: http://www.finlex.fi/fi/laki/kaannokset/1929/en19290228.pdf (Amendments followed up to: 449/1999) (Last visited 23 Oct. 2012).

[13] See e.g. Kuoppamäki, P.: Uusi kilpailuoikeus (2012) p. 94; Havu, K.; Kalliokoski, T.; Wikberg, O., Kilpailuoikeudellinen vahingonkorvaus (2010) p. – (both in Finnish).

decision *Courage v Crehan* the Court of Justice of the European Union (CJEU) held that the effectiveness of Article 101 TFEU would be "put at risk if it were not open to any individual to claim damages for loss caused to him by a contract or by conduct liable to restrict or distort competition."[14] Mirroring to some extent the approach to cases of State liability under the *Francovich* principle,[15] claimants are required to establish breach of a EU competition rule, loss suffered, and an adequate causal link. The actual scope of the right to claim compensation has, moreover, been reinforced and extended in cases such as *Manfredi*, which confirmed that the right to "full compensation" encompasses loss of profits, plus interest, in addition to actual losses;[16] and the recent *Kone* judgment, which expands the *Courage* principle to include "umbrella losses" incurred through purchases from non-cartelists in cartelised markets.[17] It is by now uncontroversial that EU law requires, exceptionally, the availability of a remedy in damages at national level where breach of EU competition law causes demonstrable harm to claimants, albeit the rules and procedures for realisation of this right lie within the purview of Member State law. Conversely, alternative antitrust remedies, such as injunctions, remain primarily within the "autonomy" of national law.[18] As further elaborated in *Manfredi*, in the absence of Community rules governing the matter, it is for the domestic legal system of each Member State to designate the courts and tribunals having jurisdiction to hear actions for damages based on an infringement of the Community competition rules and to prescribe the detailed procedural rules governing those actions. However, national provisions must not be "less favourable" than those governing actions for damages based on an infringement of national competition rules and those national provisions "must not render practically impossible or

---

[14] Case C-453/99 *Courage Ltd. v Bernard Crehan*, ECR 2001 ECR I-6297, paras. 23 and 26. It should be noted, of course, that it has been known for a long time before *Courage* that Articles 101 and 102 TFEU produce direct effects in relations between individuals and create rights for the individuals concerned which the national courts must safeguard. See already Case 127/73 BRT and SABAM [1974] ECR 51, para. 16 ("BRT I"); Case C-282/95 P *Guérin Automobiles v Commission* [1997] ECR I-1503, para. 39. The primacy of Community law requires any provision of national law which contravenes a Community rule to be disapplied, regardless of whether it was adopted before or after that rule (see, *inter alia*, Case C-198/01 CIF [2003] ECR I-8055, paragraph 48).

[15] Joined Cases C-6&9/90 *Francovich v Italy*, ECR 1991 p. 428.

[16] Joined Cases C-295-97/04 *Vincenzo Manfredi v Lloyd Adriatico Assicurazioni SpA* ECR 2006, p. 461, see in particular para. 95.

[17] Case C-557/12 *Kone AG and Others*, ECR 2014, p. 1317.

[18] See e.g. European Commission, *Staff Working Paper*. Annex to the Green Paper on Damages actions for breach of the EC antitrust rules (SEC (2005) 1732), published 19December 2005, paras. 16-17.

excessively difficult the exercise of the right to seek compensation" for the harm caused by an agreement or practice prohibited under Article 101 and 102 TFEU.[19] With the Damages Directive 2014/104/EU[20] these key principles have been codified in law to be implemented in national law by the end of 2016. We find references to these EU-law principles in Finnish case law as well.

3. The Asphalt Case

The Asphalt cartel case concerns bid rigging and other cartel activities on the Finnish road surfacing market for road construction projects.[21] The asphalt companies were found to have secretly agreed on their bids in tender contests. The cartel members violated both Finnish competition law as well as Article 81 of the EC Treaty (today Article 101 TFEU). It appears that the secret cartel was enforced with quota allocation and surveillance mechanisms. The cartel victims were mainly public customers, Finnish Road Administration (Transport agency) and municipalities from all parts of Finland (covering 70% of the population). According to the Supreme Administrative Court the asphalt cartel operated at least from summer 1994 to winter 2002.

Investigations of the Finnish Competition Authority had started in 2002. On the proposal of the Finnish Competition Authority, the Supreme Administrative Court ordered on 29 September 2009 seven companies (Lemminkäinen Oyj, VLT-Trading Oy, Skanska Asfaltti Oy, NCC Roads Oy, SA-Capital Oy, Rudus Asfaltti Oy and Super Asfaltti Oy) to pay a total of €82.55 million. The fines imposed by the lower instance, Market Court, were increased due to the severity of the infringement and the nation-wide scope of it.

---

19 See *Manfredi*, para. 62.

20 Directive 2014/104/EU of the European Parliament and of the Council of 26 November 2014 on certain rules governing actions for damages under national law for infringements of the competition law provisions of the Member States and of the European Union, OJ L 329/1, 5.12.2014, later referred to as "Damages Directive". See on the aims of the directive e.g. Mosso, C. E.; Calisti, D.; Haasbeek, L., "The Commission proposal on Antitrust Damages Actions and the Future of Private Enforcement in the EU", *Finnish Competition Law Yearbook 2013* (2014), Kilpailuoikeudellinen Vuosikirja, p. 77.

21 A similar bid rigging case has been found also in some other European countries, for instance Sweden. Fines were imposed by the Swedish Market Court. The follow-on damage case was later settled.

3.1 The Asphalt Case – Facts and Figures

The asphalt cartel[22] resulted in 41 damages claims[23] from municipalities and the State Road Administration. The 40 municipalities and the Finnish state claimed compensation from eight defendants for damages allegedly suffered due to the cartel. The plaintiffs had purchased asphalting works from the largest companies in the industry that were found to have participated in the cartel. The cases were filed between the years 2008 and 2011 at the Helsinki District Court. The plaintiffs claimed compensation from above mentioned companies and one other company for the overcharges they had paid for paving work. The total amount of the claims was €122 million. The defendants contested the claims, *inter alia* it was submitted that the cartel had been unsuccessful and no overcharges had been imposed on the customers.

As it turned out, the court proceedings became, to say the least, voluminous. After preparation in writing, the District Court arranged two joint preparatory hearings, separate preparatory hearings for each claim during spring 2012 and a joint main hearing of seven months' duration in 2012-2013. More than 2,000 documents were submitted as evidence and 66 witnesses were heard during the main hearing. The combined number of pages in the judgments comes up to about 10,000. The economic evidence related to the causes of cartel damage was also extensive. Both plaintiffs and defendants had several economic studies made. One whole month of court main hearings was spent only to cross-examine the economic experts.[24]

3.2 Decision of the District Court

The District Court of Helsinki ruled on 41 cases on 28 November 2013. The 40 municipalities had claimed a total principal amount of €66 million in damages. The District Court awarded total damages of €37.5 million. The claim of one municipality was dismissed in its entirety, as the

---

22 Supreme Administrative Court's decision, 29 September 2009, register numbers 188/3/08, 189/3/08, 190/3/08, 191/3/08, 196/3/08, 197/3/08 and 199/3/08, file copy 2389.

23 See e.g. Pohjanpalo, L., "Huomioita asfalttikartellin vahingonkorvaustuomioista, Kilpailuoikeudellinen vuosikirja" p. 89 (*Finnish Yearbook on Competition Law 2013*, in Finnish); Laurila, H.; Kalliokoski, T., "Developments in Finnish Private Antitrust Litigation: Finland Fast-Forwards into the Future?", *ECLR* 2014, p. 519.

24 The Helsinki District Court was the first in Finland to use videoconferencing during the main hearing. During the asphalt cartel trial, instead of travelling to Helsinki three to four times a week during the seven-month main hearing, attorneys from law offices from outside Helsinki took part in the hearing via video links from their own localities. Up to ten attorneys at a time took part in the main hearing in this way.

municipality in question had not shown it had suffered any damage. As a result of the applicable limitation periods, a number of municipalities' claims were furthermore dismissed to the extent they had been addressed against companies other than the contracting party.

In line with earlier case law unrelated to competition law, the District Court held that the municipalities had a right to compensatory interest from the time the overcharge was paid until the time when overdue interest started to accrue. The compensatory interest is meant to compensate for inflation – today it is the reference rate of the European Central Bank. Overdue interest started to accrue only from the time when the respondents were served the writ of summons. On average, interest increased the awarded sums by about 50%. On the first sight, the average 50% increase on the awarded amounts seems like a substantial additional deterrence. Yet, as already commented, it must be borne in mind that from the first overcharges in 1994 to the District Court's judgment in 2013 Finland's consumer price index rose by 37%, eroding much of the real value of the increased award.[25]

Also the Finnish Road Construction Agency had purchased asphalting works from the companies having participated in the cartel and thus was one of the plaintiffs. However, the Court dismissed the claims for damages of the Agency due to the new evidence that, according to the court, suggested that a state-owned asphalt constructor had participated in the cartel.

The Finnish Road Construction Agency as well as some of the defendants have appealed the District Court decision before the Court of Appeal. The case is currently pending.

3.2.1 Evaluation of Damages

According to the District Court, most municipalities could not rely on the specific damage provision, section 18 a) of the previous Finnish Competition Act, applicable in this case as they were not considered to be undertakings as defined in the said act. However, the municipalities could invoke contractual liability against their contracting parties. Against the other respondents, the municipalities could rely on general tort liability. The District Court held that the other alleged legal grounds invoked by the claimants were not applicable.

The legal grounds for the damages were considered to be both contractual as well as tort law based. Firstly, the court held that participating in the cartel was a breach of the contract in the form of violation of the

25 See Laurila; Kalliokoski, *ECLR 2014*, cit., p. 523.

duty of loyalty. Secondly, in cases where damages were claimed from defendants other than the actual contracting parties, the damages were granted based on the Finnish Tort Liability Act.

Maybe the most awaited part of the decision was the evaluation of damages. There was no prior case law on cartel damages in Finland so a new territory was entered. There was (unsurprisingly) a dispute on the amount of damages. According to the plaintiffs the asphalt companies had run hard-core cartel and had succeeded in obtaining very substantial over-charges (even 30 to 50% in some cases) as a result of the bid rigging conspiracy. Defendants, on their turn, had argued that the cartel was unsuccessful and led to price wars and no overcharges had been imposed on the customers. Both parties had their economic experts and the court evaluated the credibility of these experts in its decision.

A basic economic method used by the court was to compare the prices before the cartel, during the cartel and after it has been detected, to try to eliminate the importance of other factors. Other key evidence used by the court was testimonial witnesses (industry experts), and documents. The court went into great detail in evaluating the evidence put forward by the parties. Also the (then draft) communication of DG Competition on estimation of the damages[26] was utilised by the court.

Four types of evidence were used:

- Testimonies of the economic experts;
- Evidence put forward by the parties on price movements;
- Testimonies and estimates of damage given by industry experts who had worked in the asphalt industry;
- Indirect documentary evidence on damages.

On balance the court found that the economic experts of the plaintiff were "somewhat more reliable" as their findings were better supported by other evidence in the file. On average an overcharge of 15%, in some cases 20% was found. It is interesting to note that the case did not turn out to be a (often feared) "clash of economist" that would be "beyond control of the legal profession". Nor did the court simply "guesstimate" damages without giving clear reasons for its decision as some commentators feared before the decision was given out.

In Finland, the court will in each case assess the relevance, materiality and weight of the evidence that the parties present during the proceedings

---

[26] Communication from the Commission on quantifying harm in actions for damages based on breaches of Article 101 or 102 of the Treaty on the Functioning of the European Union (Text with EEA relevance), OJ 2013/C 167/07.

and determine the outcome by applying the law to the facts that it finds have been established by the parties. Under the Procedural Code (Chapter 17, Article 6), as a rule, Finnish courts are entitled to award damages based on what they *estimate* constitutes reasonable compensation, in the event that the plaintiff has been able to prove that violation has taken place and causality exists but proof regarding the exact amount of the plaintiffs loss cannot be obtained or would be exceptionally difficult or costly to provide. In may be reminded that the damages directive 2014/104/EU[27] requires the adoption of a similar principle to be included in national law unless it already exists.

The district court quite cleverly used several yardsticks to evaluate the damage. Not only were the economists cross-examined for a significant period of time but also the credibility of their calculations was tested by comparing their premises and conclusions with the testimonial witnesses given by the industry experts. This way the court could combine "modern economic tools" as elaborated in the Commission's working paper on the calculation of damages with "more traditional tools" of damage law. Irrespective of what one thinks of the outcome of the case, the level of granularity in the elaborations of the district court on evaluation of the damage is laudable.

According to the District Court, an infringement decision does not as such reverse the burden of proof concerning the alleged damage. Thus, the claimants have to show that they have suffered damage also in claims related to competition law infringements. If this position is upheld by higher instances, the EU damages directive will have an effect in Finland as there is a rule for shift of burden of proof in cartel cases. The Damages Directive establishes a rebuttable presumption that cartels cause harm. This will facilitate compensation, given that victims often have difficulty in proving the harm they have suffered. This will facilitate compensation, given that victims often have difficulty in proving the harm they have suffered. The presumption is based on the finding that more than 90% of cartels cause a price increase (as found by an external study). In the very rare cases where a cartel does not cause price increases, infringers can still prove that their cartel did not cause harm.

Based on an overall assessment, the District Court found that as a starting point the asphalt cartel had caused damage to the municipality claimants. As the exact damage could not be established, the Court made

[27] Directive 2014/104/EU of the European Parliament and of the Council of 26 November 2014 on certain rules governing actions for damages under national law for infringements of the competition law provisions of the Member States and of the European Union (OJ L329/1, 05.12.2014) ("Antitrust Directive").

an estimate of the overcharge. According to the Damages Directive victims should obtain full compensation for the harm suffered, which covers compensation for actual loss and for loss of profit, plus payment of interest from the time the harm occurred until compensation is paid.

In this connection the court emphasized that Finnish law is based on the principle of full compensation, but that no statutory damages can be awarded. It concluded that the overcharge had mostly been 15%. However, there were several reasons why a number of municipalities had not suffered damage for all the years they had claimed. For example, a price war prevailed in the Finnish asphalt market in 1996-1997, and according to the Court contracts concluded during these years did not usually involve overcharging.

3.2.2 Knowledge of Infringement?

The State (Finnish Transport Agency) had claimed a compensation of a total of €56.7 million from the cartel companies. The District Court dismissed the action by the State in its entirety. The District Court had received partly new evidence after the trial at the Supreme Administrative Court, and the District Court has found that the National Board of Public Roads and the Finnish Road Enterprise participated in a cartel concerning work commissioned by the State from the year 1998 at least. In addition, representatives of the National Board of Public Roads have been aware of the existence of the cartel as early as 1994. The District Court considered that no damage has been caused to the State on the basis of the activity "which the State has approved at the time when it took place, which the State has participated in, and from which the State itself considers to have benefited from". The new evidence was that two employees of the Road Production had been sharing information with the asphalt cartel member companies in 2000 and 2001, possibly in 1999 and one person had taken part in a meeting in 2000 where projects had been discussed.

The Finnish Transport Administration had been divided in two organisations in 1998 – the Road Administration (Transport Agency), which is a public authority and buys road surfacing services, and Road Production, that provides the road surfacing service and competes as a business undertaking with privately owned asphalt companies. Irrespective of the division the District court concluded that the State is "one single unit" consisting of all its parts (authorities, agencies etc.) that do not have separate legal entities. Therefore, even if the buyer (Transport agency) did not know of the cartel the State was responsible and could not obtain any damages. Furthermore, the court felt that as the biggest buyer the State should have known of the cartel since 1994 and was regarded as participant in the asphalt cartel since 1998 due to another document from 1998 that the Finnish Competition had not regarded as incriminating evidence.

It may be recalled that according to the EU-court's preliminary ruling in *Courage vs. Crehan* (453/99) a party to a contract liable to restrict or distort competition within the meaning of Article 101 of the EU Treaty can rely on the breach of that provision to obtain relief from the other contracting party. Article 101 of the Treaty precludes a rule of national law under which a party to a contract liable to restrict or distort competition within the meaning of that provision is barred from claiming damages for loss caused by performance of that contract on the sole ground that the claimant is a party to that contract. Community law does not preclude a rule of national law barring a party to a contract liable to restrict or distort competition from relying on his own unlawful actions to obtain damages where it is established that that party bears significant responsibility for the distortion of competition. It is surprising that Courage was not even mentioned by the district court when it evaluated the right to damages of the Transport Agency under these new facts. According to Courage and Crehan not every participation in an illegal agreement bars the right to damages but there needs to be a serious liability. Hence, a more detailed view of the situation is required and the court analysis is lacking in that regard. Was there a significant responsibility of the State as the legal standard in "Courage"? Does the responsibility go timely backwards (cartel period was 1994 to 2002) and where did it actually start?

Also, it seems questionable whether it is correct to treat the State as "one single entity" in terms of competition law. In competition law it is an established principle that the notion of "undertaking" is a functional one (e.g. Höfner & Elsner, C-41/90). Under this principle, part of an authority, the "business" part of it, is regarded as an undertaking whereas the other part, the "authority" part, is not. The state's asphalt paving unit was a separate organizational unit within the state but not a separate legal entity. The District Court held that since sufficiently high-ranking employees of the state knew about the cartel (towards the end of the infringement), the state as a legal entity knew about the cartel, regardless of whether the state's other units knew about it. The District Court held the state had not suffered damage since it had accepted the infringement. The court did not give any weight to the separation of roles between seller (cartel participant) and buyer (cartel victim). It was not shown in the case that anyone on the buyer's side would have known about the cartel. Does knowledge of the seller mean loss of compensation for the buyer? What is the general importance of knowledge or suspicion of a cartel by a customer? The District Court decision departs from Courage and raises questions concerning the efficiency principle. *Inter alia*, the court seems to indicate that the reason for rejecting the damage claim for the whole cartel period (1994-2002) is that as a big player the State "should have known" of the cartel even before anyone knew about it.

It must be borne in mind that hard-core cartels operate secretly. That being said, industry customers often have a *suspicion* that something strange is happening on the sellers' side but as a customer it is practically very difficult to do anything concrete about that kind of suspicion before there is a final and binding decision of the competent competition authority on the infringement. Even if the cartel victims *know* about the cartel they may be unable to improve their situation before the competent authority has used its fact finding and decisional authority to bring the infringement to an end. It is submitted that if suspicion of a cartel waives the right to damages this does not meet the legal standard of *effective right to damages* as set out in Courage, for instance.

No doubt these (and other questions) will be elaborated in the Proceeding of the Helsinki Court of Appeal that started in February 2015.

3.2.3 Binding nature of national decisions

According to Article 16 (1) of the Regulation 1/2003, when national courts rule on agreements, decisions or practices under Article 101 or Article 102 TFEU which are already the subject of a Commission decision, they cannot take decisions running counter to the decision adopted by the Commission. As regards pending matters national courts must also avoid giving decisions which would conflict with a decision contemplated by the Commission in proceedings it has initiated. To that effect, the national court may assess whether it is necessary to stay its proceedings. In order to balance the independence of courts this obligation is without prejudice to the rights and obligations under Article 267 of the Treaty. Article 16 (2) of the Regulation 1/2003 deals with national competition authorities. When competition authorities of the Member States rule on agreements, decisions or practices under Article 101 or Article 102 of the Treaty which are already the subject of a Commission decision, they cannot take decisions which would run counter to the decision adopted by the Commission.

It has been for a long time clear that courts and national authorities cannot take decisions that run counter to the infringement decisions of the Commission or the EU-courts. The supremacy of EU-law over national law means that in case of conflict EU-law "breaks" national law and the conflicting national provision cannot be applied and the principle of sincere cooperation obligates the authorities of Member States not to take actions that would jeopardize the uniform application of EU law. Arguably Finnish competition law contains a similar provision. Section 8 of the Competition Act states that if a condition which is included in an agreement, statute, decision, or other legal act or arrangement infringes section 5 or 7, or Article 101 or 102 TFEU, or an injunction, prohibition or an obligation issued by the Market Court or by the FCCA, or a temporary injunction or an obligation issued by the FCCA, such a condition shall not be applied or implemented, unless otherwise ordered by the Market Court. This section remained nearly similar in the recent law reform. References to the Articles 101 and 102 TFEU were added alongside the updated references sections 5 and 7 of national law. Furthermore, it was added that the order, injunction or obligation given by the FCCA must be followed unless the Market Court orders otherwise. While this provision has the same function than Article 101 (2), i.e. it provides for the unenforceability of contract terms that violate the prohibitions on restrictive trade practices and abuse of dominant position, section 8 has been drafted in a somewhat similar manner to Article 16 of the regulation 1/2003. Hence it can be argued that it has a wider scope of application than a mere nullity provision that affects only the contract law in a two-party relation.[28]

In many Member States the situation is uncertain concerning the status of national infringement decisions and their binding effect on civil courts. Without clear rules or precedents, the defendants in a private damage action case could deny the existence of a competition law infringement that has already been established on the public enforcement side by the national competition authorities and competent appellate courts and the plaintiff would need to prove the infringement despite there being a national infringement decision. This could jeopardize the victim's right to effective damages as all arguments regarding the infringement would need to be run from the start in the civil court. The Damages Directive aims to avoid this by mandating that final infringement decisions by national authorities and courts shall be binding in subsequent damages proceedings in the same Member State. Similarly as a Commission infringement decision, a final infringement decision of a national competition authority will constitute full proof before civil courts in the same Member State that the infringement occurred. Before courts of other Member States, it will constitute at least prima facie evidence of such infringement.

As regards the situation in Finland, in the Asphalt Cartel, in terms of *res judicata effect of infringement decision*, the District Court held that it was bound by the decision of the Supreme Administrative Court to the

[28] Among other things, the predecessor of section 8, section 18 of the Law on Competition restrictions, has been used to delineate the power between Competition Council (Kilpailuneuvosto, predecessor of Market Court) and Labour Court (Työtuomioistuin).

extent the latter had investigated and ruled on the existence of the cartel, the participants and the length of their participation. That being said it remained possible to show that the infringement lasted longer than established in the infringement decision and that there were additional infringers. In other words, the national infringement decision defined the scope of the infringement, which could not be disputed and did not need to be proven in the damages proceedings. That being said the court found it possible to accept new evidence that, in its mind, was relevant to delineate the right to damages. It also disagreed with the FCCA on the evidentiary value of certain documents. This may raise questions under the Damages Directive.

3.2.4 Joint and several liability

Under the Finnish tort law the general principle is that in case several persons have caused damage by a joint action this creates a joint and several liability. Likewise, the Damages Directive stipulates that any participant in an infringement should be responsible towards the victims for the whole harm caused by the infringement (joint and several liability), with the possibility of obtaining a contribution from other infringers for their share of responsibility. However, the directive strikes a balance to protect leniency programs that seems somewhat foreign to damage law: joint and several liability will not apply to infringers which obtained immunity from fines in return for their voluntary cooperation with a competition authority during an investigation; these companies will normally be obliged to compensate only their own customers. Furthermore, a narrow exception from joint and several liability is foreseen under certain conditions for SMEs that would go bankrupt as a consequence of the normal rules on joint and several liability.

In the Asphalt case all the infringers were held jointly and severally liable for all the damage suffered by a claimant during their participation in the cartel. The District Court argued that the cartel's effectiveness was dependent on the cartel members following the cartel agreement. Market sharing and bid-rigging were possible only through the infringers' joint efforts. In other words, every cartel member made it possible for the other members to overcharge their customers so all the members caused the overcharge together. Therefore, a causal connection existed between all the infringers and each instance of overcharging. Indeed, a cartel infringement is possible only jointly and the effectiveness of a cartel presupposes collective market power, which on its turn requires that all or at least most players adhere to the cartel agreement. The District Court held that the respondents were jointly and severally liable, but each respondent only for the time period it had participated in the infringement. If a municipality's right to claim damages against any of the participants in the infringement had become time-barred, it could thereafter claim damages only from its contracting party (provided that the claim was not time-barred against that contracting party). As to the internal division of liability between the respondents, the contracting party was held responsible for the entire damage.

3.2.5 Economic Succession or Zombie Liability?

The judgment in the Asphalt case also contains an interesting interpretation concerning the application of economic succession. Some cartel-companies had been acquired by companies with no participation in the asphalt cartel. The non-infringing companies subsequently transferred to themselves the assets of the acquired companies and continued the same business. The now empty acquired companies were put into voluntary liquidation and wound-up. In the public enforcement proceedings, the transfer of business meant that the new owners had the liability for the hidden antitrust liability. There is nothing new in this regard. It is well known that the antitrust liability passes on to the new owner in mergers and acquisition. The buyer can try to protect himself with due-diligence and covenants that protect him in case a hidden antitrust liability pops up. Supreme Administrative Court imposed *fines* on the acquiring (non-infringing) companies on the basis of economic succession. At the time, the doctrine was not codified into the Finnish Competition Act although one can pinpoint to some old Finnish precedents. The Supreme Administrative Court applied EU law directly, finding that the doctrine was well established in the CJEU's case law.[29]

In the *damage* case proceedings, the defendants argued that economic succession did not apply to damages and was not a doctrine of private law. This led to the question, whether there still is a suitable defendant left to answer the damage suits as regards the transferred business. The District Court first analysed whether the plaintiffs' right to damages had ceased when the infringing companies were wound up. It concluded that this was not the case. As the next step the court considered whether the doctrine of economic succession was part of Finnish national law in antitrust damages. It concluded that it was not. Under national law, the claimants could only bring their claims against the wound-up infringing companies. Since those companies had ceased their business activity

[29] On the public enforcement side it is known since the seminal Suiker Unie case (Coöperatieve Vereniging "Suiker Unie" UA and others v Commission of the European Communities. Joined cases 40 to 48, 50, 54 to 56, 111, 113 and 114-73, ECR 1975 p. 01663) and many EU-cases thereafter that the new owner of a company or buyer of its assets can be liable for a competition law infringement a company that has happened in the past.

and had no assets, recovery of compensation seemed very unlikely. The District Court found such relief insufficient because the national remedies available endangered the effectiveness of EU competition law. As a third step the District Court applied the efficiency principle it had found in EU-precedents, in particular in Courage. The District Court held that the non-infringing companies were held liable for the damage caused by the infringing companies whose assets they had acquired, just as they had in the public enforcement proceedings for the cartel fines. The District Court argued that the right to antitrust damages is a special type of damages remedy where priority must be given to the objectives and principles of competition law. Furthermore it stated that the public and private enforcement of EU competition law form one enforcement system with shared objectives. This enforcement system should therefore be seen as a whole. The efficiency principle can under certain circumstances necessitate economic succession in public enforcement. As a mirror image to the decision of the Supreme Administrative Court the same must therefore apply to private enforcement as well.

The District Court stated that if economic succession were applied differently in public and private enforcement, a cartel perpetrator would have to pay fines to the state but could escape paying damages to injured parties. The Court considered that such an outcome would be both strange and unacceptable. The District Court held that, taking into account the need for efficient application of EU competition law, the same principle is applicable also in private enforcement actions. Thus, the companies that had acquired asphalt businesses that had participated in the infringement could be held liable for the actions of and damage caused by the sellers.[30]

The District Court's argumentation is quite interesting because the court did not merely follow EU precedent but also created a precedent of its own. The court held that the EU-courts judgments did not prevent the application of economic succession to antitrust damages. The fact that the court – rightly or wrongly – held that economic succession was not possible under the national damage law could be contested, but the interesting part of the decision is the application of the *efficiency principle*. If "lifting the corporate veil" remains not possible, the other alternative available to the court would have been to rule that these originally infringing but subsequently empty acquired companies would have been declared as "suitable defendants". However, at this point of time the active life of these companies had ended; they were in dormant state and no longer had any assets. So going that route would mean, in practice, that the cartel

30 For the District Court's Decision see also Laurila; Kalliokoski, *ECLR 2014*, cit., pp. 521-522.

victims would most likely go empty-handed as nothing could be collected because all the assets had been moved to other (non-infringing) companies. These companies were merely empty cores left without blood, already lying in the grave. The only reason to wake them up from their eternal sleep would be to have them answer to these lawsuits. One could say that these empty companies were like a "living dead" or a "zombie". It is understandable that this kind of *liability of the living dead – zombie liability* – did not seem an appealing choice.

4. Other Finnish damage action cases

4.1 Hydrogen Peroxide Cartel

The *Hydrogen Peroxide case* is based on a cartel decision adopted by the European Commission in 2006 for a bleaching chemicals cartel. According to the findings of the European Commission in decision COMP/38.620 of 3 May 2006 – Hydrogen Peroxide, the cartel members had fixed and monitored target prices, allocated market shares and customers, exchanged confidential information and limited production. One of the fined undertakings was a Finnish company, Kemira. In 2011 CDC HP filed an action against Kemira in the District Court claiming €21 million in damages. Prior to the filing of the action, two original cartel victims, Finnish pulp and paper companies had sold their damage claims resulting from the Hydrogen Peroxide Cartel as regards hydrogen peroxide purchased from Kemira to CDC HP. CDC HP enforces these claims under its own name and on its own account and risk. It is a company specializing in cartel claims. Therefore it could use its specific technical and economical know-how in relation to the quantification of cartel-related damages in the European hydrogen peroxide market. CDC is a Belgian-registered company specialized in enforcing claims of cartel victims. As we can see, *Adam Smith's needle example on specialization* has reached the private antitrust enforcement.

In an interim judgment in July 2013, the District Court ruled e.g. on the limitation period and assignability of claims and allowed the case to proceed. The interim judgment of the Helsinki District Court deals with a number of preliminary questions raised by Kemira. The Court rejected Kemira's preliminary pleas on which the court ruled in this judgment, confirming a) its jurisdiction over the matter, b) that the damage claims are not time barred in light of the limitation periods commencing by knowledge, and c) the validity of the claims transfer. Firstly, the Court concluded that CDC HP's claims are not arising out of the supply agreements between Kemira and the pulp and paper companies, i.e. confirming the tortious nature of cartel damage claims. Based on the evidence presented, the court concluded that these claims are not subject to contractual arbitration clauses contained in supply agreements: as the cartel was secret, the parties did not explicitly agree that the arbitration clauses would also cover possible claims based on competition law infringements. In other words, the court used the secrecy of a cartel arrangement to conclude that the other party could and would not have agreed on an arbitration clause for this kind of matter. Secondly, the Court dealt with the applicable limitation periods. It concluded that the limitation periods based on knowledge did not start prior to the date of adoption of the fining decision by the European Commission on 3 May 2006. The Court thus rebutted the argument that the limitation period started prior to that date, and particularly held that knowledge could not be presumed on the basis of price increase announcements by the cartel members or press articles on the investigation, including a stock exchange release of Kemira confirming the receipt of a statement of objections. Thirdly, the Court confirmed the validity of the transfer of claims to CDC HP. The damaged pulp and paper companies had primarily tried to settle the claims with Kemira out of court. After the talks had failed, they decided to sell the claims to CDC HP which, due to its particular know-how and market knowledge, was in view of the companies better placed to successfully enforce the claims. The Court did *not*, therefore, see grounds to conclude that the transfer of the claims would amount to a "sham transaction".

Shortly before the main hearing was about to start in June 2014, Kemira and CDC HP settled the case for €18.5 million and legal costs.

4.2 Timber Purchasing Cartel

The *Timber Purchasing Cartel Case* was composed of three Finnish pulp and paper companies, UPM, Stora-Enso and Metsäliitto, that buy most of the timber in Finland. These companies operated a timber buyers' cartel.

In its decision the Market Court found the forestry companies Metsäliitto Osuuskunta, Stora Enso Oyj and UPM-Kymmene Oyj guilty of national forbidden price cooperation and sharing of procurement sources in the purchase of raw wood during 1997–2004. It was a price-fixing cartel formed by the purchasing party. The directors in charge of forestry had e.g. convened regularly to discuss issues pertaining to the availability and price of timber. The development of the procurement price of timber had been examined in the light of statistical information per forestry centre and timber assortment. The company price had been compared to average price or the price of other companies. No specific decisions were made in the meetings but they sought to influence future pricing. The regional heads had also discussed issues relating to the availability and price of timber. The price development was examined in the light of statistics per timber assortment and even per municipality. The regional heads reported their own procurement prices to each other, and these were compared to the average prices. No exact prices were agreed on in these meetings but the aim was to influence future timber trade so as to stabilise price development. The Market Court imposed a fine in 2009 following a leniency application by one of the cartel members, UPM.

The Timber Purchasing Cartel[31] initially resulted in over 700 damages claims, the total sum of which amounts to over €230 million. The majority of the claims filed were made by private individuals. However, the largest single claim, a claim for about €160 million, has been raised by Metsähallitus, which administers state-owned land and water areas. In addition, there are about forty claims made by municipalities and some by undertakings.

On 28 March 2014, the District Court of Helsinki gave 13 decisions regarding private forest owners dismissing the claims due to them being time-barred. District Court had held that the limitation period started from the date that the FCCA had stated in public that it had initiated its investigations regarding the cartel. The same court (albeit in a different composition) had found in *Asphalt*, *Hydro Peroxide* and *Car Spare Parts* that the limitation period starts to run when the public decision on competition law infringement is final, i.e. is no longer appealable. The matter regarding the statute of limitations had gone before the district court to be solved as a preliminary question. The majority of the court held that the claims were time-barred based on Section 18 a) of the Act on Competition Restrictions (480/1992) and the Act on Statute of Limitations (728/2003). One of the judges gave a dissenting opinion and would have approved the claims.[32] The majority of the District Court based its decision, among

31 Market Court's decision, 3 Dec. 2009, MAO 614/09, register number 407/06/KR.

32 Section 18 a) of the old Act on Competition Restrictions on the damages caused by competition restrictions came into force on 1 October 1998. As for the purchases of raw wood that had taken place before that date, the court held that the limitation period should have been interrupted within ten years of each payment of the purchase price instalments, since the payment was considered to be the time when the damage was incurred. As such interruption had not taken place, the claims were held time-barred. According to section 18 a), the right to receive damages will expire unless the action for damages has been filed five years from the date the injured party found out, or should have found out that the damage occurred. As for the purchases that had taken place after the enactment of section 18 a), the majority of the court held that the limitation period had started from the date of the announcement of the FCCA on 25 May 2004, according to which it investigates a suspected cartel in the procurement of raw wood. The majority of the court considered that after the announcement the plaintiffs should have had all the information in order to able to examine whether the cartel had caused them damage. The court also considered the claims expired based on Section 7 of the Act on Statute of Limitations, according to which the beginning of the

other things, on the fact that the leniency applicant (UPM) had filed a press release on the leniency application, and "UPM could expect that the limitation periods start to run from this "admission of guilt". Finnish Competition Authority had likewise informed publicly about the investigation and cartel suspicion which created "public expectation of an outcome" in the case. On the other hand, the other cartel participants, Stora-Enso and Metsäliitto, had denied their participation in a cartel in their own press releases, as well as later in Market Court. The guilt question was finally settled in the decision of the Market Court.

It is submitted that the majority view of the District Court is problematic as it would have forced forest owners to file damage actions before they can actually know whether the suspicion is right and whether they are personally harmed by the cartel or not and if so, how much. As cartels are normally secret, as a matter of practice, potential cartel victims can evaluate their position with any certainty first when the competition authority's decision finding the infringement is final because only at this stage all the relevant details become public and final in the sense that a follow-on action can be based on the final decision that defines the infringement and its scope in terms of time period, products covered and geographic scope. It is submitted that the majority view would make the claiming of damages at the very least very difficult, if not impossible. As discussed above, according to EU case law procedural rules must not render practically impossible or excessively difficult the exercise of the right to seek compensation for the harm caused by a competition law infringement.[33]

On 21 November 2014, the Court of Appeal of Helsinki repealed the decision of the District Court and unanimously held that the claims are not time-barred. According to the Court of Appeal the limitation period has started from the date that the decision of the Market Court finding the defendants having participated into the cartel has gained legal force, i.e. from January 2010. The cases have been returned to the District Court continued proceedings. Apparently the decision was reached on the basis of national law. The decision is subject to appeal to the Supreme Court.

According to news in the media the decision of the Court of Appeal has encouraged hundreds of private forest owners to take new legal actions. The issues raised in the proceedings are similar to the asphalt cartel case and include questions on statute of limitations, grounds for claiming

limitation likewise is connected to the knowledge of the damage by the injured party. The limitation period of the Act on Statute of Limitations is three years.

33 See e.g. *Manfredi*, para. 62.

damages and the amount of damages claimed. Like in the asphalt case one key question is likely to be the amount of the cartel surplus.

4.3 Car Spare Parts Cartel

In the *Car Spare Parts Cartel*, a car spare parts wholesaler claimed damages from five competitors. The claimant demanded €57 million for market foreclosure that caused the claimant's new retail chain concept to fail commercially. In the infringement proceedings, one of the defendants received leniency. The others were fined a total of €1 million by the Supreme Administrative Court in 2012 for exchanging information on future pricing behaviour regarding the claimant's retail chain. In March 2014, the District Court dismissed the claim because it found no causal connection between the infringement and the alleged harm. The Car Spare Parts Cartel Damage Case is quite different from the other 3 cases discussed above. In Asphalt and Hydrogen Peroxide cases the plaintiffs effectively sued for the overcharge (cartel surplus) caused by the cartel, i.e. the overcharge. The cartel overcharge can be evaluated by comparing prices before, after and during the cartel period. While there are many difficulties on the road, methodologically calculating the cartel surplus is a relatively "straight-forward" issue. However, damage claim was more difficult if not shaky in the Car Spare Parts case that dealt with a situation where a business plan could not be fulfilled as a result of a boycott. Also the Commission's guidance paper makes it clear that it is more difficult to establish "dynamic losses" based on claimed exclusion from the market than to calculate "cartel surplus" and the "loss of trading" partners in a price fixing case. The district court found, *inter alia* on the basis of a large number of witness statements, that the business plan of the cartel victim had been risky and had fallen apart due to other reasons than the (short lived) boycott arrangement. This case is a healthy reminder that there is no right to damages even when the existence of an Article 101 violation has been proven unless also the damage and the causality of it are proven.

The plaintiff has appealed and the case is now pending in the Helsinki Court of Appeals.

5. Conclusions on the Road

Finnish private enforcement has developed rapidly in recent years. While only a few years ago there was no case law on antitrust damages, now several important cases are pending and first big decisions are out. Finnish private enforcement has taken big steps forward and can now be regarded as one of those EU Member States where private enforcement plays a prominent role and is relatively well advanced. So far, it seems, the Finnish court system has been able to deal with the complex questions, peculiarities and challenges of the private enforcement quite well.

The Asphalt Cartel judgment contains important, yet not final interpretations of national and EU law in private antitrust damages claims. The same goes for the other judgments that have been discussed in this article. It is far too early to say what the effect of the EU Damages directive will be in Finland. This is because the case law is still emerging. Definitive answers can be given only at a point of time when there are final decisions in the pending cases. If we take a snapshot of the situation of today, it appears that the Finnish system is broadly consistent with the baseline of the Damages Directive. Of course the legislative contains also new issues. For instance, the Damages Directive aims at making it easier to access to evidence necessary in actions for antitrust damages. If a party needs documents that are in the hands of other parties or third parties to prove a claim or a defence, it may obtain a court order for the disclosure of those documents. Current Finnish rules on edition of documents seem narrower.

A lot has been written about the question whether competition law enforcement should be based on *public enforcement* or *private enforcement*. The author submits that public and private enforcement not only theoretically but also practically *complement* each other and are both very much needed. It is sometimes argued that public enforcement of antitrust law is based on "public interest" whereas private enforcement is based on "private monetary interest" of the claimants. The author thinks that the painted picture is imprecise as it is forgotten that also complainants and defendants in public enforcement cases are companies that, according to their commercial statutes, pursue "private monetary interests". So in reality while there are many obvious differences, there is little "moral difference" between private and public enforcement. In both cases it is in the hands of a public authority, an antitrust authority or a court, to have a final say.

If one has to answer the question whether competition law is in public or private interest the answer has to be *both*. In order to achieve this, "any individual" has the right to claim damages for loss caused to him by conduct that restricts or distorts competition, or to file actions based on nullity (unenforceability) of harmful competition restrictions. At the same time the existence of private rights strengthens both EU and national antitrust rules and discourages agreements or practices, frequently covert, which are liable to restrict or distort competition. Institutionally, restitution and prevention shake hands. Hence, private enforcement can and should make a significant contribution to the maintenance of effective competition. In Europe, the importance of private enforcement is possibly increased by the fact that in many EU countries public enforcement levels have gone down in recent years. In this sense private enforcement can give new energy to the at times stalling public enforcement.

Bibliography

Laurila, H.; Kalliokoski, T., "Developments in Finnish Private Antitrust Litigation: Finland Fast-Forwards into the Future?", *ECLR* 2014.

Mosso, C. E.; Calisti, D.; Haasbeek, L., "The Commission proposal on Antitrust Damages Actions and the Future of Private Enforcement in the EU", *Finnish Competition Law Yearbook 2013* (2014).

Pohjanpalo, L., "Huomioita asfalttikartellin vahingonkorvaustuomioista, Kilpailuoikeudellinen vuosikirja", *Finnish Yearbook on Competition Law 2013*, (in Finnish).

Is this really a reform to facilitate follow-on actions for antitrust damages?

Some thoughts on the Damages Directive

Anna Piszcz[1]

1. Introductory thoughts

In traditional thinking about antitrust enforcement in Europe, private enforcement was something marginal, intangible and almost hardly worth analysing. Antitrust enforcement usually meant public enforcement by competition agencies. In the 2000s, the shift to a different way of thinking about antitrust enforcement happened with the European Court of Justice judgments as well as the European Commission's Green and White Papers. It was noticed that Europe needed to improve the system of civil law redress without simply encouraging more litigation.

After years of work, on 11 June 2013 the European Commission adopted a package of measures to tackle the problem of the lack of efficient private enforcement of European Union (EU) competition law in the EU Member States. In particular a proposal for a Directive on actions for damages[2] (hereafter: Directive or Damages Directive) accompanied by the Impact Assessment and its Executive Summary, a non-binding Communication[3] and a Practical Guide to the quantification of harm in antitrust infringements,[4] as well as a horizontal Recommendation

---

1 Associate Professor, Faculty of Law, University of Białystok, Temporary on Duty of Chairman of the Department of Public Economic Law, Member of the Advisory Board to the Polish national competition authority.

2 Proposal for a Directive of the European Parliament and of the Council on certain rules governing actions for damages under national law for infringements of the competition law provisions of the Member States and of the European Union, COM (2013) 404 final, 11.06.2013.

3 Communication from the Commission on quantifying harm in actions for damages based on breaches of Article 101 or 102 of the Treaty on the Functioning of the European Union (2013/C 167/07), OJ C 167/19, 13.06.2013.

4 Commission Staff Working Document – Practical guide: Quantifying harm in actions for damages based on breaches of Article 101 or 102 of the Treaty on the Functioning of the European Union, C (2013) 3440, 11.06.2013.

on collective redress[5] were adopted to meet the need for a coherent European approach to private enforcement of EU competition law. On 26 November 2014 the Damages Directive was finally adopted.[6] Is the Directive able to create the one-size-fits-all culture when it comes to follow-on actions for damages? Is the Directive capable of facilitating such actions?

As it was rightly observed in section 10 of the Executive Summary, a private action can be brought before a court without a prior decision ("stand-alone action") adopted by a competition authority, hereafter also as CA, or once a CA has found an infringement of EU competition rules ("follow-on action"), which is more frequent. It is argued there that private and public enforcement are complementary tools for the effective application of EU competition law and they interact with each other in a few ways. The first central aspect of this interaction is the effect of antitrust decisions on civil proceedings. Its second aspect is the access to information held by the CAs. The last one is related to limitation periods on bringing a damages action.

In this chapter I set out a classification of relationships between CAs' infringement proceedings and civil proceedings for damages. I argue that the final choice of the solution to the effect of national decisions problem was not the best of three options considered. Firstly, the draft of June 2013 provided for a (German-like) cross-border binding effect. Secondly, in November 2013 the authors of the revised draft introduced the double standard and resulting: (1) non-cross-border irrefutably probative effect, (2) cross-border probative effect. Thirdly, the final version of the Directive maintains the non-cross-border irrefutably probative effect and introduces "at least half-probative" cross-border effect.

The chapter proceeds with comments to the access to information held by the CAs. Finally, I offer a short review of the real achievements of the Directive in the field of limitation periods on bringing a damages action.

2. Effect of decisions

The first set of challenges comes from the effect of decisions adopted by CAs. How are they dealt with by courts in civil proceedings for

5 Commission Recommendation of 11 June 2013 on common principles for injunctive and compensatory collective redress mechanisms in the Member States concerning violations of rights granted under Union Law (2013/396/EU), OJ L 201/60, 26.07.2013.

6 Directive 2014/104/EU of the European Parliament and of the Council of 26 November 2014 on certain rules governing actions for damages under national law for infringements of the competition law provisions of the Member States and of the European Union, OJ L 349/1, 05.12.2014.

damages? The following table summarises the range of possible options for dealing with decisions in civil proceedings for damages.

Table. Types of relationships between CAs' infringement proceedings and civil proceedings for damages

<table>
<tr><th>Model</th><th colspan="3">Relationship from the perspective of the conduct of proceedings</th><th colspan="2">Relationship from the perspective of the effect of decision</th></tr>
<tr><td>ABSOLUTE AUTONOMY
(1)+(A)</td><td colspan="3">(1) obligation to conduct both (no possibility to suspend one proceedings because of the other one)</td><td>(A) autonomy (no effect of a decision; courts conduct evidentiary proceedings as if the decision was never taken)</td><td></td></tr>
<tr><td>PARTIAL DEPENDENCE
(2)(a)(i)+(B)</td><td rowspan="3">(2) dependence of civil proceedings on a decision of CA in the form of:</td><td rowspan="2">(a) probative effect of decision:</td><td>(i) rebuttable presumptions or only evidence</td><td rowspan="3">(B) the court's obligation to suspend proceedings or temporary inadmissibility of action (it is rejected)</td><td rowspan="3">(C) court's right to choose between conducting proceedings or suspension thereof</td></tr>
<tr><td>ABSOLUTE DEPENDENCE
(2)(a)(ii)+(B)</td><td>(ii) irrebuttable presumptions</td></tr>
<tr><td>ABSOLUTE DEPENDENCE
(2)(b)+(B)</td><td colspan="2">(b) binding effect of decisions</td></tr>
<tr><td colspan="5">Model:</td><td>PARTIAL DEPENDENCE
(2)+(C)</td></tr>
</table>

Source: the author's own study

The relationship between CAs' infringement proceedings and civil proceedings for damages can be analysed from the perspective of both the effect of the decision (effect of antitrust decision on civil proceedings) and the conduct of proceedings (effect of antitrust proceedings on civil proceedings).

The absolute autonomy model should not be advised (irrespective of the jurisdiction). If the possibility of follow-on actions is not kept open, public antitrust enforcement cannot facilitate access to private enforcement. Separated and independent proceedings can lead to different outcomes for the same factual situation. Moreover, it would most likely increase the workload of civil courts (courts for civil litigation). They could not draw upon the CAs' findings although those courts are often not well equipped to look into antitrust. This might not generate cost savings.

The only efficiency which we can possibly associate with the absolute autonomy model seems to stem from an assumption that it would remove possible concerns around the doctrine of separation of powers (in this context, executive and judiciary). These concerns can be found in particular in the absolute dependence model (where the court is obliged to suspend proceedings or there is temporary inadmissibility of action and the awaited decision has a binding effect or irrefutably probative effect on civil proceedings).

With respect to the European Commission's antitrust decisions, the partial dependence model can be derived from Article 16 of Regulation 1/2003.[7] The first sentence in paragraph 1 provides that national courts, when ruling on agreements, decisions or practices under Article 101 or Article 102 TFEU which are already the subject of a Commission decision, cannot take decisions running counter to the decision adopted by the Commission. As, at the same time, the second sentence obliges them to avoid giving decisions which would conflict with a decision contemplated by the Commission in proceedings it has initiated, national courts may assess whether it is necessary to stay their proceedings. In this EU model the courts' right to choose between conducting proceedings or suspension thereof is combined with the cross-border binding effect of the European Commission's decisions.

As of 1 May 2004, responsibility for the enforcement of EU competition law has been decentralised and to some extent hived off to national competition authorities of the Member States, hereafter also as NCAs. Now NCAs take decisions about cases that transcend their borders. How do national courts treat NCAs' infringement decisions for the purpose of proceedings for damages? For example, in the UK, courts are bound by infringement decisions of the UK's CA (the Competition and Markets Authority) but there are no comparable provisions for decisions of NCAs of other Member States.[8] This is the non-cross-border binding effect of antitrust decisions. In Germany, the national courts' duty is extended to final infringement decisions by all NCAs throughout the EU.[9] This is the

---

7 Council Regulation No. 1/2003 of 16.12.2002 on the implementation of the rules on competition laid down in Articles 81 and 82 of the Treaty, OJ L 1/1, 04.01.2003.

8 See also Howard, A., "Too little, too late? The European Commission's Legislative Proposals on Anti-Trust Damages Actions", *Journal of European Competition Law & Practice*, 4 (6) (2013), p. 457. It is regulated similarly in the Czech Republic. See Uřičař, M., "Evidence in Competition Law Cases: Problems in Czech Law", in Basedow, J.; Terhechte, J.; Tichý, L. (eds.), *Private Enforcement of Competition Law*. Baden-Baden: Nomos, 2011, p. 147.

9 See §33(4) of the Act against Restraints of Competition in the version published on 15 July 2005 (*Bundesgesetzblatt* (Federal Law Gazette) I, p. 2114; 2009 I p. 3850), as

cross-border binding effect of national decisions. On the other hand, in Poland, the effect of antitrust decisions, be it decisions of the Polish NCA (President of the Office for Competition and Consumers Protection, in Polish *Prezes Urzędu Ochrony Konkurencji i Konsumentów*) or NCAs of other Member States, is not dealt with in the national legislation and even the newest jurisprudence on the effect of antitrust decisions of the Polish NCA is divergent, which creates legal uncertainty. The first, general, line of cases considers administrative decisions as only evidence which may be assessed in civil proceedings along with any other material brought by the parties,[10] the second line provides for the (non-cross-border) binding effect of national final infringement decisions,[11] and the third line suggests that the very commencement of antitrust proceedings precludes courts from independently examining the anti-competitiveness of a given market conduct (the effect of national antitrust proceedings).[12]

The German-like cross-border binding effect of national antitrust decisions was provided for in Article 9 of the draft Directive published in June 2013. However, national judiciaries prefer to enjoy discretion with regard to findings contained in infringement decisions adopted in other Member States. This seems to have been considered by the Council. After works in the Council, since November 2013 Article 9 of the draft Directive provided for the double standard, different attitude to non-cross-border (own NCA's decisions) and cross-border ("foreign"/other NCAs' decisions) effect. It offered wordings descending from previous German-like binding effect to non-cross-border (irrefutably) probative effect ("Member States shall ensure that an infringement of competition law found by a final decision of a national competition authority or a review court is deemed to be irrefutably established for the purposes of

last amended by Article 3 of the Act of 26 July 2011 (Federal Law Gazette I, p. 1554); available at http://www.gesetze-im-internet.de/englisch_gwb/englisch_gwb.html (accessed on 9.02.2015).

10 See the resolution of the Supreme Court of 9.10.2007, III CZP 46/07, LEX No. 298665.

11 In particular the resolution of the Supreme Court of 23.07.2008, III CZP 52/08, (2009) 2 *Monitor Prawniczy* 90. On the resolution see Piszcz, A., "Still-unpopular Sanctions: Developments in Private Antitrust Enforcement in Poland After the 2008 White Paper", *Yearbook of Antitrust and Regulatory Studies* 5 (7) (2012), pp. 62-66; Jurkowska-Gomułka, A., "W stronę umocnienia prywatnoprawnego wdrażania zakazów praktyk ograniczających konkurencję – glosa do uchwały SN z 23.07.2008 r. (III CZP 52/08)", 5 (2010) *Europejski Przegląd Sądowy,* pp. 43-48.

12 Judgement of the Court of Appeals in Warsaw of 25 November 2009, VI ACa 422/09, LEX No. 1120262. See also Piszcz, A., "Polish civil procedure and antitrust enforcement – recent developments from the standpoint of efficiency", in *Recent trends in economy and efficiency of civil procedure*. Vilnius: Vilnius University Press, 2013, p. 283.

an action for damages brought before their national courts") and cross-border probative effect ("Member States shall ensure that a final decision [...] given in another Member State can be presented before their national courts as evidence, among others, of the fact that an infringement of competition law has occurred").

Finally, in the last version of Article 9 paragraph 1 of the Directive the irrefutable (irrefutable, absolute) presumption of an infringement (found by NCA or by a review court) has been maintained but in paragraph 2 it is stated that "Member States shall ensure that where a final decision referred to in paragraph 1 is taken in another Member State, that final decision may, in accordance with national law, be presented before their national courts as at least prima facie evidence that an infringement of competition law has occurred and, as appropriate, may be assessed along with any other evidence adduced by the parties". This can be considered "at least half-probative" cross-border effect of national decisions.

Is this choice capable of facilitating follow-on actions? In general it is better to have Article 9 than to have nothing. But have the previous versions been less accurate? In the first version the phrase "courts cannot take decisions running counter to such finding of an infringement" could have raised doubts as to whether courts would be bound also by the finding of fault if it was made by the NCA against an infringer (defendant). The hurdle was also what, if anything, could be done if while deciding the case the other Member State's NCA did not respect fundamental procedural rights of the parties involved or obvious errors occurred. As the Committee on Economic and Monetary Affairs in the European Parliament has remarked in the draft report on the proposal for the Directive, "the binding effect shall not apply in cases where obvious errors occurred during the investigation of facts or where the rights of the defendant were not duly respected during the procedure before the national competition authority or competition court".[13] On the other hand, the wording of Article 9 was modelled on that of Article 16 in Regulation 1/2003 and therefore, in effect, its future interpretation seemed facilitated.

Is the fear of the differences in procedural standards between Member States a sufficient reason for a minimum harmonisation clause in Article 9 paragraph 2? In my opinion, the authors should have thought of the need for avoiding inducements to forum shopping. And maximum (full)

---

13 Available at http://www.europarl.europa.eu/sides/getDoc.do?pubRef=-%2F%2FEP%2F%2FNONSGML%2BCOMPARL%2BPE-516.968%2B01%2BDOC%2BPDF%2BV0%2F%2FEN (accessed 09.02.2015).

harmonisation is undeniably the way to avoid forum shopping.[14] To the contrary, the adopted minimum harmonisation clause may provoke even more forum shopping than already exists in antitrust damages cases.

An important problem here is that there may be different interpretations of the concept of "prima facie evidence" in Member States. In Poland, it is a matter of argument. One of the interpretations is that "prima facie evidence" makes the existence of certain facts only plausible.[15] If this approach was taken as a model for the interpretation of the concept of "prima facie evidence", Article 9 paragraph 2 of the Directive would not improve the claimants' position at all. To do so, a legal rule whereby decisions issued by other EU NCAs make an infringement of competition law plausible would have to be accompanied by a provision stating that making an infringement plausible is sufficient, without the need of evidence. Otherwise, decisions of other EU NCAs would only be a "beginning of the proof" and eventually an infringement of competition law would have to be proven. From this point of view, one could imagine that the version of Article 9 paragraph 2 which was devised in November 2013 and left no room for such doubts would be much easier to comply with by all Member States.[16]

As of now, it is unknown whether the Member States choose the above minimal solution ("prima facie evidence", "half-probative" cross-border effect of decisions), the highest standard solution (German-like) or one of the options in-between. However, if claimants had at their disposal a final decision adopted by any EU NCA, then, from the perspective of the effects of such decision, they would favour jurisdictions where courts are bound by such decisions (German-like). Going to a national judiciary that may freely assess the probative value of such decisions would risk that an infringement might ultimately not be proven.[17]

It seems that it would be much better if the borderline between the binding or irrefutably probative effect and probative effect was not drawn to separate own NCA's decisions from other NCAs' decisions. The borderline between the binding or irrefutably probative effect and probative effect (or rather no effect at all) could have been drawn to separate

14 The phenomenon of forum shopping is analysed in many aspects in Basedow, J.; Francq, S.; Idot, L., *International Antitrust Litigation: Conflict of Laws and Coordination*. Oxford: Hart Publishing, 2012, pp. 6-7, 46-47, 52-53, 409-410, etc.

15 See Piszcz, A. in Pais, S. O.; Piszcz, A., "Package on Actions for Damages Based on Breaches of EU Competition Rules: Can One Size Fit All?", *Yearbook of Antitrust and Regulatory Studies* 7 (10) (2014), pp. 232-233.

16 *Ibid.*

17 *Ibid.*

legitimate decisions from decisions in cases where obvious errors occurred during the investigation of facts or where the fundamental rights of the defendant were not duly respected during the procedure before the NCA or competition court (to separate a rule from exceptions). But for this purpose a national decision would have to be forwarded to the court together with NCA's files of the case.

Another issue worth noting concerns the lack of the effect of antitrust proceedings on civil proceedings in Article 9 of the Directive. In this it differs from Article 16 of Regulation 1/2003 which provides for the optionally suspending effect of the commencement of the Commission's antitrust proceedings. Moreover, it also differs from Article 18 paragraph 2 of the Directive which, with regard to consensual dispute resolution concerning the claim covered by the action for damages, obliges Member States to ensure (without prejudice to provisions of national law in matters of arbitration) that national courts seized of that action for damages may suspend their proceedings for up to two years where the parties thereto are involved in such consensual dispute resolution.

Taking this opportunity, I also would like to raise a matter of minor importance. Article 9 uses the phrase "final decision". In my opinion, this is too broadly stated and should reasonably be understood as "final infringement decision". Some could no doubt argue it results from Article 9 that a final decision is a final infringement decision as it must find "an infringement of competition law". But others could add that "infringement decision" and "final infringement decision" are defined in Article 2(11)-(12). If so, the notions defined in Article 2 should be used consistently across the whole Directive. It is worth noting that the phrase "final infringement decision" is used only in Recital 34 of the Preamble and the phrase "infringement decision" is used only in Article 10 paragraph 4 and Article 20 paragraph 2(b).

3. Access to information held by the competition authorities

Private claimants may face the difficulties in obtaining access to the evidence they need to prove a case as crucial pieces of evidence are often kept secret in the hands of defendants. Finding a solution to these problems was important not only with regard to stand-alone actions. Finally, the Damages Directive contains rules on the disclosure of evidence both included in the file of a CA and kept by a party or third party (Articles 5–8). National courts shall be able to order the disclosure of "specified items of evidence or relevant categories of evidence" (Article 5 paragraph 2). National courts shall limit the disclosure of evidence to that which is proportionate. Article 5 paragraph 3 stipulates general factors to be taken into consideration while deciding on proportionality and Article 6 paragraph 4 stipulates specific ones.

However, the new provisions create some new problems even if they solve some old ones. First, the Directive is "rolling back" effects of the judgments delivered in the Court of Justice cases *Pfleiderer*[18] and *Donau Chemie*[19] with regard to third parties' access to the CA's files. Those judgments confirmed the possibility of national courts to weigh the public and private enforcement objectives on a case-by-case basis and decide on whether to reject the request for access or give access to leniency documents. They seem to confirm that the reality of tensions between the two "cultures" of enforcement (private and public) should not be just accepted and that private antitrust enforcement should not be blocked in order to avoid or resolve those tensions.

After the transposition of the Directive, for claimants it may be more difficult to obtain some information from CAs. Contrary to the abovementioned jurisprudence, Article 6 of the Directive contains the black list[20] of absolutely protected documents[21] in paragraph 6, namely leniency statements and settlement submissions (while at the same time providing in paragraph 5 for temporary protection of the withdrawn settlement submissions, information prepared by a natural or legal person specifically for the proceedings of a CA and information drawn up by the CA and sent to the parties in the course of its proceedings).[22] By this provision, the European Parliament and the Council, in effect, confirm that the private claimant's need for evidence may not be of as much importance as the confidentiality of information delivered to CA by, *inter alia*, leniency applicants escaping the arm of competition law. Such rights of leniency applicants and settlement parties to confidentiality of submitted information, resulting from the *per se* rule of the Directive, are considered incompatible with primary law, that is the principle of effectiveness.[23]

Second, Article 5 paragraph 8 of the Directive states the following: "Without prejudice to paragraphs 4 and 7 and to Article 6, this

18 Case C-360/09 *Pfleiderer AG v Bundeskartellamt*, ECR [2011] I-05161.

19 Case C-536/11 *Bundeswettbewerbsbehörde v Donau Chemie AG and others*, ECR [2013] ECLI:EU:C:2013:366.

20 Schwab, A., "Finding the Right Balance – the Deliberations of the European Parliament on the Draft Legislation Regarding Damage Claims", *Journal of European Competition Law & Practice* 5 (2) (2014), p. 66.

21 See also Article 7 paragraph 1 of the Directive.

22 See also Article 7 paragraph 2 of the Directive.

23 Kersting, C., "Removing the Tension between Public and Private Enforcement: Disclosure and Privileges for Successful Leniency Applicants", *Journal of European Competition Law & Practice* 5 (1) (2014), pp. 3-4.

Article shall not prevent Member States from maintaining or introducing rules which would lead to wider disclosure of evidence". The first part of this provision leaves Member States with no option but to amend their national laws so that they are aligned with Article 5 paragraphs 4 and 7 and Article 6. In all other respects Member States shall be permitted to maintain or introduce rules which would lead to wider disclosure of evidence (minimum harmonisation clause). Provided that Member States shall make use of the minimum harmonisation clause, this is the second manifestation of the challenge to private enforcement of EU competition law amounting to the risk of increased forum shopping.

Third, Article 6 paragraph 9 reads: "The disclosure of evidence in the file of a competition authority that does not fall into any of the categories listed in this Article may be ordered in actions for damages at any time, without prejudice to this Article". But what is striking about the scope of this rule is that – despite the presence of leniency statements and settlement submissions on the black list of absolutely protected documents – some national documents considered as equivalents of these two categories of documents appearing in proceedings before the European Commission shall not be protected by the rules adopted as a result of the transposition of Article 6 paragraph 6. If we look into definitions contained in Article 2(16) and 2(18) of the Directive and compare them to the national concepts of leniency and settlement we may come to recognise the narrowness of the definitions introduced into the Directive.

For instance, the Directive understands settlement submission as a voluntary presentation by, or on behalf of, an undertaking to a CA describing the undertaking's acknowledgement of, or its renunciation to dispute, its participation in an infringement of competition law and its responsibility for that infringement of competition law, which was drawn up specifically to enable the CA to apply a simplified or expedited procedure. In Poland, provisions on the so-called voluntary acceptance of a fine were introduced on 18 January 2015. When legislative works were undertaken in 2012, the then President of the Office for Competition and Consumers Protection considered the introduction of the voluntary acceptance of a fine as an important target which, if reached, could show significant improvement in the area of efficiency of Polish competition law. The intended purposes of these provisions, considered as equivalent of the EU legal framework for settlements, were the simplification and acceleration of antitrust proceedings[24] (also proceedings where infringements of Article 101 or 102 TFEU are investigated in parallel to infringements of

[24] In Polish: www.uokik.gov.pl/download.php?plik=13592, pp. 13-14 (accessed 09.02.2015).

national prohibitions). In fact, the introduced "settlement" procedure is so complex that the NCA shall be incapable of accommodating and expediting it quickly and effectively. Moreover, it can be commenced only just before the end of the antitrust proceedings. Therefore, it is doubtful whether any of the documents submitted by the party to NCA within this procedure could be considered as "drawn up specifically to enable the competition authority to apply a simplified or expedited procedure". In my view, the Polish "settlement" procedure, seen from the perspective of its purposes, is going to be ineffective or even counterproductive and, therefore, unnecessary (at least in its present form). More radically, documents submitted by the party to NCA within this procedure are not required to describe the party's acknowledgement of, or its renunciation to dispute, its participation in an infringement of competition law and its responsibility for that infringement of competition law. None of them shall be a settlement submission within the meaning of the Directive. If they were submitted within the NCA's proceedings where infringements of Articles 101 or 102 TFEU were investigated, they could not be protected under legislation adopted as a result of Article 6 paragraph 6 of the Directive.

A similar problem may arise with some leniency statements. According to Article 2(16) of the Directive, such a statement is understood as an oral or written presentation voluntarily provided by, or on behalf of, an undertaking or a natural person to a CA or a record thereof, describing the knowledge of that undertaking or natural person of a cartel and describing its role therein, which presentation was drawn up specifically for submission to the CA with a view to obtaining immunity or a reduction of fines under a leniency programme, not including pre-existing information. In short, the definition of a leniency programme contained in Article 2(15) is limited to a programme concerning the application of Article 101 TFEU or a corresponding provision under national law on the basis of which a participant in a secret cartel cooperates with an investigation of the competition authority. The Polish leniency programme is, by contrast, much broader.[25] It covers all cartels (not only secret cartels) as well as other agreements, decisions or practices (including vertical ones) referred to in Article 101 TFEU or its national equivalent.

In practice, it may happen that a claimant will file an action e.g. in the German civil court and request to disclose documents submitted by the defendant to e.g. the Polish NCA within the leniency programme or

25 See also Sitarek, P., "The Impact of EU Law on a National Competition Authority's Leniency Programme – the Case of Poland", *Yearbook of Antitrust and Regulatory Studies* 7 (9) (2014), pp. 208-209.

"settlement" procedure. The court shall be obliged to assess whether their contents correspond to the definitions introduced to the Directive. Will national courts be up to such a challenge? By the way, it is worth remembering that Article 6 paragraph 7 reads: "A claimant may present a reasoned request that a national court access the evidence referred to in point (a) or (b) of paragraph 6 for the sole purpose of ensuring that their contents correspond to the definitions in points (16) and (18) of Article 2. In that assessment, national courts may request assistance only from the competent competition authority. The authors of the evidence in question may also have the possibility to be heard. In no case shall the national court permit other parties or third parties access to that evidence". How should these provisions be construed and applied? What could happen if a claimant did not request for the assessment but for the disclosure and the court had doubts as to the contents of documents? Should the rules resulting from sentences 2-4 be applied in such circumstances? The mistake of the authors of the Directive is to ignore this aspect of the future private enforcement of EU competition law.

Switching to the discussion of more general issues, I would like to ask whether the Directive was adopted too early.[26] The above examples show that as long as Member States are allowed to maintain considerable divergences in the area of antitrust procedures (e.g. with respect to national leniency programmes or settlement procedures), it will be impossible to have homogeneous conditions for private enforcement of EU competition law across the whole Union. Indeed, the EU decision-makers seem to have failed to understand that reforming private enforcement of EU competition law is not just a matter of harmonising the civil "machinery", but also of more basic questions of the need for the harmonisation of antitrust procedures and the possibility thereof.

4. Limitation periods on bringing a damages action

A third dimension of the follow-on actions problem has been concerned with limitation periods. Preambular Recital 36 of the Damages Directive stresses the importance of national rules on the beginning, duration, suspension or interruption of limitation periods which should not unduly hamper the bringing of actions for damages. This is particularly important in respect of follow-on actions. Issues of limitation periods are involved in Article 10, Article 11 paragraph 4 (last sentence) and Article 18 paragraph 1.[27]

---

26 See also Piszcz, A., "Polish civil procedure...", cit., p. 230.

27 Article 11 paragraph 4 (last sentence) refers to limitation period applicable to actions against immunity recipients and Article 18 paragraph 1 refers to the suspension of limitation periods for the duration of consensual dispute resolution process.

Article 10 paragraph 3 – being another minimum harmonisation provision – provides that limitation periods for bringing actions for damages shall be at least five years. Therefore, Member States are free to maintain or introduce longer limitation periods. Limitation periods shall begin to run where the claimant knows, or can reasonably be expected to know, of the behaviour and the fact that it constitutes an infringement of competition law, of the fact that the infringement of competition law caused harm to it, and the identity of the infringer (Article 10 paragraph 2). However, limitation periods shall not start to run before the infringement of competition law has ceased. Pursuant to paragraph 4, a limitation period shall be suspended or, depending on national law, interrupted, if a CA takes action for the purpose of the investigation or its proceedings in respect of an infringement of competition law to which the action for damages relates. The suspension shall end at the earliest one year after the infringement decision has become final (cannot be, or can no longer be, appealed by ordinary means) or after the proceedings are otherwise terminated.

Among the three issues discussed in this chapter, the limitation periods issue stands out as the one where adopted provisions seem really to be directed at facilitating follow-on actions and not just securing interests of Member States or public enforcement. Prospective claimants shall be satisfied in particular in Member States such as Poland where (1) the time limit for the statute of limitations is three years as of the day when an injured party has knowledge of harm and the identity of an infringer but cannot be longer than 10 years as of the date on which the event causing damage occurred; (2) this time limit is not subject to suspension or interruption in case of the proceedings carried out by the NCA in respect of an infringement. However, Howard justly criticised the Directive for not explaining how the suspensory effect of an appeal shall be treated in case not all infringers filed appeal against the CA's decision.[28] For example, there were two infringers and only one of them appealed the decision. Shall a limitation period run separately against each of them or it shall begin to run after decision becomes final also for an appellant? It could have been clarified in the Directive since this question is not answered satisfactorily in Member States.[29]

---

[28] Howard, A., "Too little, too late? The European Commission's Legislative Proposals on Anti-Trust Damages Actions", *Journal of European Competition Law & Practice* 4 (6) (2013), p. 462.

[29] E.g. the UK Supreme Court is of a somewhat controversial opinion that appeals against the level of the fine, will not suspend the domestic limitation periods and only an appeal against the substantive finding of infringement will have suspensory effect; see *BCL v BASF* [2012] UKSC 45, available at http://www.bailii.org/uk/cases/UKSC/2012/45.html (accessed 09.02.2015).

5. Concluding thoughts

The authors of the Damages Directive seem partly right and partly wrong. It probably will succeed in ensuring that limitation periods are reasonable and sufficient to allow injured parties to bring actions, including follow-on actions. Access to evidence will probably be better. The authors of the Directive attempted to improve some tools available to claimants and CAs; it seems they managed to do this. On the other hand, it is worth noting that there may appear increased forum shopping as a result of minimum harmonisation clauses (if Member States make use of them).

There are uncertainties in regard to what the results of the harmonisation of provisions on private enforcement of EU competition law will be. Will claimants find redress easy? Will the harmonisation result in major improvements in efficiency and effectiveness of antitrust litigation? Or, to the contrary, are the tools delivered by the Directive "blunt"?

Fortunately, the Directive does not seem to offer a culture of too ready-redress. I do not expect the increasing litigiousness as a result of the Directive. It does not seem to me that the Directive constitutes a paradigm which assumes that claimants will respond in certain ways to the harmonised system of redress. I do not think it will make the private enforcement system cheaper and quicker. Generally speaking, the Directive is cautious in many regards. It may even do more to fuel expectations than to satisfy them. So, will it fail to stimulate private enforcement?

The Directive must be transposed into national legislation by each of the Member States by 27 December 2016. It is safe to withhold opinions till the time is ripe for a sober assessment of what was achieved. I expect that any changes in the rules involved in the Directive will be off the agenda for some years. The Directive is not perfect, so instead of celebrating its adoption I would offer a few thoughts that can be shared now, without having the new framework empirically tested. Damages actions are only one element of private antitrust enforcement which alone may be as weak as the use of any other single tool. Preambular Recital 5 of the Directive mentions alternative avenues of redress, such as public enforcement decisions that give parties an incentive to provide compensation. This example shows how public enforcement can "borrow" from private enforcement and adapt its functions for public-enforcement contexts. This is how "cooperative" relations between public enforcement and private enforcement can be sustained. We could and should have "sustainable antitrust enforcement" based upon the balance of public enforcement and private enforcement in Europe.[30]

Bibliography

Basedow, J.; Francq, S.; Idot, L., *International Antitrust Litigation: Conflict of Laws and Coordination*. Oxford: Hart Publishing, 2012.

Howard, A., "Too little, too late? The European Commission's Legislative Proposals on Anti-Trust Damages Actions", *Journal of European Competition Law & Practice*, 4 (6) (2013).

Jurkowska-Gomułka, A., "W stronę umocnienia prywatnoprawnego wdrażania zakazów praktyk ograniczających konkurencję – glosa do uchwały SN z 23.07.2008 r. (III CZP 52/08)", 5 (2010) *Europejski Przegląd Sądowy.*

Kersting, C., "Removing the Tension between Public and Private Enforcement: Disclosure and Privileges for Successful Leniency Applicants", *Journal of European Competition Law & Practice,* 5 (1) (2014).

Piszcz, A., "Polish civil procedure and antitrust enforcement – recent developments from the standpoint of efficiency", in *Recent trends in economy and efficiency of civil procedure*. Vilnius: Vilnius University Press, 2013.

Piszcz, A., "Still-unpopular Sanctions: Developments in Private Antitrust Enforcement in Poland After the 2008 White Paper", *Yearbook of Antitrust and Regulatory Studies,* 5 (7) (2012).

Piszcz, A. in Pais, S. O.; Piszcz, A., "Package on Actions for Damages Based on Breaches of EU Competition Rules: Can One Size Fit All?", *Yearbook of Antitrust and Regulatory Studies,* 7 (10) (2014).

Schwab, A., "Finding the Right Balance – the Deliberations of the European Parliament on the Draft Legislation Regarding Damage Claims", *Journal of European Competition Law & Practice,* 5 (2) (2014).

Sitarek, P., "The Impact of EU Law on a National Competition Authority's Leniency Programme – the Case of Poland", *Yearbook of Antitrust and Regulatory Studies,* 7 (9) (2014).

Uřičař, M., "Evidence in Competition Law Cases: Problems in Czech Law", in Basedow, J.; Terhechte, J.; Tichý, L. (eds.), *Private Enforcement of Competition Law*. Baden-Baden: Nomos, 2011.

[30] See also Piszcz, A., *supra*, No. 10, at 76.

Private enforcement of competition law on trial – two study cases

The restitution of illegal profits and the opt-out principle relating to compensatory collective redress mechanisms

Henrique Sousa ANTUNES[1]

1. Introduction

As we have written elsewhere, recognition and protection of fundamental rights, the crisis of the Social State and growing exposure of individuals to disputes between private parties for the time being is still very scarcely mirrored in the phenomenon of the delegation of public powers. The philosophical or political ideologies and the historical and social circumstances which formed the basis for the rules separate the Anglo-Saxon family, where the individual is an important agent of social transformation, from the Roman-Germanic family, where the distinction between public action and private action appears to be clearly formulated. Yet, the complexity of today's world, and the universality, severity and repeated nature of offenses between private parties warrants that the physical person or the private legal person be rediscovered as well as the collective extent of their action within the systems of continental Europe.[2]

The caution of European jurists should not be confused with atavism. In the words of Wolfgang Wiegand, "if one can come to terms with the fact that a large number of the developments described here are commensurate with the current requirements of society but that innumerable basic concepts of our legal principles will thereby become questionable, or at least will be affected to a certain degree, then it is at least initially required that jurisprudence analyse and clarify the fundamental elements of this process. Traditional European viewpoints must then be reappraised

---

1 Assistant Professor, Católica Lisbon Law School, Catholic University of Portugal, Researcher at Católica Research Centre for the Future of Law.

2 *Disgorgement of profits: a journey between the present and the future* (report for the 19th International Congress of Comparative Law of the International Academy of Comparative Law, Wien, July 2014), p. 16.

against this background, in order to determine which of those elements should not be sacrificed to this process".[3]

In particular, the protection of intellectual property, consumer rights or the collective exercise of rights has revealed the importance of the issue of private law enforcement. That is also the case regarding competition relations. However, the choices made by European legislators reveal the distrust on solutions of other social and cultural models, condemning innovations to inefficiency. The rejection of a preventive purpose in the determination of the amount of damages and the adoption of the opt-in principle in the proposed model for the collective exercise of damages actions in Europe are two clear examples of that.

As Deborah Hensler shows, referring to a metaphor by Arthur Miller, large-scale litigation grounded on "entrepreneurial lawyers' and greedy citizens' intent on securing financial rewards for questionable claims" is not the new "monster".[4] Indeed, "if there is a new 'monster' at large, it is the rise of multinational corporations and the development of a global economy that bring with them the potential for large-scale injuries resulting from worldwide product consumption. If there is a key that has unlocked the monster's cage, it is the information science revolution and the development of the Internet, which have provided the means for people to become informed about such injuries and the tools for individuals, organizations and attorneys to organize to secure remedies".[5]

The State ought to recognize that globalization has redefined its role in applying the law and adjust sovereignty to the idea that private enforcement lends to social regulation. At a time when harmful actions have global repercussions, the exposing of illegal practices and general and special prevention of reprehensible behaviour is a path more easily trodden by the injured party, who is thus called on to exercise an important social function. Considering law from a transnational perspective means reviewing the reach of retributive sovereignty and adapting it to the geographically dispersed nature of the interests involved and, also because of this, to the essentially individual nature of the harm caused.[6]

---

3 "The Reception of American Law in Europe", *American Journal of Comparative Law* 39 (2) (1991), p. 248.

4 "Revisiting the Monster: New Myths and Realities of Class Action and Other Large Scale Litigation", *Duke Journal of Comparative & International Law*, 11 (2) (Debates over Group Litigation in Comparative Perspective – What Can We Learn from Each Other?) 2001, p. 212.

5 "Revisiting the Monster…", p. 212.

6 Antunes, H. S., *Disgorgement of profits: a journey between the present and the future*, p. 16 et seq.

2. The first study case: the restitution of illegal profits in competition law

One may read in the Explanatory Memorandum of Directive 2014/104/EU of the European Parliament and of the Council of 26 November 2014 (on certain rules governing actions for damages under national law for infringements of the competition law provisions of the Member States and of the European Union):[7] "Articles 101 and 102 TFEU produce direct effects in relations between individuals and create, for the individuals concerned, rights and obligations which national courts must enforce. National courts thus have an equally essential part to play in applying the competition rules (private enforcement). When ruling on disputes between private individuals, they protect subjective rights under Union law, for example by awarding damages to the victims of infringements. The full effectiveness of Articles 101 and 102 TFEU, and in particular the practical effect of the prohibitions laid down therein, requires that anyone – be they an individual, including consumers and undertakings, or a public authority – can claim compensation before national courts for the harm caused to them by an infringement of those provisions. [...]" (Recital 3). Also, "to ensure effective private enforcement actions under civil law and effective public law enforcement by competition authorities, both tools are required to interact to ensure maximum effectiveness of the competition rules" (Recital 6).

Notwithstanding these considerations, certain options of the legislator contradict the optimization of the principle of effectiveness. That is, in particular, the case of the prohibition of the restitution of illegal profits when the public enforcement measure proves to be ineffective in this respect ("Without prejudice to compensation for loss of opportunity, full compensation under this Directive should not lead to overcompensation, whether by means of punitive, multiple or other damages" – Recital 13 and Article 3.3).

Take Portuguese law as an example: Article 18(2) of the Administrative Offences Act, also applicable to infringements of competition law provisions, lays down that "if the agent gains from the infringement an economic benefit which can be calculated as being higher than the upper limit of the fine, and there are no other means to eliminate it, the latter may be raised up to the amount of the benefit, although this increase may not exceed one third of the upper limit established by law". The fine may, therefore, not actually disgorge the gain. Given that the determination of the sanction also depends on the seriousness of the administrative

[7] OJ L 349, 05.12.2014, p. 1.

offence, the fault and the economic situation of the agent (Article 18(1)) it is possible, at least in theory, to calculate an amount which, inclusively, is below the established upper limit.

Considering: a) the complementary scope of the classic instruments of civil law, namely civil liability, unjust enrichment and *negotiorum gestio*; b) the admissibility of the collective protection of rights (see Article 2 (4)); c) the recognition of a general preventive aim (see Article 1.1 – "(The Directive) sets out rules fostering undistorted competition in the internal market and removing obstacles to its proper functioning, by ensuring equivalent protection throughout the Union for anyone who has suffered such harm)"; d) the relevance that is given to the corresponding private enforcement of intellectual property rights (see, in particular, Article 13 of Directive 2004/48/EC), we are of the opinion that the report foreseen in Article 20 of Directive 2014/104/EU should include information regarding the impact of both public and private measures on the illegal profit exceeding the harm caused by an infringement of competition law. Also, if appropriate, a legislative proposal should follow Article 6:101 of the Draft Common Frame of Reference: "(1) Reparation is to reinstate the person suffering the legally relevant damage in the position that person would have been had the legally relevant damage not occurred; (4) As an alternative to reinstatement under paragraph (1) but only where this is reasonable, reparation may take the form of recovery from the person accountable for the causation of the legally relevant damage of any advantage obtained by the latter in connection with causing the damage"). This is the case, in special, for collective redress. Given that the harm has evident social repercussions and, also, that the lack of determination of the damage is innate to compensation of supra-individual rights or interests, we are of the opinion that the obligation to compensate should, in this situation, follow a clearly preventive function and, therefore, restitution of profits should be foreseen.

We should take a close look to the Commission Recommendation of 11 June 2013 on common principles for injunctive and compensatory collective redress mechanisms in the Member States concerning violations of rights granted under Union Law (2013/396/EU)[8], beginning with, and insofar as this harms the provision of disgorgement damages, the terms in which a prohibition of punitive damages is established (Principle 31): "The compensation awarded to natural or legal persons harmed in a mass harm situation should not exceed the compensation that would have been awarded if the claim had been pursued by means of individual actions. In

[8] OJ L 201/60, 26.07.2013.

particular, punitive damages, leading to overcompensation in favour of the claimant party of the damage suffered, should be prohibited".

The principle "prohibition of punitive damages" has a broader scope: "Collective damages actions should aim to secure compensation of damage that is found to be caused by an infringement. The punishment and deterrence functions should be exercised by public enforcement. There is no need for EU initiative on collective redress to go beyond the goal of compensation: punitive damages should not be part of a European collective redress system" ("Towards a European Horizontal Framework for Collective Redress" (COM/2013/0401 final), Recital 3.1). Yet, the sense of punishment is distorted when no more is required than the restitution of the profit illegally obtained. What justification is there to confirm the assertion of the punitive nature of a duty which puts the injuring party in the situation he would have been but for his committing the unlawful act?

It is important to note that, in Portugal, similarly to what happens in other European civil law countries, punishment and prevention are not concepts which are alien to civil liability. The affirmation is justified with regard to compensation for non-patrimonial damage, which does not, by definition, lend itself to assessment in pecuniary terms. However, the claim is also true with regard to patrimonial damage. In this area we may mention, and just by way of example, the irrelevance of hypothetical cases, the provision which allows the judge to fix the amount of damages due from the injuring party at a sum lower than the injury caused where there is negligence (Article 494 of the Civil Code), the penalty clause (the amount awarded is in addition to specific performance or recovery of damages), Article 829-A of the Civil Code, which, following the influence of the French *astreintes*, compels the judge, if so requested by the contract creditor, to order the contract debtor of a personal service to pay a sum of money per day of delay in the fulfilment of his duty or for each breach, with this amount being divided between the contract creditor and the State in equal parts, and the provisions of the Labour Law which fix or increase the damages.[9]

It is worth highlighting Law No. 83/95, of 31 August, on the right of popular action in civil liability. The passing of this law provided the civil law with the means of overcoming its proverbial lack of efficacy in compensating harm to diffuse interests or to homogeneous individual interests or rights. Interests protected by the Constitution, such as public health, the environment, quality of life, consumers' rights, cultural heritage and the

[9] See Antunes, H. S., "Once Upon a Time in America...", *Occasional Papers in Comparative Law* (Portuguese-American Comparative Law Center/Roger Williams University Ralph R. Papitto School of Law), Issue No. 2, April 2005, p. 36.

public domain (Article 1(2)) justify the specific nature of the intervention due to the nature of the protected interests or the lack of proportion between the individual impact of the harm and the collective repercussions of the damage. In this last case, the classic substantive and procedural forms of civil liability prove to be inadequate regarding compensation that only acquires expression when, due to the nature of the characteristics they take on, it is possible to combine them into a single sum.

The damages actions provided for in Law No. 83/95 relate to damage caused to transindividual and indivisible rights (for example, harm to the natural environment, which benefits all the persons in a community, due to the discharge of pollution by a company) and harm, with a common origin, to individual rights (personal or material damage suffered by the members of the aforementioned community).

Once the action has been admitted, Article 22 (2) of the law in question provides that compensation shall be fixed globally. Given that the harm has evident social repercussions and, also, that the lack of determination of the damage is innate to compensation of supra-individual rights or interests, we are of the opinion that the obligation to compensate should, in this situation, follow a clearly preventive function. In this context, and regarding homogeneous individual interests, one may read: "[...] the rules on popular action, when they define a global compensation which is intended to be shared by the injured parties, [...] are more concerned with preventing the injuring party from gaining any advantage from the harmful act than with ensuring that each of those injured parties is really compensated in the exact measure of the loss suffered. The global compensation seeks to distribute the injuring party's gains among the injured parties, although the result of this may be a certain breach of corrective justice, since this distribution cannot guarantee that all the damage suffered is effectively compensated in its exact amount. In order to quantify the global compensation the (global) gain obtained by the injuring party is used more than the (equally global) loss inflicted by him, which means that in quantifying it the criterion of restoring the hypothetical situation which is established in Article 562 of the Civil Code is not followed".[10]

In support of this conclusion, we may mention the fact that Article 31 (2) of the Securities Code provides that a decision in favour of the plaintiffs in a popular action must indicate the entity charged with receiving and managing the damages due to persons not individually identified. The following may be nominated: a guarantee fund, an association for the protection of investors or one or several holders of rights to damages

---

[10] Sousa, M. T. de, *A Legitimidade Popular na Tutela dos Interesses Difusos.* Lisboa: Lex, 2003, p. 169 et seq.

who have been identified in the action. The rule is linked, inextricably, to homogeneous individual interests: "The holders of rights who are not individually identified are the parties who are individually harmed that did not take part in the action. This is confirmed by Paragraph 3: damages which are not paid as a result of the statute of limitations or the impossibility of identifying the respective holders revert to the guarantee fund. Only individual parties may be unable to be identified".[11]

Of relevance in Portuguese law is also the transposing of European legislation allowing the judge to consider the economic advantage gained as a result of the practice of the harmful action in his calculations of the indemnity. One example is worth mentioning: according to Article 211 of the Code of Copyright and Related Rights, "when determining the amount of indemnity for loss and damage, whether patrimonial or non-patrimonial, the court should pay attention to the profit obtained by the infringing party, to the lost profits and resulting harm suffered by the injured party and the costs borne by the latter in order to protect the copyright and related rights, and also to investigate and cease the conduct which harmed his right" (paragraph 2) and "when calculating the compensation due to the injured party, it should pay attention to the amount of the proceeds derived from the unlawful conduct of the infringing party, namely the performance or performances which have been unlawfully held" (paragraph 3). Article 338-L (2) and (3) of the Industrial Property Code also provides in the same sense.

In fact, important tools of private law enforcement are to be found on European legislation, "primarily by a somewhat carefree use of boilerplate language, apparently inspired by the ECJ in its Greek Maize decision. The magic formula employed there which reoccurs like a mantra in legislation and court decisions ever since is that all sanctions shall be 'effective, proportionate and dissuasive'. Whereas probably most reoccurrences of this formula in Community legislation explicitly address 'penalties' as in the Greek Maize case and therefore do not imply that it extends to private law remedies, some provisions speak more broadly of 'sanctions' without any further qualification. Of the latter, at least some include the caveat that this should be 'without prejudice to Member States' civil liability regimes', thereby distinguishing private law remedies from the administrative or other 'sanctions' they have in mind. Yet, a few others, however, specifically address civil law remedies in general

[11] Ascensão, J. de O., "A Acção Popular e a Protecção do Investidor", *Cadernos do Mercado de Valores Mobiliários*, 11 (2001), p. 65.

or compensation payments in particular which shall be measured by the said tripartite standard".[12]

3. The second study case: the opt-out principle relating to compensatory collective redress mechanisms

There is, primarily, an underlying philosophy which, in the light of what has been written above, ought to be reconsidered.

Recital 6 of the Commission Recommendation of 11 June 2013 on common principles for injunctive and compensatory collective redress mechanisms in the Member States concerning violations of rights granted under Union Law (2013/396/EU) states: "It is a core task of public enforcement to prevent and punish the violations of rights granted under Union law. The possibility for private persons to pursue claims based on violations of such rights supplements public enforcement". Also, according to Recital 1 of the same document, the purpose of the Recommendation "is to facilitate access to justice, stop illegal practices and enable injured parties to obtain compensation in mass harm situations caused by violations of rights granted under Union law, while ensuring appropriate procedural safeguards to avoid abusive litigation". Yet, "the claimant party should be formed on the basis of express consent of the natural or legal persons claiming to have been harmed ('opt-in' principle). Any exception to this principle, by law or by court order, should be duly justified by reasons of sound administration of justice" (Principle 21).

Guaranteeing access to justice and simplifying proceedings are, certainly, two aims that the different collective justice regimes seek to achieve. The provision of procedures which group together interests, especially those which are divisible and individualized, is an expression of the sophistication of the legal system of any democratic regime. It is certainly the case that protecting diffuse interests, without individual appropriation, is a refinement to legal protection for living in community, which adds the judicialization of the collective dimension of our existence to claims to satisfy an individual aim. However, finding creative solutions to access the law is clearly necessary as a result of technological developments, imbalance in knowledge, unequal access to justice, the expansion of mass tort cases, the growth in relationships of interdependence, the dispersal of agents in commercial relationships and, especially, the crisis in the efficiency and the fair sharing of costs in most judicial

---

12 Koch, B. A., "Punitive Damages in European Law", in Koziol, H.; Wilcox. V. (eds.), *Punitive Damages: Common Law and Civil Law Perspectives*, Wien/New York: Springer, 2009, p. 200 et seq.

systems. Class actions provide an excellent example of an emerging solution for the problems that have been highlighted.

We may recall the arguments used by the European Economic and Social Committee in favour of a collective action system to protect consumer interests: "The creation of a European collective action would make it possible to provide access to justice to all consumers, irrespective of their nationality and financial situation and the amount of individual damage they have suffered. It would also be beneficial to commercial operators in view of the procedural savings which could be achieved. The costs of such an action would be lower than the costs liable to be incurred as a result of a multitude of individual actions. This procedure would also have the advantage of providing legal certainty by virtue of the fact that an extremely large number of similar complaints would be resolved under a single ruling" (Plenary Session Held on 13 and 14 February 2008 – Opinion on Defining the collective actions system and its role in the context of Community consumer law. Own initiative opinion, Recital 4.4).

A collective action system fosters interested parties' access to courts and contributes to the more efficient and fairer organization of legal disputes. It would seem that the solutions found for regulating this procedural method ought to be shaped by the essential nature of those purposes. Therein lies the advantage of an opt-out regime: it prevents lack of knowledge of the law and a lack of motivation to use the courts, above all, when the injury has less economical relevance, from providing the conditions for a harmful practice to be repeated; also, disgorgement or skimming-off illegally gained profits from wrongdoers is more likely to be compatible with an opt-out mechanism rather than with an opt-in procedure, considering the risk of affecting the right to compensation of absent parties; finally, it encourages the collective response to litigation, reducing the possibility of multiple individual claims which present a risk to the defendant, in search of a global compensation of the claimants and increasing the efficiency of the public judicial system.

As Rachael Mulheron notes, "[…] the introduction of an opt-out system within European Member States is not a 'solution in search of a problem'; indeed, the Commission specifically concurs in this view by noting that, due to 'weaknesses of the current redress and enforcement framework in the EU, a significant proportion of consumers who have suffered damage do not obtain redress' (Commission Green Paper on Consumer Collective Redress, COM (2008) 794 final, 15)".[13] Considering the English example and the practical and legal difficulties of using an opt-in

[13] "The Case for an Opt-Out Class Action for European Member States: a Legal and Empirical Analysis", *Columbia Journal of European Law*, Summer 2009, p. 451.

system, the "human reasons" which justify the preference for participating in the claim without declaring to do so, the lack of suits for compensatory redress in England, the futile attempts of claimants to join US class actions and the clear enhancement of the efficiency of the judicial resources at the state's disposal by an opt-out regime, this author remarks that "it is appropriate to conclude with a caution to English and European law-makers to take heed of 'the tale of two monsters' – that is, for many citizens, the so-called Frankenstein monster of a class action would be a more welcoming sight than the frustratingly absent Loch Ness monster of effective compensatory redress".[14]

It is not justifiable treating the choice of the opt-in or opt-out system as an option regarding a safety mechanism for collective action rather than dealing with that choice as a consideration relating to the philosophy underlying the adoption of a regime for the collective protection of rights. Standing to bring a claim and the subsequent active standing reflect the teleology of a given procedural system, the purposes that the legislator was seeking to pursue with it. The legislation on the guarantees that this provision requires, namely satisfying the constitutional standards of access to justice, is quite a different thing.

The confusion between the purpose and the means seems clear in the European Parliament Resolution of 2 February 2012 entitled "Towards a Coherent European Approach to Collective Redress". The choice for an opt-in principle lacks grounds, beginning with the assumption, which is not proven, that "a collective redress system where the victims are not identified before the judgment is delivered must be rejected on the grounds that it is contrary to many Member States' legal orders and violates the rights of any victims who might participate in the procedure unknowingly and yet be bound by the court's decision" (Recital 20) and, considering that, in an opt-in system forced to perform a guaranteeing role, the European Parliament still recognizes, however, the need for the Commission "to consider a system which will provide relevant information to all potential victims involved, increase the representativeness of collective actions, allow for the largest number of victims to seek compensation and ensure simple, affordable and effective access to justice for EU citizens, thereby avoiding excessive litigation and subsequent unnecessary individual or collective actions concerning the same infringement" (Recital 20).

The same confusion is to be found on the Communication from the Commission to the European Parliament, the Council, the European Economic and Social Committee and the Committee of the Regions

14 *Ibid.*, p. 451 et seq.

"Towards a European Horizontal Framework for Collective Redress" (COM/2013/0401 final): "The 'opt-out' system gives rise to more fundamental questions as to the freedom of potential claimants to decide whether they want to litigate. The right to an effective remedy cannot be interpreted in a way that prevents people from making (informed) decisions on whether they wish to claim damages or not" (Recital 3.4).

There is no problem with access to justice if interested parties are provided with information using appropriate means and if the judge is given the possibility of limiting the *res judicata* to those intervening in the action. Portuguese law may serve as an example. In Portugal, Law No. 83/95, of 31 August, on the right to take part in administrative proceedings and the right of popular action, grants standing in popular actions to the holders of the rights or interests at stake in the claim who have not excluded themselves from representation by the claimant (Articles 14 and 15 – opt-out regime). What this means is that the interested party is not required to make a declaration of his will in order to intervene in the claim. Any will that he does in fact demonstrate serves the purpose of excluding him from participating in the proceedings.

Reasonable notice is given by means of media or publication. The law does not require personal identification of those to whom the advertisement is directed. It is sufficient for the reference to them as holders of the interests at stake to be via briefing the claim. Decisions that become *res judicata* have *erga omnes* effect, except where these result from insufficient evidence, or when the judge should decide alternatively, based on the actual motivations of the concrete case. This may occur, for example, when the judge considers that there has been inadequate representation of absent parties.

Portuguese law provides for another important means of defending the injured parties who have not excluded themselves from the representation. The public prosecutor has the power, with regard to reviewing legality, if he or she so wishes, to replace a claimant who withdraws from the suit, or where the settlement or behaviour is harmful to the interests in question (Article 16 (1) of Law 83/95).

In aligning the opt-out system with the right to access to justice one can refer to other arguments: the absence of financial implications for those who do not exercise their option to exclude themselves from the action, the procedural and substantive obstacles which characterize the calling of injured parties to a collective action in an opt-in system and, in particular, the social benefit of the procedure in opt-out. This latter consideration becomes evident when the damages involved are for a small amount. In these cases, the fact that the damage is not particularly serious discourages recourse to the courts and the gains obtained by the agent act as an invitation for him to repeat the same behaviour. And even more so if disgorgement is excluded: "[…] an 'opt-out' system may not be consistent with the central aim of collective redress, which is to obtain compensation for harm suffered, since such persons are not identified and so the award will not be distributed to them" (Communication from the Commission to the European Parliament, the Council, the European Economic and Social Committee and the Committee of the Regions "Towards a European Horizontal Framework for Collective Redress" (COM/2013/0401 final), Recital 3.4).

On this issue, one may read in the Opinion of the European Economic and Social Committee (Plenary Session held on 13 and 14 February 2008 – Opinion on Defining the collective actions system and its role in the context of Community consumer law. Own initiative opinion, Recital 4.4): "Use of the opt-out procedure makes it possible to take account of all the persons concerned and to secure a penalty which is on a par with the level of unlawful profit which may have been made. […] Any possible infringements of constitutional principles or the European Human Rights Convention are offset by the effectiveness of the process in respect of providing redress and serving as a deterrent".

In short, the opt-out regime is the one which best fits the reasons behind a system for the collective protection of rights. The class action provides a response to the social and legal inefficiency of the traditional regimes. This being the aim, the opt-out system provides the best solution. Principle 21 of the Commission Recommendation of 11 June 2013 should, therefore, be revised, as the assessment of the implementation of the Recommendation on the basis of practical experience, by 26 July 2017, will show (Principle 41: "[…] In this context, the Commission should in particular evaluate its impact on access to justice, on the right to obtain compensation, on the need to prevent abusive litigation and on the functioning of the single market, on SMEs, the competitiveness of the economy of the European Union and consumer trust […]").

Just as is the case in the fairy-tale Cinderella, the glass slipper only fits the foot of the future princess. In this context, the guarantee of access to the courts justifies the provision of instruments which effectively promote awareness of the commencement of the proceedings and also protect the absent parties from an unfavourable *res judicata*.

4. Conclusion

We end as we began. Private law enforcement should be granted with effective tools for its purposes. This is the case with the restitution of illegal profits and with the opt-out regime in collective redress mechanisms. The European institutions seem to have missed the opportunity to be coherent with the proclaimed principle, perhaps fearing the example of American Law.

Ten years have passed, but our words are still valid:[15] in the eyes of the European jurist, attraction to the novelties of the New World has always been accompanied by a lack of trust founded on centuries of history and tradition, like a father who assents to his son's rebellion. However, the science of Law cannot ignore the phenomenon of the influence in Europe of the language, practice and teaching of American law, within an Americanization of Law which takes place alongside the Americanization of European culture. Indeed, we have only to look at Volume 45 of *Archives de philosophie du droit* on this theme ("*L'américanisation du droit*"). In the words of the introduction by Bernard Audit, "il est possible que le droit écrit et le raisonnement déductif conviennent mieux à un monde stable, comme le fut celui du XIXe siècle; tandis que l'approche de la *common law* serait mieux adaptée à un context de changement social permanent tel que nous le connaissons: en raison de l'approche inductive évoquée à l'instant, l'innovation est en quelque sorte naturelle à la *common law*, l'adaptation permanente son mode d'existence".[16] The opening up of the common law system to social evolution explains the creativity of legal solutions, even in branches with a strong historical tradition such as that of private law.

Some inspiration is also to be found in Rafael Domingo's perspective: "The new legal order must above all be a jurisdictional law and not an interstate jurisdictional model: consensual, not bureaucratic, positive, or official. It should be proposed and not imposed – based more on mutual agreement than on laws and codes and led by a civil society protected by global institutions and not by hierarchical and technocratic state entities. From this perspective, the common law system – because of its proximity to the quotidian and its own methodology and system of sources – is better suited to globalization than European civil law, which is one reason why common law finds itself at such ease in the world of international business and transnational arbitration. With the new global law, the public would be identified more with social issues than with matters of state, which certainly is not now the case in Europe and Latin American contexts".[17]

---

15 "Once Upon a Time in America…", p. 22.

16 p. 9.

17 *New Global Law.* Cambridge: Cambridge University Press, 2010, p. xviii.

Bibliography

Antunes, H. S., "Once Upon a Time in America...", *Occasional Papers in Comparative Law* (Portuguese-American Comparative Law Center/Roger Williams University Ralph R. Papitto School of Law), Issue No. 2, April 2005.

Antunes, H. S., *Disgorgement of profits: a journey between the present and the future* (report for the 19th International Congress of Comparative Law of the International Academy of Comparative Law, Wien, July 2014).

Ascensão, J. de O., "A Acção Popular e a Protecção do Investidor", *Cadernos do Mercado de Valores Mobiliários*, 11 (2001).

Audit, B., "Introduction", *Archives de philosophie du droit*, 45 (L'américanisation du droit), Ed. Dalloz, 2001.

Domingo, R., *New Global Law*. Cambridge: Cambridge University Press, 2010.

Hensler, D., "Revisiting the Monster: New Myths and Realities of Class Action and Other Large Scale Litigation", *Duke Journal of Comparative & International Law*, 11 (2) (Debates over Group Litigation in Comparative Perspective – What Can We Learn from Each Other?), 2001.

Koch, B. A., "Punitive Damages in European Law", in Koziol, H.; Wilcox. V. (eds.), *Punitive Damages: Common Law and Civil Law Perspectives*, Wien/ New York: Springer, 2009.

Mulheron, R., "The Case for an Opt-Out Class Action for European Member States: a Legal and Empirical Analysis", *Columbia Journal of European Law*, Summer 2009.

Sousa, M. T. de, *A Legitimidade Popular na Tutela dos Interesses Difusos*. Lisboa: Lex, 2003.

Wiegand, W., "The Reception of American Law in Europe", *American Journal of Comparative Law* 39 (2) (1991).

Actions for damages under Portuguese Law for infringements of the competition law

A comparative analysis of the Directive 2014/104/ EU of the European Parliament and of the Council

Agostinho GUEDES[1]

Introduction

The purpose of this paper is to perform a first analysis of Portuguese law in light of the Directive 2014/104/EU, of 26 November 2014, of the European Parliament and of the Council (hereinafter the "Directive"), determining whether or not Portuguese law complies with the Directive, mainly regarding disclosure of evidence, the assessment of damages and the limitation periods and, consequently, where I anticipate the need for adjustments of Portuguese Law to transpose the Directive.

This paper was prepared for my participation in the international conference "Antitrust Private Enforcement" which took place at the Portuguese Catholic University in Porto, Portugal, on 29 March 2014.

At the time, there was only a proposal of a Directive of the European Commission dated 11 June 2013 and my presentation was based on such proposal. However, on November 2014 the Directive was published in the Official Journal and entered into force twenty days later. This paper takes into account the Directive in its final form.

In order to better explain to the audience the issues raised specifically in an action for damages based on an infringement of competition law, I described a synoptic case (hereinafter the "Case") – a real case that is still being discussed in the Portuguese courts, which is the reason why the identities of the parties were not disclosed.

I'll begin with the description of the Case in its most relevant aspects before moving to the analysis of the Portuguese legal framework and that of the Directive.

[1] Associate Professor, Católica Porto Law School, Catholic University of Portugal, Researcher at Católica Research Centre for the Future of Law.

1. Overview of the Case: Company A holds the monopoly of the wholesale supply of a certain service (the "Service"); company A also controls company B that, in turn, holds about 80% of the retail market of the Service.

Since Company A holds the monopoly of the wholesale supply of the Service, Company A is obliged (by mandatory law) to offer the distribution of the Service to all retailers. The conditions of such offer are standardized through general conditions of contract.

Around May 2002, Company A unilaterally changed the terms of the wholesale offer, namely by raising the price of the Service. At the same time, it also offered price discounts based on conditions that, in practical terms, could only be met by its subsidiary, Company B.

As a result of this price policy and in order to offer a competitive price to their clients, the other retailers were forced to operate with negative margins (from September 2002 to April 2005), thus putting their business in jeopardy.

In practice, Company A charged Company B a lower price than that charged to the other retailers, which allowed Company B to also lower its prices to clients. However, in order to remain competitive with Company B, the other retailers were also forced to lower their prices but still paying Company A as a result of the higher price charged as of May 2002.

This is considered a typical case of abuse of dominant position, which was forbidden at the time by Art. 4, No. 1, e) of Law No. 18/2003 of June 11th (later superseded and replaced by Art. 11 of Law No. 19/2012, of May 8th).

The Portuguese Competition Authority conducted an investigation to the Case from 2003 to 2009 where it concluded that Company A had infringed the Portuguese Competition law. As a result, a fine was imposed on Company A by the Competition Authority.

Around August 2011, one of the retailers initiated legal proceedings against Company A to claim damages.

2. The general statutory provision of Portuguese law on damage claim is Art. 483 of the Civil Code.

It is commonly accepted by Portuguese doctrine and case law that anyone who claims damages based on civil liability needs to provide evidence of the existence of certain voluntary fact (the damaging act), the unlawfulness of such act (*ilicitude*), the negligence or intention to cause harm behind such act (*culpa*) and the existence of damage and the causal relationship (*nexo de causalidade*) between the unlawful act and the damage.

It is important to underline that in Portugal the concept of unlawfulness is not broadly defined (as occurs in other countries); on the contrary, unlawfulness shall arise from the infringement of certain rights (mainly personality rights or property rights) or from the breach of legal rules which aim to protect third parties' (private) interests (that protect such interests without providing "rights" to the third parties considered).

On the other hand, and although nothing is specifically written in Art. 483 on this matter, in order to claim damages based on breach of legal rules which aim to protect third parties' interests, three requirements have to be met by the claimant: (i) a breach of a certain statutory provision was detrimental to the Claimant's interests; (ii) that statutory provisions aim, in fact, to protect certain private interests; (iii) the damage occurred within the circle of private interests that the statutory provision aims to protect.[2]

The reason for this brief explanation lies in the fact that in most cases, the claim for damages based on the breach of competition law is not based on the infringement of property rights (in a broad sense), but rather on the breach of legal rules which aim to protect third parties' interests.

It is my opinion that this particular concept of unlawfulness, and the specific requirements to which it is subject, does not prevent (should not prevent) the Portuguese courts from accepting claims for damages based on the breach of statutory provisions relating to competition, since the statutory provisions that rule competition are, without any doubt, provisions that aim to protect third parties' interests. This is, precisely, the basic concept of the Directive.

Thus, on this matter I believe that Portuguese law is in line with the Directive.

3. As described in the Case above, although the change in the general conditions of the distribution contract took place in May 2002, the retailer only initiated legal proceedings in August 2011. This happened because all the Claimant attempts to obtain the relevant information to assess whether or not an abuse of dominant position was underway were barred by Company A on the grounds that such information was protected by commercial secrecy.

In other words, the information required by the retailer to claim damages from the wholesaler was held by the latter, which always refused

---

2 Although Art. 483 doesn't provide expressly for these requirements, it is commonly accepted by the Portuguese doctrine that they have to be met in order to support the claim for damages. Varela, J. A., *Das Obrigações em Geral*, Vol. I. 10th ed. Coimbra: Almedina, 2000, pp. 539-542.

its disclosure. Although the retailer suspected that it was being a victim of an unlawful conduct by the wholesaler it was not completely sure of such facts and could not bring the wholesaler to justice based simply on suspicions and assumptions it could not prove.

As stated in the preamble of the Directive, actions for damages "*for infringements of Union or national competition law*" typically require a complex factual and economic analysis. The evidence necessary to prove a claim for damages is often held exclusively by the opposing party or by third parties and is not sufficiently known by or accessible to the claimant. In such circumstances, strict legal requirements for claimants to assert in detail all the facts surrounding their case at the beginning of an action and to offer precisely specified items of supporting evidence can unduly impede the effective exercise of the right to compensation.

To address this issue in general terms, Art. 417 of the Portuguese Civil Procedure Code sets out a broadly defined "duty to cooperate". Under this statutory provision, all persons, whether or not involved in the proceedings, are bound to cooperate with the court by answering any question, allowing any necessary inspection, delivering anything required and performing every act determined as necessary by the court. However, in the small number of judicial cases where the court was asked to provide the claimant a compensation for damages arising from the breach of competition law there is no information on whether or not the claimants explored the possibilities allowed by Art. 417.

The Directive addresses this issue in Art. 5.

Art. 5, para. 1, instructs the Member States to "ensure that in proceedings relating to an action for damages in the Union, upon request of a claimant who has presented a grounded justification containing reasonably available facts and evidence sufficient to support the plausibility of its claim for damages, *national courts are able to order the defendant or a third party to disclose relevant evidence which lies in their control*", on a need-to-disclose basis, of course, and subject to proportionality and adequate protection of confidential information.

I underline that this third party to whom the court is able to order the disclosure of evidence may be (and will certainly be in many cases) the national competition authority, in which case, this disclosure shall be also subject to the limitations set out in Art. 6, that apply in addition to Art. 5.

It is my belief that the "duty to cooperate" set out in Art. 417 of the Portuguese Civil Procedure Code is in line with arts. 5 and 6 of the Directive and, if duly interpreted by the court (according with the Directive), won't restrict the purposes of the Directive on this issue. On the other hand, the broadly manner in which Art. 417 is drafted will surely impose on the Portuguese lawmaker the need to safeguard the boundaries, particularly those set out in articles 6 and 7.

Also important in this context, and still related to the assessment of the relevant facts, is the rule whereby the "infringement of competition law found by a final decision of a national competition authority or by a review court is deemed to be irrefutably established for the purposes of an action for damages brought before their national courts under Article 101 or 102 TFEU or under national competition law" – Art. 9, para. 1, of the Directive.[3]

In other words, if the competition authority (or a review court) has carried out an investigation and has concluded that an infringement of competition law has occurred, then those entities who suffered damages as a result thereof shall be able to claim damages without bearing the burden of proof in what concerns the content of the final decision.

In the Portuguese Civil Procedure Code, the statutory provision that addresses this issue (Art. 623) refers only to court decisions on criminal matters. This provision determines that, in a civil procedure, a decision of a criminal court whereby a certain person was convicted constitutes only a rebuttable presumption of the facts on which the conviction was based. Thus, it is rather unlikely that a decision of a competition authority would be taken into account, in any manner, in a claim for damages brought before the civil courts.

This is surely a matter where the Portuguese lawmaker will need to make important changes, I believe even beyond the limits of competition law taking into account the Principle of Equality (Art. 13 of the Portuguese Constitution).

4. In matters concerning breach of competition law is also important to remember that, in some cases, the liability arising from such wrongful conduct may trigger breach of contract and the inherent contractual liability, whenever the duty to comply with statutory provisions (statutory competition provisions, in this matter) was included in the contract whether expressly or implicitly. It is generally accepted in the Portuguese legal system that the performance of contract includes the compliance

---

3 On a similar line, Art. 9, para. 2, determines that the "Member States shall ensure that where a final decision referred to in paragraph 1 is taken in another Member State, that final decision may, in accordance with national law, be presented before their national courts as at least prima facie evidence that an infringement of competition law has occurred and, as appropriate, may be assessed along with any other evidence adduced by the parties."

with mandatory legal rules, a duty included in the general duty to act in good faith set out in Art. 762 of the Civil Code.[4]

The qualification of this liability as contractual or tort is important in the matter of burden of proof, since, in the former, it is the debtor who has to prove that there was no intention or negligence on its part (Art. 799 of the Civil Code); it is also important in the matter of limitation periods: if the liability is of tort nature, the claimant has only three years to bring his claim before the court (Art. 498 of the Civil Code), whereas it would have twenty years to do so if the claim arises from the breach of contract (Art. 309 of the Civil Code).

In the Case, the wholesaler unilaterally changed the terms of an existing contract giving rise to an abuse of dominant position. Not only should such unilateral change be considered null and void due to violation of a mandatory law, but such act should also be considered a breach of the general duty to act in good faith when performing the contract and the liability arising thereof qualified as of contractual nature.[5]

The issue of the limitation period shall be addressed below.

5. Under Portuguese law, and except in very special circumstances (expressly determined by a statutory provision), the claimant has the burden of proof of all the legal requirements in order to obtain compensation for damages.

As stated above, the claimant has the burden to prove the damaging act, the unlawfulness of the same (*ilicitude*), the negligence or intention to cause harm (*culpa*), the existence of damages and the causal relationship between the unlawful act and such damages (*nexo de causalidade*). As mentioned previously, whenever the claim is based on contractual liability, the claimant does not have to prove the negligence or intention but solely the other four requirements, namely the damage and the causal relationship between the act and the damage.

In what concerns the damage, Art. 562 of the Civil Code entitles the claimant to full compensation for all damages suffered; the defendant is obliged to place the claimant in the position in which the latter would have been if the infringement had not occurred, and that includes the right to claim compensation for loss of profit (Art. 564 of the Civil Code).

Portuguese law does not allow punitive damages or any other form of overcompensation of damages.

---

4 Varela, J. A., cit., pp. 125-128.

5 Almeida, C. F. d, *Responsabilidade civil pelo abuso de posição dominante: em especial, os prazos de prescrição*, (not published) p. 29 et seq.

On this matter, the Directive provides that "Member States shall ensure that any natural or legal person who has suffered harm caused by an infringement of competition law is able *to claim and to obtain full compensation for that harm*" (Art. 3, para. 1). In the following paragraph, the Directive clarifies that "Full compensation shall place a person who has suffered harm in the position in which that person would have been had the infringement of competition law not been committed. It shall therefore cover the right to compensation for actual loss and for loss of profit, plus the payment of interest".

At the same time, paragraph 3 provides that full compensation cannot "not lead to overcompensation, whether by means of punitive, multiple or other types of damages".

I dare to say that in this area Portuguese law is perfectly in line with the Directive.

Art. 17 of the Directive establishes two interesting rules concerning the proof of damages.

On the one hand, the "Member States shall ensure that the national courts are empowered, in accordance with national procedures, *to estimate the amount of harm if it is established that a claimant suffered harm* but it is practically impossible or excessively difficult precisely to quantify the harm suffered on the basis of the evidence available" (Art. 17, para. 1). On the other hand, it "shall be presumed that cartel infringements cause harm", being this presumption rebuttable by the infringer (Art. 17, para. 2).

These two paragraphs address different, although complementary, issues. On one side the proof of the damage (of the harm) and on the other side the quantification of such damage or harm.

As to the first issue, the presumption of damage arising from cartel infringements, there is no similar provision in Portuguese law, and this will be one field where the intervention of the Portuguese lawmaker will be required. It must be underlined, however, that this presumption, by itself, does not solve the entire problem, since the damage must be proved *and quantified* in order to entitle the claimant to compensation.

But this presumption combined with paragraph 1 will surely become very useful, since once the existence of damage is established (although through a presumption) the court will have the power to quantify such damage, even if such quantification must be made "on the basis of the evidence available".

It is important to underline that Portuguese law already confers a similar power to the court. In fact, Art. 566, para. 3, of the Civil Code, provides that in the cases where it is not possible to determine the exact value of the damages, the court shall determine such value on the basis of considerations of equity (*ex aequo et bono*) within the limits of the evidence obtained.

6. Of course the plaintiff is not entitled to compensation for all damages claimed, but solely for damages resulting from the infringement.

This principle is clearly stated in Art. 3, para. 1: the person "who has suffered harm *caused by* an infringement of competition law is able to claim and to obtain full compensation for *that* harm". This same principle underlies paragraphs 2 and 3.

Paragraph 2 sets out that the person who has suffered harm shall be placed "in the position in which that person would have been had the infringement of competition law not been committed"; paragraph 3 excludes overcompensation, "whether by means of punitive, multiple or other types of damages".

The Directive establishes this principle but leaves to the Member States the issue of how to establish a causal relationship between the infringement and the damage; however, the "Member States shall ensure that neither the burden nor the standard of proof required for the quantification of harm render the exercise of the right to damages practically impossible or excessively difficult" (Art. 17, para. 1).

Although this provision seems to be mainly directed to the proof of the damage and its quantification, I would dare to say that the same principle should be applicable to the causal relationship, since all these issues are closely tied.

Art. 563 of the Civil Code refers to causal relationship and sets out that the duty to indemnify will cover the damages that the injured party probably would not have suffered had the infringement not occurred.

The Portuguese doctrine sees in this rule the acceptance, by the lawmaker, of the "theory of the adequate causality" (*teoria da causalidade adequada*), in its negative formulation. According to this formulation, a damage is an adequate consequence of a certain act if the latter was a condition of the damage, or at least one of the conditions (even if such damage wasn't foreseeable), and there were no exceptional circumstances which may have caused the act to become irrelevant for the damage. Even in this case, that is, if exceptional circumstances occurred that made the act irrelevant for causing the damage, an "adequate causality" is considered to exist if such exceptional circumstances were known by the defendant or should be have been known by him if acting diligently.[6]

---

[6] Telles, I. G., *Direito das Obrigações*. 7th ed. Coimbra: Coimbra Editora, 1997, p. 405.

In my view, it is fair to say that Portuguese law accepts a broad concept of causal relationship, which is in line with the concept of the Directive on this matter.

7. Going back to the Case, the defendant argued that any liability from its part would have to be qualified as tort; being that the case, and taking into account that the alleged infringement had occurred from 2002 to 2005 and the legal suit was filed in 2011, the defendant would have to be discharged from any liability, since the applicable limitation period is three years.

In fact, Art. 498 of the Civil Code determines a limitation period of three years for damage claims based on tort liability, which is counted from the moment the claimant became aware of his/her right to compensation, even if the claimant didn't know the identity of the infringement party and/or the extension of the damages suffered.

In the Case, the claimant argued that the liability arising from the abuse of dominant position should be qualified as contractual, in which case the limitation period is extended to twenty years, but this Art. 498 poses an important problem for anyone who claims damages arising out of an infringement of competition law, taking into account all the difficulties related to the finding of the relevant facts and the disclosure of evidence.

The Directive addresses this issue in two ways.

Firstly, the limitation period for claiming damages arising out of an infringement of competition law is set at five years *at least* (Art. 10, para. 3). It's also important to point out that the limitation period shall not begin to run before the infringement of competition law has ceased and the claimant knows, or can reasonably be expected to know, of the behaviour, of the fact that it constitutes an infringement of competition law, of the fact that the infringement of competition law caused harm to it and the identity of the infringer (Art. 10, para. 2).

Secondly, the limitation period shall be suspended or, depending on national law, interrupted "if a competition authority takes action for the purpose of the investigation or its proceedings in respect of an infringement of competition law to which the action for damages relates". Such suspension "shall end at the earliest one year after the infringement decision has become final or after the proceedings are otherwise terminated" (Art. 10, para. 4).

This simple comparison between Portuguese law and the Directive shows that the transposition of the Directive into Portuguese law will result in a provision dramatically different from the rule presently in force.

I don't know whether the Portuguese lawmaker will choose to adopt a specific rule for infringements of competition law or rather to change Art. 498 of the Portuguese Civil Code in order to extend the provisions of the Directive to all cases of damage claims based on tort liability.

Should the Portuguese lawmaker decide to follow the first route mentioned above, I suspect that this may trigger a problem of conformity of such rule with the Constitution – the principle of equality set out in Art. 13 – unless it is possible to demonstrate that the claims for damages based on infringement of competition law are legally different from all the other claims, and that such difference justifies such a specific legal framework.

In this regard, I come back to the Case underlining that a legal regime in line with the Directive would have rendered the discussion about the contractual or tort nature of the liability useless, since the investigation of the Portuguese competition authority would have suspended (or interrupted) the limitation period which would lead to an expiration of the latter only in 2014 (the investigation was initiated before the infringement had ceased).

Bibliography

Almeida, C. F. d, *Responsabilidade civil pelo abuso de posição dominante: em especial, os prazos de prescrição*, (not published).

Telles, I. G., *Direito das Obrigações*. 7th ed. Coimbra: Coimbra Editora, 1997.

Varela, J. A., *Das Obrigações em Geral*, Vol. I. 10th ed. Coimbra: Almedina, 2000.

Part II

Exclusionary abuses: recent trends

Upside down: The EU jurisprudence on aftermarkets

Paul Nihoul[1]

Introduction

This paper is devoted to aftermarkets, considered under Article 102 TFUE. The term "aftermarkets" may appear complicated in the first instance. But it means, in substance, what it refers to. "After"-"markets" are markets coming after (an)other one(s). In this contribution, we will designate these aftermarkets with the symbol "M2" or "M3", depending on their number. They will be called "secondary" or "third" market(s). These markets intervene, in business models, as well as in competition law instruments, after "primary" or "M1" markets.

Suppose you are buying a printer. The latter will constitute, for our analysis, the primary market – or M1. In connection with that object, you may acquire all sorts of goods or services relating to that primary market. For instance, with a printer, you would have to buy consumables. In case of defect, you would have to buy spare parts. You could also order improvements – in case the printer works with software in need to be upgraded or updated. Accessories can be purchased – for instance cords. Services can even be ordered – like maintenance services, repair services or coaching services (in this latter case, if the printer is sophisticated and you need explanations to use it properly).

Business model

That sort of situation has a particular relevance for businesses seeking to maximize profits. One man who knows a lot in that regard is Michael Porter – a Harvard academic who spent his academic life investigating the most successful companies and trying to find out what the key was

---

1 Chair of Academic Society for Competition Law (Ascola); General Editor of JECLAP – Journal of European Competition Law & Practice; Professor of law at the Université Catholique de Louvain (UCL), Belgium.

for their success.[2] That key, he stated, was to protect oneself against competition. Whenever companies are protected from competitors, they can charge higher prices. With such prices, they can increase profits.[3] By contrast, companies living on competitive markets can hardly make a living. They must maintain prices close to costs. Would they charge higher prices, consumers would flee to alternative suppliers.

The theory developed by Porter has particular relevance for aftermarkets. The latter provide businesses with opportunities to protect themselves against competitors. They can do so by locking consumers in – compelling the latter to purchase their products or services on aftermarkets by organizing a link or dependency with the primary market.

A typical example is the purchase of printers. Such equipment requires, for its use, ink cartridges. These last years, printer manufacturers have adopted all sorts of practices aimed at ensuring that customers purchasing their equipment would buy the cartridges and ink of the same brand – theirs. Some of these practices are technical in nature. For instance, printer manufacturers have inserted, on cartridges, microchips ensuring a dialogue between the cartridge and the printer. That dialogue makes it possible for the printer to start printing. Cartridges not equipped with such chips, that is, cartridges produced by other manufacturers, cannot be used – or hardly.

Other mechanisms are: design protection impeding the duplication of cartridges by independent producers; frequent changes of form for cartridges, making it more difficult for such producers to adapt their line of production; collection systems whereby empty cartridges are returned to the brand manufacturer, thereby preventing independent manufacturers from buying them and filling them with their ink; rebates and discriminatory pricing in favour of distributors participating to the system, etc.

In these situations, customers are locked in. Whenever they purchase a primary product from a given firm, they must buy, in substance, the secondary ones from that same supplier. On the secondary market, they enjoy limited alternatives. Their choice is restricted. If they are unhappy with the conditions proposed by the firm on the aftermarket market, their only possibility in terms of reaction is to decide that, next time, they will

---

2 See mainly Porter, M., *Competitive Strategy. Techniques for analysing industries and competitors*. Amsterdam: Free Press, 1980. Porter, M., *Competitive advantage. Creating and sustaining superior performance*. Amsterdam: Free Press, 1985. More recently, see discussions on http://www.aftermarketeurope.com/ where a recurring theme is the importance of aftermarkets to generate profits.

3 Doing so, they can attract capital – which, in turn, helps them establish positions where, if they behave properly, they will not suffer from competitors.

purchase another brand.[4] The consequence is that, absent immediate pressure, the firm may be tempted to charge, on these aftermarkets, higher prices – prices higher than those that could be charged on competitive markets.

Typically, the strategy, for firms, could then be formulated as follows. Design products requiring accessories or secondary supplies. Sell the primary product at a low price – attracting the attention of customers, ensuring that that product is chosen by preference to those supplied by competitors and causing the dissemination of the product in society. Once you have a substantial installed base, charge, for accessories, higher prices. In setting the level of these prices, take two elements into account. Firstly, the price for accessories should not be overtly excessive, for clients may otherwise stop using the primary product. Secondly, it should, however, compensate, at least, the losses incurred, or the low revenues obtained, on the primary market. This will be easier, in practice, on aftermarkets where a large quantity of small accessories can be sold – for instance nails to be used on nail guns. On such markets, a tiny price increase may generate huge profits as such products are used by millions and is resented as not being unacceptable by customers.[5]

Should society react?

So much for the business model carried out by firms that want to maximize their profits on conformity with the reason why they were created. Should this be accepted, however, by society? How should society react when confronted with such behaviour?

- Should authorities accept such behaviour and consider that, on the markets concerned, the possibility that higher prices may be charged is the reward to be paid for firms able to attract customer in the first instance?
- Or should it react, considering that, in all circumstances, consumers should have the possibility of exercising a choice – even on secondary markets where generic producers ought to have the

4 They can also threaten the brand manufacturer by telling him/her that, next time they must purchase a product pertaining to the relevant market, they will turn to alternatives. Another possibility, for unsatisfied customers, is to disseminate information on the "bad" behavior adopted by the manufacturer in question.

5 In the literature, see Farrell, J.; Klemperer, P., "Coordination and lock-in: competition with switching costs and network effects", in Armstrong, M.; Porter, R. (eds.), *Handbook of Industrial Organization*. Amsterdam: Elsevier, 2007, pp. 1967-2072. See also Katz, M. L.; Shapiro, C., "Systems competition and network effects", *The Journal of Economic Perspectives*, 1994, pp. 93-115.

possibility of presenting their goods or services to customers – thus empowering the latter to choose, among available supplies, what best corresponds to their needs?

In the European Union, interventions by authorities must be founded, in the context of competition law, on a legal basis. On what provisions could such interventions be based, as regards aftermarkets? In the context of competition law, interventions by authorities can be based on Article 101 TFUE, Article 102 TFUE and Merger control. In this paper, we concentrate on the treatment given under Article 102 TFUE.[6]

Leading case: *Hilti*

More than the other provisions, it is the application of Article 102 TFUE which has attracted attention in the context of aftermarkets. The leading case in that context is *Hilti*. The case is not very old – with a decision by the Commission in 1987,[7] a judgment by the Court of First Instance in 1991[8] and a judgment by the Court of Justice in 1994.[9] It is repeatedly cited in ulterior jurisprudence. For these reasons, one can probably consider that case constitutes, for the analysis of the jurisprudence, a solid precedent.

In that case, the company – of which the case bears the name – was manufacturing nail guns to be used in construction works. In these guns, cartridges were inserted with, in them, nails.

- The nail guns made by Hilti were relatively sophisticated. They involved complex technology in which Hilti, on the basis of its experience, had acquired an edge on rivals.
- That edge also existed for cartridges, which were specifically designed for use in the guns made by the company. The design of such cartridges was protected by intellectual property rights. As a result, these tools could not be duplicated by other manufacturers.
- Although still comfortable, the situation was different for nails. Such products are rather basic, and involve little (if any)

6 For a survey of alternatives opened to authorities as regards the regulation of aftermarkets, see Schulz, L., "The economics of aftermarkets", *Journal of European Competition law and Practice*, 2015, pp. 123-128; OFT, The Economics of Secondary Product Markets (OFT1471), 2012, available at http://webarchive.nationalarchives.gov.uk/20140402142426/http:/www.oft.gov.uk/OFTwork/research/economic-research/completed-research.

7 Decision of the European Commission, of 22 December 1987, relating to a proceeding under Article 86 of the EEC Treaty (IV/30.787 and 31.488 – Eurofix-Bauco v. Hilti), OJ L 65/19.

8 Arrêt *Hilti v Commission*, T-30/89, EU:T:1991:70.

9 Arrêt *Hilti v Commission*, C-53/92 P, EU:C:1994:77.

technological component. The consequence is that they can be manufactured, relatively easily, by generic producers.

To conduct its business, Hilti considered these products as forming a system. In line with explanations provided in the previous section, the strategy was to ensure that users equipped with Hilti nail guns would use the nails produced by the firm – thereby allowing the firm to maximize profits as millions of nails were used with such guns on a yearly basis.

To carry out that strategy, the firm sought to prevent independent nail manufacturers to find, on the market, empty cartridges which they could fill with their nails. To that effect, it resorted to a variety of practices. In substance: Hilti refused to license the necessary IP rights to those manufacturers so as to prevent them from producing cartridges on their own; forbad subsidiaries and independent distributors to sell empty cartridges; provided discounts to firms abiding by that policy; refused to repair damaged nail guns whenever it appeared that the latter could have been used with nails manufactured by independent producers.

In substance, thus, Hilti sought to impede the emergence of a separate market for cartridges, and nails, compatible with its primary products, and to promote the idea, and the perception, that these products were to be considered as belonging to the same market.

Position of the Commission

The case came to the European Commission, which decided otherwise. For that institution, three products were involved. Three markets were thus to be distinguished.

- One for nail guns, where Hilti was in competition with other nail gun producers. (M1)
- Another for cartridges. On that market, the sole cartridges to be considered were those compatible with the nail guns made by Hilti. The cartridges made for other nail guns were not substitutable. They could not be used as an accessory to the nail guns made by Hilti. (M2)
- And a last market for nails. On that market, only the nails compatible with the cartridges to be used on Hilti nail guns could be taken into account. Indeed, other nails would not fit into these cartridges and could not, as a result, be used as substitutes by customers. (M3)

Analysing then the structure of the market, the Commission observed that Hilti possessed a dominant position on M1. That position was due to the technological hedge acquired by the company throughout its history. The company had been the first to imagine the possibility of using such a mechanism to attach materials. It had created the market and had been able to sustain the interest of customers with continuous innovation – remaining, as a result, lead on the market.

What was the position of Hilti on M2? On that market, the firm was the only one producing cartridges compatible with its nail guns. As indicated, these cartridges were protected by IP rights. These rights were not licensed to any other company – the firm refused to do so. The consequence was that the firm possessed, on that secondary market, a monopoly.

On M3, there were, by contrast, competitors. Technically, market entry was relatively easy as manufacturing nails did not involve significant technological components. In practice, however, selling such nails was difficult since, as a result of the practices used by the firm, manufacturers could not find empty cartridges in to insert their nails.

For the Commission, in doing so, Hilti abused its dominant position. Such exclusionary policies produced a situation where independent manufacturers could not present their products to customers who would then have been in a position to choose the nails best corresponding to their needs – presumably nails cheaper than those proposed by Hilti.

That analysis made by the European Commission was confirmed by the European courts and seems in line with the general jurisprudence developed by these institutions in the field of competition. In the case, the notion of abuse was applied in conformity with the general jurisprudence. In that jurisprudence, many cases prohibit dominant firms to use the dominance they possess on a primary market in order to extend that domination on related ones.

The structure of the markets involved was also analysed in conformity with the tools generally used in other cases. Among these tools are, in the first place, the market share held by the company on the relevant market. In this case, no specific indication was provided on that point as the firm considered that these figures were confidential. But the case provides a reasonable certainty that that market share was significant on the primary market – and total on the secondary one. The relative capacity of competitors to react was taken into account – particularly on the market for cartridges where the Commission noted that potential entrants could not find anywhere empty cartridges. It was also considered on the market for nails where, for the same reason, it was observed that independent manufacturers were not in a position to supply purchasers with nails made by them in the absence of cartridges available on the market.

Markets were also defined using criteria such as the existence of a specific demand, and a specific supply, for the products in question. For the Commission, nail guns, cartridges or nails are not necessarily manufactured by the same firm. There is a desire, on the part of independent suppliers, to manufacture nails independently.

Microsoft

Hilti is often cited as the leading case for aftermarkets. The position adopted in that case by the European institution has been confirmed in other situations – some also involving the Court of Justice, which, in last resort, decides about the interpretation to be given to the rules of competition, in particular of those formulated in the Treaties.

One of these ulterior cases involved the US firm Microsoft. Among others, Microsoft had integrated, apparently for free, into its operating system, multimedia software Windows Media Player. The consequence of that integration was that, if they needed multimedia software, customers did not need to seek other software. As a result, competitors could not present their software to potential buyers or acquirers. And the latter were denied any real, realistic possibility of choosing the multimedia software which they considered corresponded to their needs.

Again, that case can be considered as containing stable and solid jurisprudence positions as it attracted much attention both in Europe and the United States, given the involvement of an EU company. In practice, the case affected 95% of personal computers worldwide as this was at the time the market share held by the company on the market for the operating system. This is to say that a significant portion of the world population was concerned – and this has certainly contributed to the Commission revising several times its copy to make sure it conformed to ideas shared by the Commissioners.

In that case, the position adopted by the Commission,[10] and confirmed by the General Court,[11] was similar, in substance, to that provided in *Hilti*. In the decision, the Commission devotes considerable efforts to market definition. In conformity with its business model, the firm defended the idea that the two products were to be considered jointly as part of a broad market consisting as software systems used on personal computers. That position was set aside for the same reasons as those provided in *Hilti*. For the Commission, a specific, separate supply existed for multimedia software.

- Indeed, such software had been developed by others firms – and it was precisely in reaction against these initiatives that Microsoft had designed its own software and integrated it in Windows.

---

[10] Decision of the European Commission, of 24 March 2004, relating to a proceeding under Article 82 of the EEC Treaty, Case COMP/C-3/37.792.

[11] Arrêt *Microsoft v Commission*, EU:T:2007:289.

- The Commission also provided indications that, similarly, there existed a specific, separate demand for other multimedia software. Surveys were provided, showing that part of the users preferred the software made by other firms as it was found of better quality. In such a context, it was important they be provided with choice opportunities allowing them to select the software corresponding to their needs.

Other cases

Beyond *Hilti* and *Microsoft*, other cases deal with aftermarkets. As an example: in the car market, two vehicle manufacturers were sued for charging excessive prices on the market of spare parts meant for the vehicles of their brand.[12] Here again, markets were defined as being separate. The general car market was dissociated from the market for spare parts. On the primary market, these manufacturers did not enjoy any form of dominant position. On the contrary, they were confronted with heavy competition as users do not hesitate to change brands whenever they must purchase a new car. By contrast, each of these manufacturers was found to have a dominant position, in fact a monopoly, on the market for spare parts corresponding to their vehicles. No spare part made for one type of care can be deemed substitutable, as regards demand, to spare parts meant for another one. And no substitutability existed as regards the supply side because, as in many similar markets, the car manufacturers owned IP rights on the design of the spare parts and refused to license such rights to allow the production of such products by independent manufacturers.

The consequence was that, once they had bought a car of a specific brand, customers were locked in. In case of accident, or need for repair, they had to purchase the spare parts made by the car manufacturer of the same brand. These manufacturers were taking advantage of the situation, by charging tariffs which could be deemed excessive. The case went to the Court of Justice, which considered that the car manufacturers held a dominant position on the secondary market (spare parts) and were abusing their position by charging excessive tariffs.[13]

12 Arrêt *Volvo*, C-238/87, EU:C:1988:477. Arrêt *Renault*, C-53/87, EU:C:1988:472.

13 In *Hilti*, the firm could charge higher tariffs on nails because they had little effects on customers. Typically, nails used in nail guns are charged to final consumers by construction workers. And even a small variation of price has a tremendous effect on profits as nails are sold by millions. In *Volvo* and *Renault*, the final price for spare parts was also charged, in most instances, to consumers who could not react. In cases of accidents, repair costs are charged to insurance companies and there is no related effect on insurance clients. Whenever they have some responsibility in the accident, the latter

New approach proposed

Despite its well established character, the case law presented above is being challenged. The challengers primarily come from the business side – particularly the side which, as a result of the position adopted by the European institutions, is being prevented from using the business strategy delineated above: charging high prices on aftermarkets after selling the primary product at a reasonable tariff. That is the side of the dominant firms, which can carry out that strategy because they dominate the aftermarket.

That position has been echoed in various publications – some of which are economic and others are legal in nature. In the European Union, the main paper on that subject matter comes from John Temple Lang – a former DG COMP director currently working as an attorney in a prestigious law firm and defending, in that capacity, firms which, in his former career, were opposed to the Commission.[14]

For M. Temple Lang, a distinction must be made between two categories of cases as regards aftermarkets. In a first category are the cases where the firm dominates the secondary but also the primary market. That is, typically, the situation in *Hilti*, and also in *Microsoft*. In those cases, for M. Temple Lang, the current jurisprudence should be upheld. Indeed, the position of M1 dominance involved in those situations implies that customers do not really enjoy choice possibilities. The firm being an obligatory partner on that primary market, they must purchase, in substance, the primary product coming from that firm. They cannot turn to M1 alternatives if they are not satisfied with the prices charged on the secondary market or if they do not want such secondary product.

By contrast, the situation would be different, and should thus be treated differently, when the firm does not dominate the primary market. The lack of dominance, on such markets, would imply that customers can turn to alternatives when they are not satisfied. Would prices be excessive on the secondary markets? Customers could then turn to alternatives when they buy a new product on that primary market – and we can suppose they would do so. According to M. Temple Lang, that possible reaction of M2 unsatisfied customers would discipline the firm on the secondary market. Knowing that it would lose M1 customers if it was charging M2 excessive prices, the firm would behave reasonably on this secondary market.

---

see their premiums being increased. But no connection can be established because the price for spare parts and these increases.

14 Lang, J. Temple, "Practical Aspects of Aftermarkets in European Competition Law", *Competition Policy International*, 2011, pp. 191-241.

Of course, that possible reaction by unsatisfied customers (turning to alternatives) would only produce effects the next time they purchase a new product. But another element would contribute to disciplining the firm. Without waiting for the next occasion to buy an M1 product, dissatisfied customers could voice their anger – and this would cause current purchasers to turn to alternatives. Thus, firms would adopt reasonable M2 behaviour not only because they could lose customers in the future but also because they could lose some now already as a result of information provided by angry users.

In the publication by J. Temple Lang, the proposal is based on four ideas.

(a) Firms should be free to organize their activities as they consider appropriate. They know better than authorities how to conduct their business. If they consider that their operations should turn around systems rather than products, authorities should let them do so.

(b) In the context of aftermarkets, the organization of competition around systems makes it possible for producers to sell primary products at discount prices. This is interesting, according to J. Temple Lang, for the dissemination of innovation. As these products are sold at low prices, they are purchased by more customers. That dissemination, in turn, is important as it brings about, from firms, additional resources that they will be able to invest in research for the development of new innovations.

(c) The organization of activities around systems has one disadvantage – that the use of the equipment is more expensive as it is on the sale of consumables of accessories that profits must be made. But that disadvantage is only apparent. Transferring the cost to secondary products ensures that pricing strategies are more equitable. Such strategies indeed ensure that costs depend on usage. In the context of printers: those printing more will pay more than those who hardly make use of their equipment.

(d) The price for accessory products or services will always remain reasonable. Firms will not abuse their position on that market, as charging excessive prices would induce customers not to purchase a new primary product when the one they have will have to be replaced – or, if they decide to replace that product, to shift to another supplier charging lower prices for the use of its product.

1995: Lack of dominance

These ideas have received some credit within the Commission. In 1995, that approach was used in *Pelikan v Kyocera* – a case concerning a claim made by producer Pelikan that printer manufacturer Kyocera was abusing a dominant position by refusing to let independent ink manufacturers to place cartridges in its equipment.[15]

As it did in *Hilti* and the other cases mentioned above, the Commission considered that the consumables meant for Kyocera equipment form a market separate from that for printers. The arguments are the same as those used in those cases. For the Commission, there is a specific demand for consumables on the part of the people owning Kyocera equipment. There is also a specific supply for that sort of product as other producers, independent from Kyocera, commercialize that sort of supply.

The analysis is the same as regards the structure of the primary market. In its decision, the Commission notes that, on that primary market, no dominance exists. The manufacturers of printers are in competition against one another – and that competition, according to the Commission, is intense.

Where the difference appears is where the Commission analyses the possible existence of a situation of dominance on the secondary market – corresponding to the consumables to be used in Kyocera equipment. On that market, Kyocera holds a factual monopoly. Filled cartridges usable on such equipment can only be found with Kyocera. No alternatives exist – as a result of the strategy used by the firm which has consistently opposed the emergence of independent manufacturers of consumables compatible with its equipment.

Despite that factual monopoly, the Commission denies the existence of a dominant position. That position is based on the fact that, on that secondary market, Kyocera, according to the Commission, could not behave independently from competitors, or consumers. That constraint weighing on its behaviour was due, for that institution, to the degree of competition existing on M1. That competition implies the possibility, for M2 customers, to turn to an M1 alternative in case they are not satisfied with the strategy carried out on M2 by the firm.

In the decision, the presence of competition on M1 is thus the reason for considering that no dominance exists on M2 despite the presence of a factual monopoly on that latter market. That analysis is based on the following elements.

- Customers can make informed choices on lifecycle printing whenever they purchase a printer.
- They are likely to make their choices on the basis of the information they have been able to gather.

[15] Decision of the European Commission, of 22 September 1995, Case No. IV/34.330 – Pelikan/Kyocera, SG(95) D/11872.

- There are reasons to believe that a number of customers would shift to an M1 alternative if they realize that M2 prices are excessive – and that number would be sufficient to cause problems to the firm if it was really taking place.
- That shift would occur in a relatively short period of time.

In its reasoning, the Commission considers two shifting possibilities. The first is the possible exodus of current printer owners to another brand, next time they must make such purchase, if they realize that their printer is expensive in usage. The second is the possible shift of current purchasers who would normally buy Kyocera equipment but refrain from doing so on the basis of information provided by unsatisfied Kyocera users.

1997: Different markets

A related position was adopted by the Commission in another case decided two years later – in 1997.[16] The case concerned, this time, Ricoh photocopiers. These machines were used with cartridges containing ink. Only the cartridges made by the equipment manufacturer could be used. Their form and functionalities could not be duplicated without authorization by the manufacturer (IP rights). No authorization to that effect had ever been given by the manufacturer. As part of the same strategy, Ricoh was refusing to sell empty cartridges. As a result, independent ink manufacturers could not find cartridges to fill with their ink.

Under *Hilti*, the case would have been analysed as containing three markets: one for the equipment, another for the cartridges and a third for the ink.

Ricoh's market share was small on the primary market (photocopiers). But it was total on the secondary one as the firm was the only one supplying cartridges and ink. Despite that situation, the Commission concluded that the firm did not dominate the secondary market. To reach that conclusion, that institution used the four criteria established in *Kyocera*. For the Commission, information was available on the lifecycle cost of the equipment; as information was available, it was likely to be used by customers; the latter would shift to M1 alternatives, next time, if they were not satisfied by M2 conditions; current buyers would make the same shift, now, on the basis of information provided by angry users.

The conclusion was that the request made by the competing undertaking (Info-Lab) was to be rejected. As it did not dominate the market for consumables, the equipment manufacturer could not be deemed to abuse

[16] Decision of the European Commission, 1997, Case No. IV/E.2/36.431 – Info-Lab/Ricoh.

a dominant position by refusing to sell empty cartridges to independent ink manufacturers.

Interestingly, the Commission provides, in its decision, a second argument to justify its position. That argument is founded in a definition of market which is different from the one proposed in *Hilti*, *Microsoft*, *Volvo*, or *Renault*. In those cases, each product is considered a market. The argument is that there exists a separate demand, and a separate supply, for each of them.

This is independent of whether, at the time of the case, it was effectively possible to purchase and/or produce these products independently. Otherwise, the definition of markets would depend on the strategy carried out by the firm. For instance: in *Hilti*, the firm wanted to avoid any competition on the market for nails compatible with its cartridges and nail guns. For that reason, it made sure that independent nail producers would not be able to find empty Hilti cartridges to fill. That decision cannot determine the definition given to markets by competition authorities. If so, firms would be allowed to decide themselves how the rules of competition apply to their behaviour.

In *Kyocera*, the Commission distinguished a market for printers and a market for consumables. There was no request, on the part of the challenging party, to divide the latter in two markets – one for cartridges and one for ink. That party was asking the permission to sell Kyocera compatible cartridges that it would have manufactured and filled itself.

The demand was different in that second case, where the challenging party requested the right to fill, with its ink, cartridges made by Ricoh. For the Commission, the market for consumables could not be divided in two (cartridges, ink). This was due to the fact that Ricoh was the only firm providing cartridges for its photocopiers.[17] Thus, there was no separate supply for that sort of product on the market. Similarly, there existed no separate demand for empty cartridges. The consequence, for the Commission, was that cartridges and powder were sold as a single product and constituted, for that reason, a single market.

For the Commission, the request made by the challenging party could not be accepted because the market could not be divided in two. This was an argument supplementary to the one regarding the absence of dominance on the secondary market, due to the discipline imposed on the firm by M1 shifting possibilities.

---

17 In fact, it was the only firm having the right to provide such cartridges. No other company held the right to supply cartridges which would suit the copiers made by Ricoh as the adaptation was protected by IP rights.

2008: Back to dominance

In 2008, the issue of aftermarkets emerged again – this time in a case concerning the possibility, for independent watch repairers, to obtain spare parts in order to carry out their activities.[18] The case concerned, specifically, luxury watches. At this stage, the decision has not been made public. But the case gave rise to a judgment by the General Court, which contains elements about the content of the decision.

In the case, the Commission rejected the claim as it had done in Kyocera and Info-Lab. In substance, the argument was the same as the one analysed above in the context of Kyocera and Info-Lab. For the Commission, the behaviour of luxury watch manufacturers was constrained on M2 as a result of the possibility, for current and future watch owners, to shift to other brands, on M1, if the manufacturers engaged in abusive behaviour.

In *Kyocera*, that argument had been used to conclude that the firm did not dominate the aftermarket. The same approach had been adopted in *Info-Lab*, where the division of consumables in submarkets was also rejected. This time, arguments on dominance and markets are combined. For the Commission, the possibility for watch owners to shift to M1 alternatives on case of M2 behaviour implies that there is no need to define separately a market for watches, a market for spare parts and a market for repair services.

In the judgment,[19] these arguments made by the Commission were rejected flatly. Firstly, the General Court found that different markets must be distinguished. The existence of a specific supply of repair services is a sign that those activities are considered, on the supply side and, as a result, on the demand side as being separate. Secondly, the General Court ruled that no evidence had been provided about the possibility, for current or future watch owners, to shift to M1 alternatives in case of M2 abusive behaviour.

2009: Lack of dominance again

The last case concerning aftermarkets was again started by Pelikan – and addressed, this time, against printer manufacturers Hewlett Packard, Lexmark, Epson and Canon.[20] The allegation was that these firms held dominated the markets corresponding to their consumables and, on these

---

18 Decision of the European Commission, 10 July 2008, Case AT.39097, Watch repair.

19 Arrêt *Confédération européenne des associations d'horlogers-réparateurs (CEAHR) v. European Commission*, T-427/08, EU:T:2010:517.

20 Decision of the European Commission, 20 May 2009, Case COMP/C-3/39.391 EFIM, SG-Greffe(2009)D/2924.

markets, abused their position through restrictive patenting strategies, the use of microchips and of recollection programs to shorten the supply of empty cartridges – thereby making the purchase of such cartridges by independent ink producers impossible.

Here again, the Commission rejected the claim. In the case, it did not discuss the possible existence of separate aftermarkets. The rejection was based on the idea, seen in the previous cases, that dominance on aftermarkets can be excluded if competition on the primary market results in "effective" discipline on the secondary market. The Commission states that the primary and secondary markets are closely linked. This leads to the conclusion that no dominance can be found on the aftermarket – impeding the finding that an abuse has been committed.

Departing from jurisprudence

In the previous sections, we have analysed four cases where the Commission takes a certain distance from earlier case law: *Kyocera*, *InfoLab*, *HP e.a.* and *Watch Repair*. The extent of the distance is presented, by the supporters of such decisions, as being limited in scope.

- In substance, the jurisprudence would not change as regards situations where primary markets are subject to domination. In cases involving such situations, the firms dominating the primary market cannot be disciplined on the secondary market as customers cannot turn to M1 alternatives. Corresponding to that situation are the cases *Hilti* and *Microsoft* seen above.
- By contrast, the jurisprudence would change, or would have to change, for situations where the firm does not dominate the primary market. In these situations, the existence of M1 alternatives disciplines the firm on M2 and the consequence is that that firm cannot be said to dominate that M2 market.

Currently, these second situations are ruled under *Volvo* and *Renault*. These cases, adversaries contend, were decided in the context of preliminary procedures. Such procedures do not really grant Courts ample opportunities to review, satisfactorily, the facts of the case. The consequence is that, when deciding the case, the Court was, probably, not aware of the scope of the ruling it would issue.

Another precedent for this second type of situations is *Hugin*, where a UK distributor was denied access to spare parts necessary to maintain, lease and repair cash registers manufactured by Hugin. On the primary market, the latter firm had a market share of circa 12%. This did not prevent the Commission from considering that an abuse had been committed on the secondary market. For the Commission, that market corresponded to the spare parts meant for equipment made by Hugin.[21] The consequence was that the latter firm could be found, on that market M2, as being dominant. The refusal to supply the necessary spare parts was then deemed abusive, particularly in a context where it broke a long standing business relationship.

By the supporters of the new approach, the case is dismissed, formally, as having been annulled by the Court of Justice. They are right to the extent an annulment was ordered. But the reason why the decision was annulled lies elsewhere – the situation only concerned the UK and the Court considered that the condition relating to the internal market being affected had not been satisfied. European law, for the Court, could not, thus, apply.

A final critique frequently heard from supporters of the new approach is that the solution provided by the European institutions in *Volvo*, *Renault* and *Hugin* should not be based upon the application of modern competition law. It should rather rely on rules derived from consumer protection, as regards the former. For the latter, it ought to be founded on rules prohibiting B2B unfair practices. This supposes, of course, that one type of objective only can be assigned to the rules of competition – and that there is, somewhere, an intellectual instance that would have the scientific authority to impose that objective, worldwide, to all competition law systems.

Issue 1 – Relevant markets

In the new approach proposed, a first issue regards the combination of products to consider that they form a single market. That combination was made in *Info-Lab*, where the Commission refused to consider that cartridges and ink could constitute separate markets.

In doing so, the Commission adopted a position which can hardly be justified. According to case law, separate markets exist where there is a separate demand, and a separate supply, for them. That is the case for cartridges – and for ink. Admittedly, the photocopiers sold by Ricoh had always been used with cartridges made by Ricoh and filled by that firm. But this cannot be used as an argument to question the existence of separate markets. The absence of independent ink supply alternatives was due to the refusal, by Ricoh, to commercialize empty cartridges and to allow independent manufacturers to producer compatible cartridges.

That behaviour cannot be distinguished from the one at stake in *Hilti*. In that latter case, three products were involved – nail guns, cartridges,

---

[21] Arrêt *Hugin v. Commission*, case 22/78, EU:C:1979:138.

and nails. They were identified with different product markets. In the case, Hilti was using different practices to avoid the market availability of empty cartridges. These practices were deemed abusive, because they were preventing the emergence or development of an independent offer which would have been beneficial to customers. In *Info-Lab*, the Commission adopts an opposite view – it proposes to consider these practices as the reason why the consumables should not be divided in two markets corresponding, respectively, to cartridges and nails.[22]

Issue 2 – Dominance

The second issue is to what extent domination is requested, on the part of the firm, to apply the prohibition enshrined in Article 102 TFUE. As indicated, the zone of discussion regards cases where the primary market is subject to competition. In those cases, the question is to assess the power detained by the firm on the secondary market. On that market, the share detained by the firm is generally very substantial and amounts, even, in most cases, to 100%. That was, at least, the market share detained in all four decisions reported above.

Despite that factual monopoly, the argument made by the Commission in those decisions is that the firm in question does not dominate the market. Its behaviour, it is contended, is constrained by the possibility of an M1 shift – today by informed current purchasers and later by installed based users when they need to make a new purchase on the same market.

The reasoning developed by the Commission is that customers "can" find information on life cycle costs of printers and photocopiers. Is this realistic? Large end users can probably seek and find that type of information. But it is doubtful that final consumers would. Where would that information be available? It could be provided on the internet site or display signs presented by the manufacturer. But the information would then be provided by the firm itself. All users know that such information cannot really be considered trustworthy – even if it is not, probably, completely out of range with reality.[23]

Another element in the reasoning of the Commission is the idea that, where they have access to information, customers are "likely" to behave accordingly. Suppose that they realize that cartridges are expensive for a

---

[22] For the evaluation of market definition, *Hilti*, just as *Microsoft*, are relevant precedents. Market definition is independent from the assessment of dominance. As a step leading to the application of competition law, the former comes before the latter.

[23] Specialized journals or newspapers sometimes compare the performances of products. But a limited portion of consumers probably consult these sources of documentation, particularly where the product to be purchased is not extremely expensive.

given brand. Customers, the reasoning goes, would then shift to an alternative next time they must buy a like product.

That perception amounts to a "belief" and runs counter to the notion of "consumer apathy", which is widely recognized. Unsatisfied customers do not necessarily choose other brands. This is because changing brands requires a form of investment – in time, energy and sometimes also money. Customers are not necessarily prepared to make that sort of investment. Another reason for them not to change is that they are never sure that what they could get with a new supplier will be better than what they have with the current one. When it comes to changing suppliers, the grass is not necessarily greener for the neighbour…

Another interesting element in the demonstration made by the Commission is the idea that unsatisfied consumers would voice their discontent, that that expression of lack of satisfaction will reach current purchasers, that such purchasers will take that view into account and that they will, as a result, purchase from another firm the product or service needed.

Each and every internet user knows that it hardly feasible to find one internet site providing unanimous support for a given product or service. Typically, blog or comment gatherers would attract unsatisfied comments. Reading about various brands, you, as an internet user, learn about all negative experiences gone through by fellow customers around the globe – and on that enumeration of complaints, it is very difficult to build a relative certainty as to the type of good or service that ought to be purchased.

Remedies first

As indicated in the previous sections, markets have not been defined entirely in conformity to the accepted methodology in the cases applying the new approach – and the Commission has also been elliptic, somehow, in those cases, for the determination of dominance on the secondary market. The question is why it did so in a context where it is generally so cautious, when introducing variations to the existing jurisprudence, to avoid possible annulments by the European courts. The answer may lie in *Info-Lab* where, somewhat surprisingly, the Commission relates the case to the doctrine of essential facilities. For that institution, one should avoid the application of that doctrine in the cases involving aftermarkets.

In principle, all decisions applying Article 102 TFUE start with a definition of the relevant markets, an examination of the possible existence of market power, an analysis of the practices adopted by the firm to determine whether such practices can be deemed abusive and a determination of the remedies to be imposed to ensure that those abuses, if established, will stop.

In *Info-Lab*, the Commission starts with… the end. It qualifies the case as involving the issue whether the firm (Ricoh) could be obliged, on the basis of competition law, to cooperate with another (Info-Lab) which will be a rival on a secondary market. Further down in the decision, the issue is reformulated in whether Ricoh could be forced to sell empty toner cartridges with the sole purpose of enabling a prospective market-player (Info-Lab) to compete with it on the market for filled toner cartridges. That is starting with the conclusion – that is, analysing the case in view of whether it would be legitimate to impose on a firm an obligation to deal.

For the Commission, an obligation to cooperate can only be imposed where there is a compelling need for consumers. The condition would not be satisfied in cases applying the new approach as the firm could not be found dominant on the aftermarket. That position was criticized by the challenging party. The latter was claiming that, if allowed to enter the market, it would charge customers a lower tariff for ink. This would be, it claimed, to the benefit of customers. Indeed, the principle underlying competition is that, where customers are provided alternatives, they exert on firms a pressure that has a downwards effect on prices.

Interestingly, that claim, which corresponds to the heart of the mechanism inherent to competition, was set aside by the Commission as being irrelevant. For that institution, the fact that higher tariffs are possibly charged by the firm on the secondary market does not provide an indication of domination. Furthermore, such higher prices do not imply that competition should be introduced as a way to provide benefits to consumers.

> The Commission is of the opinion that such […] a forced cooperation with prospective market-players would only be envisageable if there was a compelling consumer's need, which presupposes the existence of a dominant position in the consumables market. This however is not the case here […] Even if Info-Lab could actually offer filled toner cartridges at a lower price than Ricoh, this would not be in itself sufficient to conclude that a dominant position in filled cartridges, which could perhaps justify an obligation on Ricoh to sell empty toner cartridges to Info-Lab, existed (para. 49).

The Commission was also arguing, in the same case, that customers were thinking in terms of "systems" composed of equipment, cartridges and ink made by the same producers. Such systems are, according to the Commission, in competition against one another (inter-brand competition). There would be no need, as a result, to start decomposing, or fragmenting, the system into separate products, and markets.

Against that argument, the challenging party was arguing that, if they were granted opportunities to do so, customers would assess, for their purchases, separately, the price for the main equipment, and the price of consumables. That party was thus claiming that the current attitude by customers, which was indeed to compare system based prices, would change if the markets were separated – like in the telecom sector where services were distinguished from networks with the liberalization process in an attempt to increase the value customers were obtaining from operators which, earlier, proposed a system composed of access to a network, the possession of a terminal equipment and the possibility to use these products to contact correspondents.

Again, the argument was set aside by the European Commission. According to the decision, granting customers improved possibilities for cost analysis may be useful. But it is not sufficient to justify the imposition of an obligation to deal with another firm.

> "Info-Lab admitted that consumers' purchase decision on a photocopier may focus on the price per copy. However, according to Info-Lab consumers would perhaps adjust to a more sophisticated cost analysis by separately assessing the machine itself and the toner cartridge supply if given the opportunity. This is merely Info-Lab's hypothesis and even if the customer could make a more sophisticated cost analysis [...] if Info-Lab sold Ricoh compatible toner cartridges, this does not lead to the conclusion that a dominant position in filled cartridges exist. Improved possibilities for cost analysis might be useful for consumers, but this is not sufficient to justify imposing an obligation on Ricoh to co-operate with a prospective market player".

Conclusion

In many regards, the jurisprudence developed by the European Commission regarding aftermarkets has and valleys. To a certain extent, it can even be stated that, in some decisions belonging to that jurisprudence, what previously appeared certain is suddenly taken away all form of credit.

Currently, the only certainty is the acceptance, by the Commission, of the current jurisprudence for cases where primary markets are subject to dominance. Where competition exists on such markets, the point of view of the Commission is not stable – despite the existence of a clear jurisprudence developed by the European courts. Until recently, there was a tendency, within the Commission, to consider that a firm could not reserve for itself ancillary activities corresponding to aftermarkets. Another position has started to emerge, where competition is analysed in terms of systems. In that position, producers should be free to control the sales of products and services on aftermarkets even if the consequence is higher prices, as regards such products or services, for consumers – and barriers to entry for competitors.

The reason underlying that new position lies, apparently, in a desire to limit the application of the so-called "doctrine of essential facilities". Under that doctrine, firms must provide rivals with access to resources essential for the exercise of activities on secondary markets. In the four cases belonging to that new trend, the conclusion seems to come in the first place. It is as if the people in charge of these cases had decided that equipment manufacturers should be free to exercise their activities as they wish. It is thus, as if, *a priori*, no obligation of cooperation could be imposed – or else in extreme, hardly materialized, circumstances.

Starting with that decision, the authors of these decisions seem to have used technicalities belonging to competition law. In one decision, the market has been defined in a way which makes the emergence of competition on the aftermarket concerned (*Info-Lab*) impossible. In the other ones, the markets concerned were clearly distinguished by business actors. The Commission then developed a complex demonstration with the conclusion that the aftermarket could not be dominated as customers could shift to alternatives on… another market.

In *Luxury Watches*, that reasoning was characterized, by the General Court, as theoretical in nature. The judgment issue in that case has the merit of bringing back some sense of reality in that "upside down" jurisprudence. Just alleging that consumers "can" access information and are "likely" to seek alternatives is just not credible where an authority must justify a decision with effects on hundreds of millions of customers…

Bibliography

Farrell, J.; Klemperer, P., "Coordination and lock-in: competition with switching costs and network effects", in Armstrong, M.; Porter, R. (eds.), *Handbook of Industrial Organization*. Amsterdam: Elsevier, 2007, pp. 1967-2072.

Katz, M. L.; Shapiro, C., "Systems competition and network effects", *The Journal of Economic Perspectives*, 1994, pp. 93-115.

Lang, J. Temple, "Practical aspects of aftermarkets in european competition law", *Competition Policy International*, 2011, pp. 191-241.

Porter, M., *Competitive advantage. Creating and sustaining superior performance*. Amsterdam: Free Press, 1985.

Porter, M., *Competitive strategy. Techniques for analysing industries and competitors*. Amsterdam: Free Press, 1980.

Schulz, L., "The economics of aftermarkets", *Journal of European Competition law and Practice*, 2015, pp. 123-128.

Distinguishing legitimate price competition from unlawful exclusionary behaviour

Reconciling and rationalising the case-law

Alison JONES[1]

1. Introduction

Ever since its judgment in *Hoffmann-La Roche* in 1979, the EU Courts (the Court of Justice (ECJ) and the General Court (GC)) have consistently defined an (exclusionary) abuse as:

> an objective concept relating to the behaviour of an undertaking in a dominant position which is such as to influence the structure of a market where, as a result of the very presence of the undertaking in question, the degree of competition is weakened and which, through recourse to methods different from that which condition normal competition in products or services on the basis of the transactions of commercial operators, has the effect of hindering the maintenance of the degree of competition still existing in the market or the growth of that competition.[2]

The conundrum with which EU competition law has struggled with since is how to construct a test, or tests, to identify abusive behaviour which strengthens dominance and hinders the maintenance or growth of competition (unlawful exclusionary behaviour) and to distinguish it from normal competition based on traders' performance (competition on the merits). In seeking so to identify abusive conduct, the EU courts have not generally utilized a single test but have adopted conduct-specific

---

1 Professor of Law at King's College, London; Solicitor at Freshfields Bruckhaus Deringer LLP.
See also Jones, A.; Sufrin, B., "The European Way – reflections on the *Intel* judgment", *Competition Law & Policy Debate* 1 (1) (2015), p. 32.

2 Case 85/76 *Hoffmann-La Roche & Co AG v Commission* [1979] ECR 461, para. 91. Since Case 6/72 *Europemballage Corporation and Continental Can Company Inc v Commission* [1973] ECR 215, the ECJ has made it clear that TFEU Art. 102 covers not only practices that directly cause harm to consumers (exploitative abuses), but also practices that cause consumers harm through their impact on competition (exclusionary abuses).

tests applicable, for example, to predatory pricing, margin squeeze and rebates, respectively.[3]

A concern which has been mounting, however, is that the tests adopted by the EU Courts are not all consistent with each other or with the objective underpinning the rules. In addition, that, partly perhaps because of the special responsibility imposed on a dominant firm not to allow its conduct to impair genuine undistorted competition on the common market,[4] some of the tests developed to identify abusive practices are excessively broad[5] and/or unclear. In the context of pricing practices there is a concern that such rules risk chilling aggressive low-cost pricing, "the very conduct the antitrust laws are designed to protect".[6] These types of anxiety triggered a vigorous debate in the EU, actively engaged in by the Commission,[7] on the goals of Article 102 and the nature of an exclusionary abuse of a dominant position. This debate culminated in the Commission's publication in 2009 of "Guidance on its Enforcement Priorities in Applying Article 82 [102 TFEU] to Abusive Exclusionary Conduct by Dominant Undertakings" (the *Guidance Paper*),[8] in which the Commission explained that it would focus its resources only on cases where the exclusionary conduct of the dominant firm impairs effective competition by "foreclosing their competitors in an anti-competitive way, thus having an adverse impact on consumer welfare"[9] and proposed tests

---

3 A number of tests have been proffered in the search for a coherent predictable and workable mechanism for identifying all abusive conduct (such as the profit sacrifice test, the equally efficient competitor test and the consumer welfare effects test), but the truth seems to be that none of these are ideal. Although a perfect test in theory might be one that consistently and accurately condemns all, but only, conduct which leads to a net decrease in consumer welfare it seems that "[n]o such test exists in the real world", H. Pate, Testimony before the Antitrust Modernization Commission, 29 September 2005.

4 Case 322/81 *NV Nederlandsche Banden-Industrie Michelin v Commission* [1983] ECR 3461, para. 57.

5 In particular, there is excessive reliance on presumptions of illegality, see further *infra*.

6 *Matsushita Electric Industrial Co v Zenith Radio Corp* 475 US 574, 594 (1986).

7 See in particular, DG Comp Staff Discussion Paper on the Application of Article 82 [102 TFEU] of the Treaty to Exclusionary Abuses' *DG Competition Staff Discussion Paper*, December 2005, available at http://ec.europa.eu/competition/antitrust/art82/index.html, proposing that Article 102 should be applied only to exclusionary behaviour that harmed consumer welfare and had a market distorting foreclosure effect.

8 "Guidance on the Commission's Enforcement Priorities in Applying Article [102 TFEU] to Abusive Exclusionary Conduct by Dominant Undertakings" (the *Guidance Paper*) C(2009) 864 final, [2009] OJ C 45/7.

9 European Commission, *Guidance Paper*, *Ibid.*, para. 19. Anticompetitive foreclosure is defined as "a situation where effective access of actual or potential competitors to supplies or markets is hampered or eliminated as a result of the conduct of the dominant undertaking whereby the dominant undertaking is likely to be in a position to

for identifying such conduct. Although the *Guidance Paper* is explicitly not intended to constitute a statement of the law – rather, in some areas, it proposes a different approach from that set out in the case law of the EU courts – some have hoped that it will trigger a gradual evolution in, and recalibration of, the jurisprudence of the EU courts.[10]

This paper analyses the cases on abuse dealing with low cost pricing by a dominant firm to determine: (i) whether they are consistent with each other and the goals underpinning the EU competition laws; (ii) whether any evolution in the case-law can be detected; and (iii) what changes can be anticipated in the future and would be desirable to ensure the law's coherence. In particular, in part 3 it considers the implications of the judgment of the GC in *Intel.*[11] This judgment was eagerly awaited as many wondered whether it might embrace a more "modernised" effects-based approach to loyalty rebates – that is, rebates designed to encourage the customer to buy exclusively or quasi-exclusively from the supplier and whose grant is conditional on the customer obtaining all, or most, of its requirements from the undertaking in a dominant position.[12] Although the original complaint in the Intel case had been lodged, and the Commission's investigation launched, well before the publication of the *Guidance Paper*, the Commission's final decision[13] was adopted in May 2009, five months after its publication, and took account of the methodology set out therein. The case consequently reignited the debate[14] about the philosophical basis

profitably increase prices to the detriment of consumers". See also e.g. speech of Philip Lowe, "Consumer Welfare and Efficiency – New Guiding Principles of Competition Policy?" 27 March 2007.

10 See e.g. Kroes, N., "Preliminary Thoughts on Policy Review of Article 82" Speech at the Fordham Corporate Law Institute New York, 23 September 2005 ("As far as I am concerned, I think that competition policy evolves as our understanding of economic evolves. In days gone by, 'fairness' played a prominent role in section 2 enforcement in a way that is no longer the case. I don't see why a similar development could not take place in Europe").

11 Case T-286/09 *Intel v Commission* 12 June 2014.

12 *Ibid.*, para. 76.

13 Case COMP/C-3/37.990 *Intel* [2009] OJ C 227/13, [2010] 4 CMLR 314.

14 See e.g. Ibáñez Colomo, P., "*Intel* and Article 102 TFEU Case Law: Making Sense of a Perpetual Controversy", LSE, *Law, Society and Economy Working Papers* 29 (2014); articles by A. Jones & B. Sufrin, D. Crane, B. Allan, C. Ahlborn & D. Piccinin, M. Dolmans & T. Graf and D. Neven, in "Symposium: Intel", *Competition Law & Policy Debate* [2015] 1(1) pp. 28-96; Nihoul, P., *Journal of European Competition Law & Practice* 5 (8) (2014), p. 521; Peeperkorn, L., "Conditional pricing: Why the General Court is wrong in Intel and what the Court of Justice can do to rebalance the assessment of rebates", *Concurrences Journal* 1 (2015), p. 43; Venit, J., "Case T-286/09, *Intel v Commission – the Judgment of the General Court: All Steps Backward and No Steps Forward*", *European Competition Journal* 10 (2014), p. 203; Whish, R.,

of EU competition law and the question of how "abusive" conduct can or should be identified. As, however, the GC in *Intel* followed the traditional approach to rebates it has dampened the hopes held by some that the approach towards case prioritisation set out in its *Guidance Paper* might eventually encourage and spark a change in the law.

The paper commences, in section 2, by setting out some background to the issues – in particular it analyses the objectives of Article 102 (and EU competition law) and outlines the challenges involved in achieving its objectives. Section 3 then analyses the cases dealing with abuses of a dominant position through pricing practices, focusing on predatory pricing, selective price cuts, margin squeeze and loyalty rebates, and draws out the similarities and inconsistences between them. Section 4 concludes that there is a need to rationalise the case law and for the ECJ to explain more fully the policy underpinning the cases, when it is legitimate to rely on presumptions of illegality in the context of Article 102, how the various types of abuse relate to each other and how case-law under Article 101 can, or should, impact on the development of principles under Article 102. As the ECJ will have the opportunity to address the question of how Article 102 applies to loyalty rebates in the appeal from the GC's judgment in *Intel*[15], the paper examines some of the important issues which require assessment in that judgment (it also touches on relevant aspects of the judgment in *Post Danmark II* which deals with standardized retrospective rebates).[16]

2. The background: a need for modernisation?

2.1 The objectives guiding and underpinning EU competition law

It has been seen that a frequent complaint is that EU competition law applies excessively broad rules against single-firm conduct under Article 102, and to pricing conduct and above-cost loyalty rebates in particular. The rules, it is claimed, may chill aggressive low-cost pricing (because the EU courts have been too willing to presume or assume that low-cost pricing practices are abusive) and are *ad hoc* and

Editorial "*Intel v Commission*: Keep Calm and Carry on!", *Journal of European Competition Law & Practice*, [2014]; Wils, W., "The Judgment of the EU General Court in Intel and the So-Called 'More Economic Approach' to Abuse of Dominance", *World Competition: Law and Economics Review* 37 (4) (2014) 405 and Zenger, H., "*Intel* and the future of Article 102", *CRA Competition Memo* June 2014.

15 Case C-413/14 P. The grounds of appeal are set out in [2014] OJ C 395/25.

16 Case C-23/14 *Post Danmark A/S v Konkurrencerådet* 6 October 2015 (the Danish Court asked the ECJ what guidelines should be used to decide whether the application by a dominant undertaking of a rebate scheme with a standardised volume threshold constitutes an abuse of a dominant position).

inconsistent with the policy goals of the law. Crucial issues are, therefore, what objectives underpin, and guide, the interpretation and development of Article 102[17] and whether they explain the rules developed.

The EU competition provisions were designed to put in place a system to ensure that competition in the internal market is not distorted.[18] Although the EU's commitment to "undistorted competition" could, arguably, enshrine multi-faceted goals which permit non-competition, or public policy, factors to play an influential role in the development of EU competition law,[19] for a number of years, the Commission has articulated its clear view that the overarching goal of the competition laws is not to protect the process of competition as such (a process objective) but "to protect competition on the market as a means of enhancing consumer welfare and of ensuring an efficient allocation of resources"[20] (an outcome objective).[21] Although this interpretation accords with the current mainstream economics consensus and it is true that many judgments of the EU Courts have relied upon mainstream economic tools to shape and interpret EU competition law, the case law of the EU Courts does not unambiguously endorse it as the ultimate objective of EU competition law. Rather, their judgments have placed emphasis on the need to protect not only the interests of consumers but the interests of competitors and the structure of the market and competition as such;[22] the function of the Treaty competition rules being "to prevent competition from being distorted to the detriment of the public interest, individual undertakings and consumers, thereby ensuring the well-being of the European Union."[23]

---

17 For the view that the identification of such a principle is crucial to prevent Article 102 from "becoming a series of ad hoc and unpredictable rules [...]" see Vickers, J., "Abuse of market power" Speech to the 31st annual conference of the European Association of Research in Industrial Economics, Berlin, 3 September 2004.

18 See now, TEU, Art. 3(3) and Protocol No. 27 on the internal market and competition, annexed to the Treaty of Lisbon.

19 Indeed, Art. 120 TFEU specifically states that "the Member States and the Union shall act in accordance with the principle of an open market economy with free competition, favouring an *efficient allocation of resources*" but no specific reference is made to an efficient allocation of resources in the EU competition rules.

20 Commission guidelines on the application of Article 81(3) [now Article 101(3)] of the Treaty [2004] OJ C101/97, para. 13. Former Competition Commissioner Joaquín Almunia stressed that consumer welfare is not just a catchy phrase; rather it "is the cornerstone, the guiding principle of EU competition policy" SPEECH/11/803 "Competition – what's in it for consumers?" 4 November 2011.

21 See Peeperkorn, L., "Conditional pricing...", cit.

22 Case C-501/06 P *Commission v GlaxoSmithKline Services Unlimited* [2009] ECR I-9291, para. 63.

23 Case C-52/09 *Konkurrensverket v TeliaSonera Sverige AB* [2011] ECR I-527, para. 22.

The important weight attached in the cases on the structure of competition has led some to stress the importance in the EU of competition as a mechanism not simply for achieving consumer welfare and efficiency, but for ensuring the freedom to conduct a business and equal and undistorted access to the market which will result in variety and safeguard consumer choice.[24] This interpretation places greater emphasis on the importance of undistorted competition as a process in itself than on competition simply as a mechanism for achieving the outcome of benefiting consumers. Others, however, reject this view and adhere to the view that changes to the structure of the market are important only in so far as they are likely to harm competition. "This focus on consumer harm gives orientation and consistency to competition law enforcement, something that cannot be expected from the goal of preserving a certain (not defined) structure of the market or the goal of protecting the competitive process itself."[25]

In spite of these differences in interpretation, there seems little doubt that the ECJ considers that the welfare of consumers forms at least part of the EU competition law fabric, even if it is not its sole or preponderant objective. In *Post Danmark I*,[26] the Grand Chamber of the ECJ gave a judgment which, although containing no express statement about the objectives of the law, did focus heavily on the effects of the conduct on consumers, and in *Groupement des cartes bancaires v Commission*,[27] it placed emphasis on the poor allocation of resources to the detriment, in particular, of consumers that results from certain types of collusive behaviour between firms liable to infringe Article 101.

2.2 Rules and Standards

A second question is how the objectives of EU competition law are to be achieved; how can competition law identify and prohibit conduct which will thwart its goals?

Because of the difficulty of measuring in any individual case how conduct affects competition, all competition law systems have to devise legal rules or standards aimed at distinguishing anticompetitive from

---

24 Wils, W., "The judgement…", cit., pp. 16-17. See also Behrens, P., "The Ordoliberal Concept of 'Abuse' of a Dominant Position and its Impact on Article 102 TFEU" in Nihoul. P., and Takahashi, I., *Abuse Regulation in Competition Law*, Proceedings of the 10th ASCOLA Conference (2015).

25 Peeperkorn, L., "Conditional pricing…", cit., p. 48.

26 Case C-209/10 *Post Danmark v Konkurrencerådet (Post Danmark I)*, 27 March 2012.

27 Case C-67/13P *Groupement des cartes bancaires v Commission*, 11 September 2014.

procompetitive conduct.[28] Those chosen generally involve a trade-off between, on the one hand, the application of more complex standards, requiring detailed factual and economic analysis, which are more difficult and costly to apply, both by undertakings and decision-takers, and less predictable and transparent; and, on the other hand, application of clearer bright-line rules, requiring less sophisticated analysis and less emphasis on expert economic evidence and which are therefore easier to administer and for firms to self-assess, but which may be less accurate in some cases.[29] A challenge is therefore to devise an approach which provides sufficient clarity and accuracy, that is to put in place rules which reflect the economics underlying them, but which are at the same time administrable by agencies and the courts and sufficiently clear to allow firms to comply with them. Because it may be impossible to devise a test that consistently and accurately condemns all, but only, conduct which harms competition[30] and workability may entail a certain crudeness in the tests adopted, an important issue is frequently whether tests utilised achieve the objective articulated or whether, in particular, they might at times be either over-inclusive – so sometimes condemning legitimate business practices (creating a risk of false positives or "Type 1" errors), and so potentially chilling procompetitive conduct which benefits consumers, or under-inclusive – allowing anticompetitive practices which harm consumers to escape antitrust prohibitions (creating a risk of false negatives or "Type 2" errors).

Competition law frequently demands that decision-takers engage in intricate analysis to determine the effects of the conduct of an undertaking (or undertakings) in the legal and economic context in which it occurs; in particular through defining relevant markets and then assessing whether the conduct at issue facilitates, or will facilitate, the strengthening or exercise of market power (whether it results in actual, or is likely to result in, anticompetitive effects) and whether countervailing efficiencies for the conduct at issue exists. This is often referred to as a "rule of reason" style analysis or effects based or a consumer-welfare balancing approach. Because of the complexity and time-consuming nature of such assessments, most competition law systems also allow for shortcuts to be taken which sidestep such a full analysis, in particular, in cases where

---

28 See e.g. Kaplow, L., "Rules Versus Standards: An Economic Analysis" (1992-1993) 42 Duke LJ 556 (using the following definitions of rules and standards – a rule entails an advanced determination of what conduct is permitted leaving only factual issues to be determined by the adjudicator whilst a standard leaves specification of both what conduct is permissible and factual determinations to the adjudicator, pp. 559-560).

29 See e.g. *OECD Policy Roundtables*: Resale Price Maintenance (2008), available at http://www.oecd.org/daf/competition/43835526.pdf.

30 See Pate, H., "Testimony…", cit.

anticompetitive effects are very likely (or where they are very unlikely); for example by utilising presumptions or assumptions of illegality as a mechanism for clearly prohibiting, deterring, and facilitating prosecution of manifestly anticompetitive conduct.[31] Setting out a clear rule against obviously pernicious conduct may be considered acceptable as it eradicates the need for a claimant to prove, at cost, its adverse consequences.

Article 101(1) explicitly allows for a (rebuttable) presumption of illegality to be applied,[32] as it prohibits both agreements which have as their *object* the restriction of competition as well as those which have such an effect. The Court has made it plain that the words "object or effect" are alternative,[33] not cumulative, requirements: so if the object of the agreement is found to be "sufficiently deleterious", it need not be established that it also has a restrictive effect. Complex market analysis and proof of actual or likely effects on competition and consumers are thus avoided,[34] and an assumption that the agreement restricts competition applies; the burden then shifts to the parties to the agreement to justify it under Article 101(3). This heavy burden of demonstrating that Article 101(3) is satisfied is, however, notoriously difficult to discharge, especially in object cases. The wording and structure of Article 102 is different but the approach adopted under it nonetheless mirrors that adopted under Article 101. Even though therefore it does not itself explicitly permit presumptions of illegality to be applied (it simply prohibits any "abuse" of a dominant position), such presumptions are utilised in practice.[35] In

31 See Case C-67/13P *Groupement des cartes bancaires*, cit., Opinion of Advocate General Wahl. Presumptions of legality may also be used for conduct, which is very unlikely to have anticompetitive effects, perhaps because the undertaking(s) lacks market power or the impact of the conduct is likely to be insignificant, see Commission Regulation (EU) No. 330/2010 of 20 April 2010 on the application of Article 101(3) of the Treaty on the Functioning of the European Union to categories of vertical agreements and concerted practices.

32 In the US, in contrast, a conclusive presumption of illegality is applied in *per se* cases, the presumption is irrebuttable; an assumption of an unreasonable restraint of trade is made.

33 See e.g. Case C-9/92P *Commission v Anic Partecipazioni SpA* [1999] ECR I-4125, para. 123.

34 Even in these cases, however, some assessment of the relevant market is required under EU law to demonstrate that the jurisdictional element of Art. 101 TFEU is satisfied – that the agreement appreciably affects trade between Member States; see Case C-439/11 P *Ziegler SA v European Commission*, judgment of 11 July 2014.

35 See e.g. Case C-*AstraZeneca*, para. 361 ("the Commission applied Article [102 TEFU] correctly in taking the view that the submission to the patent offices of objectively misleading representations by an undertaking in a dominant position which are of such a nature as to lead those offices to grant it SPCs to which it is not entitled or to which it is entitled for a shorter period, thus resulting in a restriction or elimination of

its *Guidance Paper*, the Commission recognises that, in the context of Article 102, there is no need for a demonstration of anticompetitive effects in the case of conduct "that can only raise obstacles to competition and [...] creates no efficiencies";[36] such practices are, by their very nature, abusive (or abusive by object). Further, although Article 102 contains no equivalent of Article 101(3), it has long been recognised that conduct which is prima-facie abusive[37] may be objectively justified and it is now clear that this may be either because the conduct is objectively necessary or because the abusive conduct is counterbalanced, or outweighed, by objective economic justifications, advantages in terms of efficiency that also benefit consumers.[38] The ECJ has thus recognised "what is, in effect, a full blown 'Article 102(3)' defence".[39]

An important question is when, instead of conducting an analysis which considers actual or likely anticompetitive effects, an assumption of anticompetitive effects can (or should) be relied upon and the burden shifted to the undertaking(s) to justify their conduct? Best practice suggests that any such rule (or presumption) should be drawn on the basis of the objectives underpinning it if it is to yield minimal error costs (especially from over-inclusive presumptions of illegality which may lead to false positives).[40] For example, few would quibble with the application under Article 101 of a presumption of illegality to cartel activity. As there is growing international acceptance that such activity poses a serious threat to economies and consumers most antitrust systems treat such conduct as an "automatic"

---

competition, constituted an abuse of that position") and discussion of *AKZO* and *Intel* below.

36 *Guidance Paper*, cit., para. 22.

37 See e.g. Case C-53/03 *Syfait v GlaxoSmithKline plc* [2005] ECR I-4609, Opinion of Advocate General Jacobs, para. 72 (noting that the two-stage analysis suggested by the distinction between an abuse and its objective justification is somewhat artificial. "Article [102], by contrast with Article [101], does not contain any explicit provision for the exemption of conduct otherwise falling within it. Indeed, the very fact that conduct is characterised as an 'abuse' suggests that a negative conclusion has already been reached, by contrast with the more neutral terminology of 'prevention, restriction, or distortion of competition' under Article [101]. In my view, it is therefore more accurate to say that certain types of conduct on the part of a dominant undertaking do not fall within the category of abuse at all. However, given that the Commission has, in the light of some previous Community case-law, developed its submissions in terms of objective justification, it may be convenient for present purposes to assume that structure").

38 Case C-209/10 *Post Danmark I*, cit., para. 41. As with Article 101(3) TFEU, this burden is also difficult to discharge.

39 See Peeperkorn, L., "Conditional pricing...", cit.

40 See Case C-67/13P *Groupement des cartes bancaires*, cit., Opinion of Advocate General Wahl.

violation of the rules. Parties to cartels deliberately set out to interfere with free competition, to contradict the principles of the free market economy and to act instead to protect the prosperity of the participants as a whole. Such agreements are costly to create and enforce, harm efficiency and consumers and are "*naked*" – "[t]hey seek to restrict competition without producing any objective countervailing benefits".[41] The direct interference with the free operation of competition justifies an assumption that the agreement restricts competition (is restrictive by object), whatever the parties' market shares, the level of the market at which the cartel operates, the product or service involved and whether or not it can be demonstrated that the cartel has in fact harmed consumer welfare or final consumers. In *Groupement des cartes bancaires*, the ECJ recognised that since horizontal price fixing by cartels "may be considered so likely to have negative effects, in particular on the price, quantity or quality of the goods and services, that it may be considered redundant, for the purposes of applying Article [101(1)], to prove that they have actual effects on the market [...].[42]

The extent to which analysis of anticompetitive effects should be sidestepped in situations other than this, for example in relation to vertical agreements or to single firm conduct which may conceivably be designed to achieve efficiencies is, however, much more controversial.[43] In the US, rules of illegality are applied sparingly and "rule of reason" is the presumptive and prevailing standard. The EU courts have also frequently stressed the need for rigorous assessment of the actual or potential anticompetitive effects of conduct which is not obviously anticompetitive under Article 101, 102 and/or the EU Merger Regulation and might be designed to realise efficiencies. For example, in *Delimitis*[44] the ECJ stressed that because beer supply agreements (incorporating an exclusive purchasing or exclusive dealing obligation – a commitment on behalf of the buyer to obtain all (or most) of the contract products exclusively

---

41 Monti, M., "Fighting Cartels Why and How? Why should we be concerned with cartels and collusive behaviour?", 3rd Nordic Competition Policy Conference, 11-12 September 2000. See also Peeperkorn, L., "Conditional pricing...", cit. ("Even if a cartel is formed, by mistake, by a group of producers who collectively are too small to control the market – and who will thus fail to produce an appreciable negative effect on the market as any price rise they initiate will be met by customers going to the non-participating competitors resulting in serious loss of market share for the cartel participants – not allowing such a cartel does not risk destroying any efficiencies").

42 Case C-67/13P *Groupement des cartes bancaires*, cit., para. 51. In the US, cartel arrangements are, because of their pernicious effect on competition and lack of any redeeming virtue, considered to be illegal *per se* under section 1 of the Sherman Act of 1890, *Northern Pac R Co v United States*, 356 US 1, 5 (1958).

43 The scope of the category thus depends on the objectives considered to underpin the competition law rules, see discussion in Part 2.A.

44 Case C-234/89 *Delimitis v Henninger Bräu* [1991] ECR I-935.

from the supplier)[45] entailed advantages to both supplier and buyer, such agreements did not have the object of restricting competition within the meaning of Article 101; it was therefore necessary to ascertain whether they had the effect of preventing, restricting or distorting competition. In addition, and importantly, the ECJ emphasised in *Groupement des Cartes Bancaires* in 2014 that, in the context of Article 101, the category of agreements restrictive of competition by object must be interpreted restrictively and applied only to situations where an agreement inherently reveals a "sufficient degree of harm to competition";[46] the category should therefore be confined to conduct which by its very nature can be seen to be harmful to the proper functioning of normal competition. Where such a restrictive object does not exist, more detailed analysis of effects is required.

These issues are particularly important in the area of pricing by a single firm. An overly-draconian rule against low pricing might deter beneficial low cost pricing and provide the wrong incentives for competitors to complain about the conduct of their more successful rivals. Indeed, some commentators take the view that "[g]iven the enormous stake that antitrust has in low prices, and our extraordinary difficulties assessing predation claims", under-deterrent rules in this area are preferable, even if it means that some anticompetitive conduct goes unchecked.[47] Others, however, are more cautious and are concerned that an under-inclusive rules in this area might make "the world of predatory pricing [...] a monopolist's paradise. Even though many respected scholars believe it is not rare, successful predatory pricing judgments are exceedingly rare [...] If we expand the world of predatory pricing analysis to encompass dis-

45 In its *Guidance Paper*, cit., para. 32 the Commission refers to exclusive dealing as arrangements whereby a dominant firm tries to foreclose its competitors by hindering them from selling to customers through use of exclusive purchasing obligations or rebates (which it refers to together as exclusive dealing),

46 Case C-67/13P *Groupement des cartes bancaires*, cit., para. 58. See also Peeperkorn, L., "Conditional pricing...", cit. ("Usually restrictions and conduct are defined as 'by object' based on sufficient experience that the restriction or conduct in question will normally have an overall negative effect on consumers. In the case of a truly new type of restriction or conduct, it thus seems prudent to first acquire sufficient experience before classifying the new restriction or conduct. However, in some cases it may be clear enough, based on investigating in theory what the effects could be, that the new type of restriction or conduct can safely be defined to be by object. Examples of the latter are provided in pt 22 of the Article 102 Guidance: not allowing customers to test competitors' products (an example based on the *Tomra* case) or to pay a customer to delay the introduction of a competitor's product (example based on the *Intel* case, where this was described as a 'naked restriction'). For both types of restriction, it is difficult to imagine what efficiency could be reached with that restriction").

47 See e.g. Hovenkamp, H., *Antitrust Enterprise*, pp. 161 and 172; Carlton, D. W., "Should 'Price Squeeze' be a Recognized form of Anticompetitive Conduct?", *Journal of Competition Law and Economics* 4 (2) (2008), pp. 271, 273.

counting practices, we are implicitly making the conservative empirical judgment that this is an area of law that we want to make almost per se legal. Why should policymakers make this decision without backing it up with a reasonable amount of evidence suggesting that it is the appropriate approach?"[48]

3. Identifying unlawful pricing abuses

3.1 Predatory pricing: pricing below cost

Although there may be some sceptics,[49] there is now generally "a broad consensus that, in certain circumstances, temporarily charging prices below a firm's costs can harm competition and consumers";[50] a firm with market power (or hopes of acquiring it) may lower its prices[51] with the purpose of eliminating or disciplining its competitors[52] and, following the predatory siege, charge supra-competitive prices.[53] There is less consensus, however, on how frequently predatory pricing is likely to be tried and to succeed and how an appropriate antitrust standard for identifying predatory pricing can be constructed, which does not deter low cost pricing.

Article 102 itself does not prescribe any legal rule to define when price cutting by a dominant firm may become abusive. In the context of predation, however, a legal price-cost test has been developed

48 Lande, R. H., "Should Predatory Pricing Rules Immunize Exclusionary Discounts", *Utah Law Review* 2006, p. 863.

49 See e.g. Bork, R. H., *The Antitrust Paradox: A Policy at War with Itself*. N.Y.: Basic Books, 1978, reprinted with a new Introduction and Epilogue, 1993, pp. 144-155 and McGee, J., "Predatory Pricing Cutting: The Standard Oil (NJ) Case", *Journal of Law and Economics* (1958), p. 137.

50 Department of Justice, *Competition and Monopoly: Single-Firm Conduct under Section 2 of the Sherman Act* (2008) (now withdrawn), p. 49, relying on e.g. Areeda, P. E.; Hovenkamp, H., *Antitrust Law*. 2nd ed. Aspen: Aspen Law & C Business, 2002, para. 723b; Posner, R. A., *Antitrust Law*. 2nd ed. Chicago: Chicago University Press, 2001, p. 214 and Areeda P.; Turner, D. F., "Predatory Pricing and Related Practices Under Section 2 of the Sherman Act", *Harv L Rev* 88 (1975), p. 697.

51 Although low prices are of course good for consumers (a core competitive activity which may benefit consumers in the short run), the concern with predation results from the fact that as the dominant firm has a deep pocket, it can invest in a strategy which will exclude its competitors.

52 The lower prices may be applied across the board or targeted at certain customers (those that would be most likely to switch their custom to a competitor) or in certain areas, see discussion of selective price cuts below.

53 The price reduction is thus profitable only because of the added market power that the predator acquires as a result of excluding or disciplining existing and potential competitors.

by the ECJ, starting with its landmark ruling in *AKZO Chemie BV v Commission*.[54] In this case, the ECJ appeared to draw on the debate sparked by Areeda and Turner's seminal article on predatory pricing to craft relatively well-defined tests governing predation.[55] The ECJ clarified that not all competition by means of price can be considered to be legitimate, and that:

- prices below average variable cost (AVC) are regarded as abusive;
- prices above AVC but below average total cost (ATC)[56] are abusive where they form part of a plan for eliminating a competitor.[57]

To assess the parameters of lawful low-prices the court thus made use of criteria based on the dominant firm's prices and costs as well as on its strategy. It adopted a dual approach. First, it assumes that conduct is predatory where the dominant firm is pricing below its average variable costs (AVC) prices. This assumption is, arguably, justifiable as if the dominant firm is not covering its variable costs it makes no sense for it to be selling extra units at all;[58] the conduct has "no conceivable economic purpose other than the elimination of a competitor, since each item produced and sold entails a loss for the undertaking".[59] It seems reasonable therefore in this context to shift the burden to the dominant firm to provide an objective justification for its behaviour.

In contrast, where prices are between AVC and ATC, a presumption is *not* applied. Rather such pricing will only be held to be abusive where it can be demonstrated that it forms part of a deliberate strategy to exclude a competitor or where anticompetitive effects can be demonstrated. In *Post*

54 Case C-62/86 *AKZO v Commission* [1991] ECR I-3359.

55 Areeda, P.; Turner, D. F., "Predatory Pricing and Related Practices", cit.

56 There has been considerable debate as to whether, if a price-cost based test is appropriate, AVC and ATC are the correct cost-benchmarks. AVC was adopted by Areeda & Turner. Although they preferred a test based on marginal cost (the increase in total cost of increasing output by one unit), they accepted that marginal costs are hard to determine in practice and that such a test would not be workable; AVC (variable costs being much easier to distil from accounting records) was thus adopted as a proxy. The question of which price-cost test(s) should be adopted to conduct an AEC test is controversial, in particular whether short-run and/or long run costs should be utilised and whether the correct standard should be average or incremental costs, see e.g. Ridyard, D., "Interpreting the As-Efficient Competitor Test in Abuse of Dominance Cases", *CompLRev* 10 (2) (2014), p. 125.

57 Case C-62/86 *AKZO*, cit., paras. 71-74.

58 See, for example, Allan, B., "Article 82: A Commentary on DG Competition's Discussion Paper", *Competition Policy International* 2 (1) (2006), pp. 42, 57.

59 Case C-333/94 P *Tetra Pak II* [1996] ECR I-5951, para. 41.

Danmark I,[60] the ECJ reaffirming this conclusion stressed that an assumption of anticompetitive effects is not appropriate in these circumstances. "Indeed, to the extent that a dominant undertaking sets its prices at a level covering the great bulk of the costs attributable to the supply of the goods or services in question, it will, as a general rule, be possible for a competitor as efficient as that undertaking to compete with those prices without suffering losses that are unsustainable in the long term".[61] The ECJ thus applied an as efficient competitor (AEC) test, clearly articulating its view that Article 102 does not generally "seek to ensure that competitors less efficient than the undertaking with the dominant position should remain on the market. Competition on the merits may, by definition, lead to the departure from the market or the marginalisation of competitors that are less efficient and so less attractive to consumers from the point of view of, among other things, price, choice, quality or innovation."[62]

Although the Court requires some further analysis of the strategy of the dominant firm where its prices are between AVC and ATC, it has not demanded proof that recoupment of losses is feasible after the predatory siege. On the contrary, it has held that "demonstrating that it is possible to recoup losses is not a necessary precondition for a finding of predatory pricing".[63] This does not mean that the likelihood of recoupment is completely irrelevant, however. Rather, it seems implicit in at least some of the rulings that a *dominant* firm, having disciplined or excluded its rivals from the market, will be able to raise prices, recoup losses made during the predatory period and harm consumers. The risk of consumer harm from the predatory strategy is thus assumed. Actual proof that it is likely to be successful and, consequently, that consumers will be harmed is not required.

3.2 Pricing above cost: selective price cuts, margin squeeze and rebates

A further (and even more) controversial question which arises is whether, and if so when, *above cost* pricing can be abusive and how tests to identify any such anticompetitive conduct can be constructed (whilst

60 Case C-209/10 *Post Danmark I*, cit. In this case the Danish authorities had referred to average incremental costs rather than AVC, see Ridyard, D., "Interpreting…", cit. In Case C-23/14, *Post Danmark II*, cit, para. 61, however, the CJ described the test as 'one tool amongst others'.

61 *Ibid.*, para. 38.

62 *Ibid.*, paras. 21-22.

63 Case C-202/07P *France Télécom SA v Commission* [2009] ECR I-2369, para. 113. But see e.g. Strader, J. M., "*Post Danmark's* Recoupment Test", *Comp L Rev* 10 (2) (2014), p. 205.

complying with the aims of accuracy and administrability). In the EU, three separate strands of case-law indicate that above-cost pricing can be abusive in certain circumstances: (1) where, in exceptional circumstances, price cuts are targeted at specific categories of customers; (2) where the pricing practices can exclude equally (or reasonably) efficient competitors and produce anticompetitive effects (in particular, margin squeeze cases); and (3) where certain rebates are used.

3.2.1 Selective price cuts

The Commission recognizes in its *Guidance Paper* that it is easier for a dominant firm to engage in predatory conduct if it selectively targets specific customers with low prices, as this will limit the losses incurred by the dominant undertaking. It also states that normally only pricing below ATC or Long Run Average Incremental Costs (LRAIC)[64] is capable of foreclosing as efficient competitors from the market.[65] This suggests that to establish predatory pricing generally, prices must be below cost and that the law is not concerned with pricing practices which are capable of excluding only less efficient competitors. Two judgments of the EU Courts, however, *Compagnie Maritime Belge v Commission* and *Irish Sugar*, have held that even above cost price cuts may be abusive if they form part of a deliberate plan to eliminate competitors and are specifically targeted to meet the prices of a competitor.

A rightful concern is that as these judgments expand liability for low pricing broadly, without clearly articulated limitations, they have the potential to chill beneficial price cutting by dominant firms. Such concerns are, however, somewhat allayed by the exceptional factual scenarios that existed in the cases (and which were referred to in the judgments), in particular, that both involved collectively dominant firms holding quasi-monopolistic positions engaged in practices designed to exclude or discipline a competitor. A narrow construction of the cases is supported by the ECJ's judgment in *Post Danmark I*,[66] which specifically held that in the circumstances of that case prices offered by *Post Danmark I* which were higher than ATC "cannot be considered to have anti-competitive effects".[67] This highly significant conclusion seemed to flow from its prior statement that the purpose of Article 102 was not to ensure that

64 See Ridyard, D., "Interpreting…", cit.

65 *Discussion Paper*, cit., para. 67.

66 Case C-209/10 *Post Danmark I*, cit.

67 *Ibid.*, para. 36. The ECJ did not refer to the *Compagnie Maritime Belge* or *Irish Sugar* cases in this context in the judgment. Advocate General Mengozzi did, however, find that they were only marginally relevant to that case (in particular he referred to the fact that in both cases there was documentary evidence of intention to exclude, near

competitors less efficient than the undertaking with the dominant position should remain on the market.

3.2.2 Margin squeeze

A margin squeeze (or price squeeze, as it is known in the US) occurs when a vertically integrated firm, which is dominant in an upstream market, supplies the upstream input to its rivals at such a high price that, when compared to the price the dominant firm charges on the downstream market, it does not allow an as efficient (or perhaps a reasonably efficient) competitor sufficient margin to trade profitably. The vertically integrated firm can, therefore, simultaneously raise the upstream price of inputs and cut the retail price of the finished good, so "squeezing" the profit margins of rivals in the retail market.[68]

A margin squeeze has some similarities to predatory pricing in that it involves an allegation that a dominant firm is pricing at a level which a competitor cannot match. There are also some core differences, however. First, and critically, in a margin squeeze case, the dominant firm may not need to price below cost overall to be able to exclude an equally efficient competitor on the downstream market (so there may be no short-run benefit to consumers). Take, for example, the following hypothetical example, in which broadband is made available using new equipment plus associated services over a traditional network. Suppose a sole firm provides the traditional network but that a number of firms (including the monopolist) are engaged in providing the equipment and services enabling broadband. Assume the cost of providing the network is €12 per month. Assume the cost of the broadband equipment plus other services is €8 per month. Assume also that the dominant firm sells the broadband service (involving both traditional network and additional broadband costs) at €25 per month but sells the network input to other rival broadband suppliers at €18 per month. Clearly this pricing structure will "squeeze" a rival broadband provider with the same broadband costs as the dominant firm (an equally efficient competitor). The dominant firm

---

monopoly positions and that pricing was one of a series of practices which constituted abuses – circumstances which did not exist in *Post Danmark*), paras. 91-94.

68 Although there are some older cases in the EU dealing with margin squeezes, these types of claims have proliferated in regulated utility markets. Despite liberalization of the telecommunications and energy markets and privatization of many of the state-owned monopolies operating in these sectors, previous incumbents have retained large market shares and, frequently, the control of networks or infrastructures necessary to provide retail services. This has enabled dominant firms to engage in pricing practices on the wholesale and retail markets which make it extremely difficult, or impossible, for rivals to operate and compete on downstream retail markets in the long-run.

is, however, making a €5 per month profit on its broadband service. Its pricing can only be considered to be "below" cost, if the downstream arm of the vertically integrated firm is hypothetically assumed to pay the same cost for the network input as its rivals (that is, it is also paying the 50% mark-up on network costs from €12 to €18 per month).

Second, although in a traditional predatory pricing scenario the below cost pricing occurs in the market in which the predator is dominant and is designed to protect and preserve its market power in that market,[69] in margin squeeze cases the allegation is that the pricing practice is designed to exclude competition in a downstream market. A margin squeeze, like a refusal to deal, involves a form of "leveraging", in which a dominant firm is able to use its market power in a dominated market to affect competition or gain a competitive advantage in a neighbouring or downstream market. Although a margin squeeze is, of course, distinct from the situation where the dominant firm simply refuses outright to supply an essential input to a downstream competitor, forcing them to exit the downstream market, the squeeze may eventually operate in the same way as a refusal to deal; in the long-run, rivals are not able to remain on the downstream market but will have to exit from it.

The question of whether, and if so when, margin squeezes are, or may be, anticompetitive and how they may be identified has caused controversy and provoked many different views. It seems clear that margin squeezes can, by foreclosing competition on downstream markets, cause anticompetitive effects (by, for example, protecting the position of dominance in the upstream market or removing the incentive for competition in the downstream market); but should it be analysed as excessive pricing, a form of predation, discriminatory pricing, a form of constructive refusal to deal or an independent offence? Initially the Commission supported the view that there should be an independent margin squeeze offence, based simply on the "margin" between the upstream and downstream prices. Indeed it developed a broad theory of abuse. In *Napier Brown-British Sugar*,[70] for example, it found that a dominant supplier of raw and granulated sugar had sold its sugar at prices which left "insufficient margin for a packager and seller of retail sugar, as efficient as [British Sugar] itself in its packaging and selling operations, to survive in the long-term".[71] Subsequently, in *Deutsche Telekom*,[72] the Commission used the margin

69 But see, e.g., Case C-333/94 P *Tetra Pak*, cit.

70 [1988] OJ L284/41. See also *National Carbonising* [1976] OJ L35/6 and Case T-5/97, *Industrie des poudres sphériques SA v Commission* [2000] ECR II-3755, para. 178.

71 *Ibid.*, para. 65.

72 [2003] OJ L263/9.

squeeze theory to condemn the behaviour of Deutsche Telekom (DT), the operator of the German fixed telephone network, which had a statutory obligation to offer retail access to the local loop and whose wholesale and retail prices were regulated by the German national regulatory telecoms authority (NRA), RegTP. Despite the existence of the regulatory system the Commission investigated and held that DT had committed an abuse of its dominant position in the form of a margin squeeze generated by an inappropriate spread between wholesale charges for local loop access services and retailer charges for end-user access services. It held that a margin squeeze exists if the difference between the retail prices charged by a dominant undertaking and the wholesale access prices it charges its competitors for comparable services is negative, or insufficient to cover the product-specific costs to the dominant operator of providing its own retail services on the downstream market. Importantly, it also held that proof of the margin squeeze was *in itself* sufficient to establish the existence of the abuse.[73]

These decisions led to concern that the simple, standalone margin squeeze offence constructed by the Commission (a presumption of illegality for margin squeezes) was too broad and incompatible with predation and refusal to deal cases. As it concentrated solely on the potential for the pricing conduct to foreclose competition and not on its actual effect, it was liable to be "over-inclusive" and consequently to have the potential to chill competition. In particular, it did not, (i) require a plausible theory of harm resulting from the exclusion of the equally efficient competitor downstream (a consideration of whether anticompetitive effects may result upstream or downstream); (ii) take account of possible efficiencies that might be generated (for example, by allowing the primary level monopolist to realize efficiencies from carrying out its second-level activities and/or by allowing the monopolist to squeeze out a second-level firm which is itself a monopolist and eliminate double marginalization); or (iii) allow for account to be taken of the fact that intervention might undermine firms' incentives to invest and innovate. The approach was thus criticized for being too formalistic and for risking substituting a rule of competitor welfare for consumer welfare.[74] A growing view has been that, rather, as margin squeeze operates "effectively" as a refusal to deal

[73] However, it went on to say that even if it had to establish that DT's conduct had restricted competition by raising barriers to entry, such barriers did exist in this case.

[74] Carlton, D. W., "Should 'Price Squeeze' be a Recognized Form of Anticompetitive Conduct", *Journal of Competition Law and Economics* 4 (2008), p. 271 and Hovenkamp, H. J.; Hovenkamp, E.N., "The Viability of Antitrust Price Squeeze Claims", *University of Iowa Legal Studies Research Paper*, 08-33 (2009), available at http://ssrn.com/abstract+1156974, 28.

to rivals downstream, it should be analysed as such and the principles and standards applied should be the same ("competition law should treat economically-equivalent actions in an identical manner"):[75] if the dominant firm does not have a duty to deal it should not have a duty to deal on specific terms. Were this correct, the question of whether the pricing is squeezing rivals then would simply constitute one step in the process which requires proof *both* that the margin does not allow an equally efficient competitor to operate profitably at the downstream level *and* that the "constructive" refusal to deal is unlawful.[76]

The Commission accepts this approach in its *Guidance Paper* where it states that it will generally only consider a margin squeeze to be an enforcement priority if: it relates to an upstream product or service that is indispensable, or objectively necessary, to be able to compete effectively downstream; and the margin squeeze is likely to lead to the elimination of effective competition on the downstream market and consumer harm, for example, by preventing foreclosed rivals from bringing innovative goods or services to market, by stifling follow-on innovation or by extracting monopoly profits in an unregulated downstream market where the upstream market is regulated.[77] The Commission envisages a *less cautionary* approach, however, in a sector where regulation already imposes an obligation to supply and/or where the upstream product of the dominant firm has been developed through state protection or state financing (as was the situation in the *Telefónica* case);[78] in such cases imposing an obligation to supply, or prohibiting a margin squeeze, is not capable of having

---

75 *OECD Policy Roundtables*, Margin Squeeze DAF/COMP(2009)36, p. 29. The margin squeeze could also be analysed, alternatively, as excessive pricing or price discrimination.

76 See, e.g., *Ibid.*, p. 21 ("[T]his paper argues that, with one possible exception, nearly all the behaviour that can be characterised as a margin squeeze can be equivalently characterised as one of the other forms of abuse of dominance. This observation suggests that when margin squeeze is recognised as a distinct form of abuse, the principles and standards applied in prosecuting margin squeeze cases should be identical to the principles and standards applied if the case were prosecuted as the equivalent alternative form of abuse of dominance. For example, if the margin squeeze case could be characterised as a case of, say, refusal-to-deal or predatory pricing, the margin squeeze case should be prosecuted using the established principles and evidentiary standards of refusal-to-deal or predatory pricing cases, respectively").

77 *Guidance Paper*, cit.

78 *Ibid.*, para. 82. This suggests that in regulated markets, the margin squeeze will be presumed to harm consumers (as the purpose of the obligation to grant access was designed to increase competition downstream without creating disincentives to innovate upstream) and will therefore in practice be prohibited unless the dominant firm can objectively justify the conduct or demonstrate that it produces efficiencies that outweigh the consumer harm.

a negative effect on the input owner's incentive to invest and innovate upstream.

In its judgment in *Deutsche Telekom*[79] the ECJ appeared to reflect on concerns that the standalone margin squeeze offence articulated by the Commission might be overly broad. Although therefore it affirmed the Commission's view that margin squeeze constitutes an offence independent of other abuses, it made it clear that such conduct is not, by its very nature, abusive. Two hurdles must therefore be passed before an infringement is established. First the existence of a margin squeeze must be established. This is determined by reference to the upstream and downstream prices of the dominant firm and, generally, its downstream costs.In principle, therefore, an abuse is only committed if the pricing practice is capable of excluding an as efficient competitor from the downstream market – an AEC test is applied. The ECJ indicated, however, in *TeliaSonera*[80] that in exceptional circumstances the costs of a downstream competitor may be relevant, for example, where the level of the dominant undertaking's costs is specifically attributable to the competitively advantageous situation in which its dominant position places it. The ECJ thus appeared to indicate that a margin squeeze may occur where the pricing operates to exclude reasonably efficient operators, perhaps where their costs are higher than those of the dominant firm but only because of their smaller scale of operation or because of the unavoidable extra costs they incur, to compete downstream.[81]

Second, some anticompetitive effects (actual or potential) have to be demonstrated. It must be shown that the pricing practice resulting in a margin squeeze of equally efficient competitors would create barriers to the

---

79 Case C-280/08 P *Deutsche Telekom v Commission* [2010] ECR I-9555.

80 Case C-52/09 *TeliaSonera*, cit.

81 See also, e.g., *OECD Policy Roundtables*, Margin Squeeze, cit., 11: ("Where competition is just being introduced into these sectors there may be a justification for applying the reasonably efficient entry rather than equally efficient test. Firms may need to gain efficiency through experience and potential investors may be more readily scared away if early entrants fail due to aggressive competitive responses"). A difficulty with this approach, however, is that it is not easy to reconcile with the general principle of "legal certainty" and, in particular, the view of the General Court in *Deutsche Telekom* that a test focusing on the costs of a competitor would be contrary to it, Case T-271/03, *Deutsche Telekom v Commission* [2008] ECR II-477, para. 192, cited with approval by the ECJ, Case C-280/08 P, cit., para. 202. Indeed the *TeliaSonera* judgment itself is somewhat lacking conviction and clarity on this point as, when summing up its findings, the Court stressed that the general rule was that the relevant prices and costs should be those of the dominant firm and that "only where it is not possible [...] to refer to those prices and costs should those of competitors on the same market be examined", *Ibid.*, paras. 46 and 113.

growth of products and the degree of competition in the retail market. It must therefore be capable of making more difficult, or impossible, the entry of equally efficient competitors onto the downstream market.[82] Such anticompetitive effects do not, however, have to be concrete but it is sufficient to demonstrate that there is an anticompetitive effect which may *potentially exclude competitors who are at least as efficient as the dominant undertaking*.[83] Even where anticompetitive effects can be demonstrated, counterbalancing efficiencies proffered for the conduct must be considered.

Although the interpretation of an actual or potential anticompetitive effect is rather expansive,[84] the judgments of the EU courts have been welcomed for their application of the AEC test and their recognition that (a) anticompetitive effects must be demonstrated and that (b) anticompetitive effects may be counterbalanced by efficiencies. It is disappointing nonetheless that in the cases the ECJ did not utilize, as the Commission did in its *Guidance Paper*, the opportunity to reflect more fully on the similarities, differences and relationship between margin squeeze, predation and refusal to deal cases and to harmonize and rationalize the legal tests in this area. Rather, in both *TeliaSonera*[85] and *Telefónica*[86] the ECJ ruled that the criteria established in *Oscar Bronner*[87] were not applicable in a margin squeeze case as it constituted an independent form of abuse distinct from refusal to supply. In the former case the ECJ expressed con-

---

82 Although anticompetitive effects are likely where a regulatory regime mandates access to the upstream market with the objective of opening access and introducing competition into the downstream market or where access is not mandated, but the upstream product is indispensable to entry into the downstream market. A violation cannot be ruled out, however, simply because access to the upstream product is not mandated or indispensable. Indeed, the ECJ held that it is not necessary that the undertaking is "super-dominant" upstream, nor that it holds a dominant position downstream, nor that it cannot be established that it will be able to recoup its sacrifice in the pricing scheme. Rather, the cases indicate that, in absence of an objective justification, a margin squeeze will generally be designed to prevent the development of competition downstream and to allow dominance downstream to be acquired or strengthened.

83 Case C-52/09 *TeliaSonera*, cit., para. 65. A potentially exclusive effect is probable where the pricing is negative (that is where the input price is higher than the dominant undertaking's retail price to end users, paras. 73-74).

84 Although ECJ was readily prepared to assume anticompetitive effects in *Deutsche Telekom*, the facts were important to that conclusion. The regulatory regime established that access upstream was indispensable to penetration at the retail level and that a clear (EU) policy choice had been made to open up the downstream market and to develop competition on it.

85 *Ibid.*, paras. 55-58.

86 Case C-295/12 P, 10 July 2014.

87 Case 7/97 *Oscar Bronner v Mediaprint Zeitungs- und Zeitschriftenverlag GmbH & Co KG* [1998] ECR I-7791.

cern that harmonisation of the tests would require the *Bronner* criteria to be established "before any conduct of a dominant undertaking in relation to its terms of trade could be regarded as abusive", a condition which it thought would reduce the effectiveness of Article 102.[88]

In the margin squeeze cases, the ECJ has therefore stressed its independence as a form of pricing abuse which is distinct from others, including predation and refusal to deal. It is seen in the section below that in contrast, the EU courts treat loyalty rebates not as an independent pricing abuse but as a form of exclusive dealing.

3.2.3 Exclusivity (or loyalty or fidelity) rebates

In *Intel* the GC distinguished between three different types of rebate which are treated in different ways under Article 102:

- Quantity rebates;[89]
- Loyalty or fidelity rebates which it referred to as exclusivity rebates,[90] such as those at issue in *Intel* itself;[91]
- Other conditional rebates, such as target rebates which are not directly linked to a condition of exclusivity or quasi-exclusivity but which may have a "fidelity-building" or "suction effect" (the rebates at issue in *Post Danmark II* - standardized retroactive rebates - fell within this category).

The category of rebates which it treated (and is treated) most strictly under EU law and which have consequently attracted greatest attention and controversy are the second category referred to – loyalty, fidelity or exclusivity rebates. In 1979 in *Hoffmann-La Roche* the ECJ laid down a rule that both exclusive dealing obligations and loyalty (or fidelity) rebates by their very nature abusive; in other words, they constitute object abuses.

> An undertaking which is in a dominant position on the market and ties purchasers – even if it does so at their request – by an obligation or promise on their part to obtain all or most of their requirements exclusively from the said undertaking abuses its dominant position within the meaning of Article [102], whether the obligation in question is stipulated without further qualification or whether it is undertaken in consideration of the grant of a rebate. The same applies if the said undertaking, without tying the purchasers by a formal

88 *Ibid.*, para. 58.

89 Case T-286/09 *Intel*, cit., para. 75 and Case 85/76 *Hoffmann-La Roche*, cit., para. 90.

90 The Commission in its decision refers to these as "fidelity discounts within the meaning of the *Hoffmann-La Roche* case law", see *Intel* decision, cit., paras. 922-923.

91 Case T-286/09 *Intel*, cit., paras. 125-137.

> obligation, applies, either under the terms of agreements concluded with these purchasers or unilaterally, a system of fidelity rebates, that is to say discounts conditional on the customers obtaining all or most of its requirements – whether the quantity of its purchases be large or small – from the undertaking in a dominant position.[92]

Although this approach has been reaffirmed by the EU courts,[93] its application to loyalty rebates, an ubiquitous business practice,[94] has been subjected to savage criticism. In particular, arguably that the assumption is *not* justified as, (i) it is based only on the potential for such loyalty-inducing rebates to foreclose the dominant undertaking's competitors and to restrict customers' freedom to choose their source of supply (without an assessment of whether they are in fact liable to foreclose competitors);[95] (ii) it does not require an examination of whether competition will be distorted through any foreclosure of competitors' access to the market; and (iii) it ignores the efficiency rationales that a voluminous literature records[96] might underpin them (and which are recognised in the Article 101 jurisprudence). Consequently, it has been advocated that a less rigid approach should be adopted which focuses more closely on the question of whether the rebates are actually capable of tying customers and foreclosing rivals' access to the market and harming consumers. They should not be assumed to have, or to be intended to have, an anticompetitive object as they do not automatically reveal a "sufficient degree of harm to competition".[97] Consequently, as the test first set out in *Hoffmann-La Roche* is not empirically grounded in economics[98] or on a calculated study of whether such rebates are manifestly anticompetitive, the application

---

92 *Ibid.*, para. 89.

93 See especially e.g. Case T-65/89 *BPB Industries and British Gypsum v Commission* [1993] ECR II-389 and Case T-57/01 *Solvay SA v Commission* [2009] ECR II-4621, *aff'd* Case C-109/10 P [2011] ECR I-10329.

94 Single-product discounts conditional on the quantity or percentage of a product purchased, and designed to encourage loyalty to the supplier, are ubiquitous business practices which may often be procompetitive and justified by efficiency objectives. For example, discounts may be designed to allow the supplier to engage in long-run output planning, to pass on cost savings, to sell more (increase output), to bring down prices to larger purchasers or loyal clients; they may provide a mechanism to break oligopolistic pricing and, like exclusive dealing agreements, may encourage dealers to promote the supplier's products. Further, they may be granted as a response to buyer pressure or buyer power.

95 See e.g. Venit, J., cit., Zenger, H., cit.

96 See e.g. Peeperkorn, L., "Conditional Pricing…", cit.

97 See Case C-67/13P *Groupement des cartes bancaires*, cit.

98 See Case C-67/13P *Groupement des cartes bancaires*, cit., Opinion of Advocate General Wahl.

of the rule creates a significant risk of false positives and an "intolerable risk" of chilling legitimate procompetitive price competition.

It has been seen that in other more recent above-cost pricing cases the ECJ has recognised the need for caution in the application of Article 102. In *Post Danmark I*, it clarified that price discrimination does not "itself suggest that there exists an exclusionary abuse" and that it cannot be assumed even that pricing *below* ATC (where it is above AVC)[99] is abusive. Further, the ECJ confirmed that even where it has been demonstrated that a pricing practice may result in a margin squeeze of an equally efficient competitor (independent of any finding of a pricing abuse at the wholesale or retail level), some anticompetitive effects have to be demonstrated. Two reasonable questions, therefore, are whether some form of AEC test should be applied in the context of loyalty rebates and/or whether their actual ability to foreclose competitors in a way which is liable to harm competition and consumers should be considered.

The AEC test

In its *Guidance Paper* the Commission accepts that vigorous price competition is generally beneficial to consumers[100] and that conditional rebates may stimulate demand and benefit consumers.[101] It thus recognises that enforcement should be focused on cases where loyalty rebates are most likely to have anticompetitive foreclosure effects, both where: (i) rival suppliers cannot compete with the dominant firm to supply the entire demand of the customer (for example, where the customer must carry a certain percentage of the dominant firm's products because it is a "must stock item" or where competitors are capacity constrained); and (ii) the discounts are designed to induce customers to purchase the rest (or most) of their other requirements from the dominant firm – in particular where it enables the dominant firm "to use the 'non contestable' portion of the demand of each customer (that is to say, the amount that would be purchased by the customer from the dominant undertaking in any event) as leverage to decrease the price to be paid for the 'contestable' portion of demand (that is to say the amount for which the customer may prefer and be able to find substitutes)".[102] Like margin squeeze the concern is about leverage; in this case not from one market to another but from one portion of the market to another. The Commission thus states in its *Guidance*

99 In that case the Danish authorities had referred to average incremental costs rather than AVC, see Ridyard, D., cit., and Case C-209/10 *Post Danmark I*, cit.

100 *Guidance Paper*, cit., para. 23.

101 *Ibid.*, para. 37.

102 *Ibid.*, para. 39.

Paper that it "will normally only intervene where the conduct is capable of anti-competitive foreclosure of as efficient competitors"[103] and advocates a test for identifying such conduct which involves calculation of the effective price for the contestable portion taking the rebate into account.[104]

An effects-balancing test

Not all agree, however, that adopting a price-cost test provides an ideal mechanism for distinguishing anti- from procompetitive use of rebates or that it provides a panacea to promote administrability. In many cases such a test may be fiendishly difficult and impracticable to apply (especially given the need to ascertain the non-contestable and contestable shares of the market);[105] indeed, application of the test appeared to present acute problems for the Commission in *Intel*, even when applying it *ex post*.[106] In addition, some have argued that such an approach does not fully reflect the different nature of the exclusionary conduct in loyalty rebates cases; in such cases price is not used as the sole mechanism of excluding competitors (through lowering prices below cost as in predation cases) but as a mechanism for encouraging (or mandating) exclusive dealing with the dominant firm and raising their equally efficient (or reasonably (or potentially equally) efficient) rivals' costs of entry by preventing them from entering the market at an efficient scale and leading them to reduce output and raise prices (so permitting the dominant firm to raise or maintain its price and harm consumers).[107] Price-cost tests may not therefore accurately predict consumer impact as below-incremental cost pricing is not necessarily required for the strategy to be successful.[108] Rather, harm may occur because rivals "are never given an opportunity to compete, despite their ability to offer products with significant customer demand."[109]

---

103 *Ibid.*, para. 23.

104 *Ibid.*, paras. 40-47 (to determine whether loyalty rebates are using the non-contestable portion of the dominant firm's supply as leverage to decrease the price in the contestable portion). But see n. 60. See also e.g. Ridyard, D., cit.

105 But see Peeperkorn, L., "Conditional pricing…", cit.

106 Jacobson, J., "A Note on Loyalty Rebates", *The Antitrust Source*, June 2010, p. 1.

107 See e.g., Krattenmaker, T. G.; Salop, S. C., "Anticompetitive Exclusion: Raising Rivals' Costs to Achieve Power Over Price", *Yale LJ* 96 (1986), p. 209 and Salop, S. C., "Exclusionary Conduct, Effect on Consumers, and the Flawed Profit-Sacrifice Standard", *Antitrust LJ* 73 (2006), p. 311.

108 See e.g. Salop, *Ibid.*; Wright, J. D., "Simple but Wrong or Complex but More Accurate? The Case for an Exclusive Dealing-Based Approach to Evaluating Loyalty Discounts", 3 June 2013. See also Case C-52/09 *TeliaSonera*, cit. (in *TeliaSonera* the ECJ accepted that a reasonably efficient competitor test can exceptionally be applied in margin squeeze cases).

109 *ZF Meritor LLC v Eaton Corp*, 696 F3d 254 (3d Cir. 2012), p. 45.

This would suggest that an alternative might be to conduct an effects-based assessment similar to that proposed by the ECJ in *Delimitis*.[110] It has been seen that in this case the Court stressed that, given the procompetitive explanations for exclusive dealing arrangements and the potential advantages that they produced for suppliers and resellers, they could not be held to have as their object the restriction of competition (within the meaning of Article 101(1)); a careful market analysis had therefore to be adopted to determine whether the effect of the exclusive arrangements is to restrict competition by foreclosing access to the market. This requires an assessment of whether there is a concrete possibility for new competitors to enter the market, or for existing competitors to expand, taking account of the number and size of the producers on the market, the existence of networks of agreements, the saturation of the market, and brand loyalty, etc.

Although the Commission in its *Guidance Paper* does propose the use of the AEC test in rebates cases, it accepts that even if "the data suggest that the price charged by the dominant undertaking has the potential to foreclose equally efficient competitors, then the Commission will integrate this in the general assessment of anti-competitive foreclosure [...]",[111] which includes the position of the dominant undertaking and its competitors, the conditions of the relevant market, the position of customers or input suppliers, the extent of the allegedly abusive conduct, possible evidence of actual foreclosure and direct evidence of any exclusionary strategy.

The Intel Judgment

In the lead up to the GC's judgment in *Intel* there was considerable speculation as to whether the GC might consider "modernising" and develop its approach to loyalty rebates as the Commission has done in its *Guidance Paper*.[112] Indeed, in assessing the loyalty rebates in its decision in *Intel*, the Commission, besides applying the principles derived from the existing case law, also applied an AEC test, reflecting the methodology set out in its *Guidance Paper*.[113] The Commission's conclusion was that, on either basis, Intel should be sanctioned for abuse of a dominant position and imposed a fine of €1.06 billion, the largest ever imposed on a single undertaking.

---

110 Case C-234/89 *Delimitis*, cit.

111 *Guidance Paper*, cit., para. 27.

112 Case T-286/09 *Intel*, cit., para. 76.

113 *Guidance Paper*, cit., paras. 37-46.

The GC in *Intel* did not, however, retreat from the orthodox approach to loyalty rebates. Rather, it upheld the Commission's decision, making it clear that it did so on the basis of established case law. It held that exclusivity (or loyalty) rebates,[114] because of their innate capability of tying customers, do not have to be examined in context before concluding that, in the absence of objective justification, they infringe Article 102.[115] Because it concluded that such rebates are "inherently capable" of making access to the market more difficult for competitors,[116] it held that the amount of the rebate,[117] the short duration of the supply contracts,[118] the (small) portion of the market concerned in the relevant conduct[119] and the fact that the rebates were granted in response to customers requests and buying power[120] were all irrelevant. It also rejected the argument that in respect of one customer (HP) the rebates did not qualify as "exclusive" as they covered only 28% of HP's total requirements for x86CPUs, on the grounds that the rebates did cover 95% of its requirements in a certain market segment.[121]

In treating exclusivity rebates as presumptively illegal the GC in *Intel* rejected the view that an AEC test should be applied, holding that such a test was neither necessary nor dispositive (if passed) in an exclusive rebates case. On the contrary, it considered that anticompetitive foreclosure may occur even if the price/cost test is satisfied (on the basis that the AEC test shows impossibility to match, not absence of foreclosure effect); "an AEC test only makes it possible to verify the hypothesis that access to the market has been made impossible and not to rule out the possibility that it has been made more difficult."[122]

---

114 The Commission, in its decision, refers to these as "fidelity discounts within the meaning of the *Hoffmann-La Roche* case law", see *Intel* decision, cit., paras. 922-923.

115 Case T-286/09 *Intel*, cit., paras. 76-77, 86.

116 *Ibid.*, para. 179.

117 *Ibid.*, paras. 108-109.

118 *Ibid.*, para. 111.

119 *Ibid.*, paras. 116-124.

120 *Ibid.*, paras. 138-139.

121 *Ibid.*, paras. 125-137. In contrast it held that quantity rebates are deemed to reflect gains in efficiency and economies of scale and are presumptively legal (para. 75 and Case 85/76 *Hoffmann-La Roche*, cit., para. 90) and that other conditional rebates, such as the target rebates, are unlawful only if it is shown by a consideration of all the circumstances that they are capable of restricting competition – proof of actual effects is not necessary, *Ibid.*, paras. 78 and 103.

122 Case T-286/09 *Intel*, cit., para. 150 ("It is true that a negative result means that it is economically impossible for an as-efficient competitor to secure the contestable share of a customer's demand. [...] However, a positive result means only that an as-efficient competitor is able to cover its costs [...] That does not however mean that there is no

The GC rather equated loyalty rebates with *de facto* exclusive dealing. Exclusive dealing is, however, unlike the position in the US, for example, where courts tend to apply similar rule of reason analysis to exclusive dealing arrangements under both section 1 and section 2 of the Sherman Act, treated in fundamentally different ways depending upon in the EU whether it is adopted by a dominant or non-dominant firm (see Table 1 below).[123] Where a firm is dominant, it has been seen that in *Hoffmann-La Roche* the ECJ held that the anticompetitive effects of the conduct are assumed. In contrast, where a firm is *not* dominant a permissive approach is adopted, reflecting such agreements' scope to generate efficiencies and inability to restrict competition in many instances. Where the supplier's and buyer's market shares do not exceed 30% of the relevant market, a presumption of legality applies so long as the non-competition provision[124] does not last longer than five years.[125] Even where these market share thresholds are exceeded, *Delimitis*[126] requires a careful market analysis to be conducted.

foreclosure effect. The mechanism of the exclusivity rebates [...] is still capable of making access to the market more difficult for competitors of the undertaking in a dominant position, even if that access is not economically impossible [...]").

123 See Ibáñez Colomo, cit.

124 Which includes an obligation on the buyer to purchase from the supplier or from another undertaking designated by the supplier more than 80% of the buyer's total purchases of the contract goods or services and their substitutes on the relevant market, calculated on the basis of the value or, where such is standard industry practice, the volume of its purchases in the preceding calendar year, see Commission Regulation (EU) No. 330/2010 of 20 April 2010 on the application of Article 101(3) of the Treaty on the Functioning of the European Union to categories of vertical agreements and concerted practices, Art. 1(d).

125 See Reg. 330/2010 *Ibid*. Where the parties market shares do not exceed 15% it is unlikely that an exclusive dealing commitment, however long it lasts, will be found to restrict competition appreciably; see the Commission's Notice on agreements of minor importance which do not appreciably restrict competition under Article 101(1) of the Treaty on the Functioning of the European Union (De Minimis Notice) [2014] OJ C291/01.

126 Case C-234/89 *Delimitis*, cit.

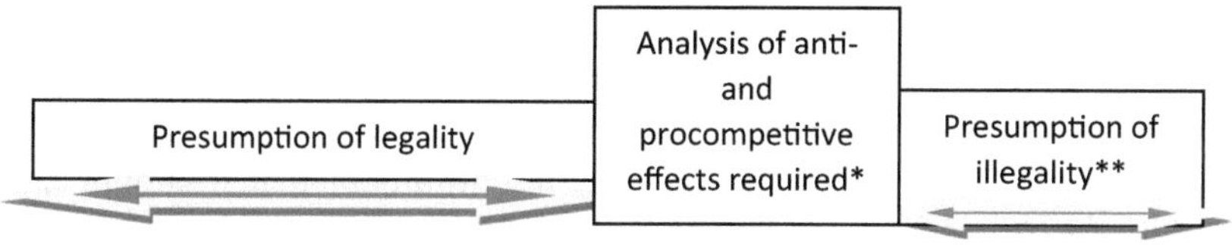

Table 1

Supplier's Market Shares	0–15%	16–30%	31–39%	40–100%
Assessment of exclusive dealing contract under EU Competition Law	Unlikely to restrict competition appreciably if buyer's market share also does not exceed 15%	Even if the agreement infringes Article 101(1), presumed to satisfy Art. 101(3) if buyer's market share does not exceed 30% and duration of agreement does not exceed 5 years	Market analysis must be undertaken to determine if agreement has as its effect the restriction of competition	Where firm is dominant, it abuses its dominant position (unless the conduct is objectively justified)

* A finding of dominance is unlikely but not impossible at market shares of less than 40%
** If the supplier is found to hold a dominant position

It is legitimate to ask, therefore, whether it is justifiable to dispense with market assessment entirely, and simply to assume anticompetitive effects of exclusive dealing and loyalty rebates simply because a firm reaches the dominance threshold, without any assessment of the degree of the supplier's market power, the portion of the market covered by the exclusive dealing commitments, the degree of market foreclosure and the impact of the contracts on competitors and on prices and choice offered to final consumers; is a dominance or market power screen an appropriate or relevant tool for distinguishing by object and by effect restrictions?[127] In *Van Den Bergh*[128] the GC appeared to be edging towards the view that a market analysis is required under Article 102,[129] and the approach of the

[127] See Peeperkorn, L., "Conditional pricing...", cit.
[128] Case T-65/98 *Van den Bergh Foods Ltd v Commission* [2003] ECR II-4653.
[129] See also *Guidance Paper*, cit., paras. 34-36.

ECJ in *Post Danmark I*,[130] *Deutsche Telekom*[131] and *TeliaSonera*[132] added force to the view that some assessment of anticompetitive effects should be conducted in (non-predatory) pricing cases.

In *Intel*, however, the GC rejected the argument that it should harmonise its treatment of exclusivity under Article 102 and Article 101. It distinguished the situation of a dominant undertaking offering exclusivity conditions from that of a supplier operating on a "normal competitive market" (as was the situation in *Delimitis* which fell to be judged under Article 101)[133] holding that the supplier in a dominant position is to a large extent an "unavoidable trading partner"; consequently its grant of an exclusivity rebate makes it structurally more difficult for a competitor to submit an offer at an attractive price and gain access to the market. Although therefore the GC did, using language reminiscent of that adopted in the *Guidance Paper*, recognise the risk that the grant of exclusivity rebates would enable the undertaking in a dominant position to use its economic power on the non-contestable share of the demand of the customer as leverage to secure the contestable share, it assumed that such a result would ensue so depriving customers of their right to choose and making access to the market more difficult for a competitor.[134]

In so ruling, the GC[135] placed central emphasis on the notion of the "special responsibility" of dominant undertakings, the cornerstone of the jurisprudence on Article 102 since *Michelin I*.[136] Dominant undertakings have a responsibility not to allow their conduct to impair genuine undistorted competition and are therefore under a positive duty towards the competitive process which puts them in a different position, not only to non-dominant undertakings, but also to firms subject to section 2 of the Sherman Act. It is a peculiarly European concept. It has been suggested[137] that paragraph 23 of *Post Danmark I*[138] reined in the "special responsibility" doctrine indicating that it may apply *only* to dominant positions having their origin in former legal monopolies. That judgment, however, having recited the usual mantra about the special responsibility, simply said in a separate sentence, with no linking word or phrase, that when the dominant position has such an origin "that fact has to be taken into account". The GC,

130 Case C-209/10 *Post Danmark I*, cit.

131 Case C-280/08 P *Deutsche Telekom*, cit.

132 Case C-52/09 *TeliaSonera*, cit.

133 Case T-286/09 *Intel*, cit., para. 89.

134 *Ibid.*, para. 93.

135 *Ibid.*, para. 90.

136 Case 322/81 *Michelin*, cit., para. 57.

137 See e.g. Venit, J., cit., p. 209.

138 Case C-209/10 *Post Danmark I*, cit.

in *Intel*, clearly did not consider that the special responsibility concept has been restricted. Quite on the contrary. In its view the special responsibility imposed on a dominant firm explains the different treatment to conduct which may be legitimate on the part of non-dominant undertakings. The very distinction between Article 101 and Article 102 is based on an "in-consistency" of treatment accorded to the two types of undertakings. On this basis it is perfectly valid to judge exclusivity practised by dominant undertakings by different criteria to those applied to non-dominant firms.

The GC also did not consider that it was acting inconsistently with other judgments dealing with above cost pricing under Article 102. Rather it distinguished case law applying the AEC test in the context of both selective low pricing (*Post Danmark I*) and margin squeeze (*Deutsche Telekom* and *TeliaSonera*) on the basis that exclusivity rebates are about rebates which are conditional on exclusive, or quasi-exclusive supply, not pricing. "Different treatment of exclusivity rebates and pricing practices is justified by the fact that, unlike an exclusive supply incentive, the level of a price cannot be regarded as unlawful in itself".[139] The GC thus appeared to consider that the fact that the dominant undertaking uses pricing, in the form of rebates, as a mechanism for achieving exclusivity is irrelevant.

4. Conclusions

The GC's decision in *Intel* not to reject the orthodox approach and, like the ECJ in *TeliaSonera*,[140] not to follow the approach proposed by the Commission for its case prioritisation in the *Guidance Paper* has been a particular disappointment to those promoting a need for a more modernised approach to Article 102 and consistency in treatment of conduct with similar effects.[141] From this standpoint, it has been criticised for taking "all steps backward."[142] An important issue, therefore, is whether the "modernisation" of Article 102 is mortally wounded.

A first point to make is that in spite of *Intel* some evolution in the case-law under Article 102 can be detected. In both *Post Danmark I* and the margin squeeze judgments the EU Courts have demonstrated caution about condemning low pricing by dominant firms and clearly indicated that the competition law rules are not generally designed to protect less efficient

---

139 Case T-286/09 *Intel*, cit., para. 99.

140 Which declined to align the treatment of margin squeeze with the law on refusal to deal as the Commission has done in its *Guidance Paper*, cit., para. 80.

141 Despite its use of language reminiscent of that adopted in the *Guidance Paper*, cit., see Case T-286/09 *Intel*, cit.

142 See the title of Venit's article, cit., "Case T-286/09, *Intel v Commission* – the Judgment of the General Court: All Steps Backward and no Steps Forward".

competitors. In addition, as is the context of Article 101, in these cases the ECJ has expressed caution about applying presumptions of illegality and has demanded that a predatory strategy or anticompetitive effects be established in cases involving selective price cuts above AVC and margin squeeze.

There is concern, nonetheless, that the case-law on loyalty rebates is out of line with these cases, the principles underpinning them and the jurisprudence developed in relation to exclusive dealing obligations under Article 101. These issues will now have to be addressed by the ECJ in its forthcoming ruling in *Intel*.

In this case the ECJ will have to consider whether it will agree with the uncompromising stand of the GC (and keep calm and carry on)[143] or whether it will propose moving to an approach which requires some assessment of such agreements' potential to produce anticompetitive effects in the legal and economic context in which they operate (even if it does so without endorsing the use of the AEC test[144] but proposes another approach, for example, one more closely aligned to that adopted in *Delimitis*). A fundamental question which the ECJ should address, therefore, is whether it thinks the approach set out 35 years ago in *Hoffmann-La Roche* is still consistent with the objectives underpinning Article 102 and the approach it has set out in later cases, especially *Post Danmark 1*, its margin squeeze cases and its more recent ruling in *Groupement des Cartes Bancaires*, which suggest that presumptions of legality should be applied sparingly under EU competition law and that in general reference to anticompetitive effects should not be mechanical; the likely existence of such exclusionary effects should not be merely assumed but should be assessed and demonstrated.[145] Although it might not agree fully with the objectives articulated, and the methodology pursued by the Commission in its *Guidance Paper*, it is hard to disagree with the ideals that the case law should be consistent and reflect the underlying objective of the rules and that presumptions of illegality should be based on the premise that the object of the conduct, or its intent, is to restrict competition. Although in *Intel* the GC might have felt reluctant to depart from an entrenched body of case law,[146] as there is no doctrine of stare decisis in EU law it would be

---

143 See Whish, R., cit.

144 See e.g. articles by Allan and Neven, cit.

145 See the Opinion of Advocate General Mazák in Case C-549/10 P, *Tomra* 2 February 2012, para. 44.

146 Although it seems that the GC is not bound by precedent or the judgments of the ECJ (see Arnull, A., "Owning up to fallibility: Precedent and the Court of Justice", *CMLRev* 30 (1993) p. 247) in Case T-168/01, *GlaxoSmithKline Services Unlimited* [2006] ECR II-2969 the ECJ considered that the GC had made an error of law by departing from the established line of cases (and taking an unashamedly consumer

open for the ECJ to depart from previous case-law if it felt it was necessary to reflect a change in opinion or circumstances.[147]

In reflecting on the question of whether a change of approach is appropriate, the ECJ may consider whether such fundamentally different approaches to exclusive dealing under Articles 101 and 102 is justified by reference to the objectives underlying the competition law rules and, if so, whether it is legitimate to assume that exclusivity rebates will operate as *de facto* exclusive dealing and that (*de facto*) exclusive dealing will ordinarily distort competition by foreclosing competitors without any assessment of the dominant undertaking's market share (which may range from 40-100%), the degree of foreclosure or the volume of custom tied to it through the exclusivity rebates; that is, whether it is reasonable to assume anticompetitive effects and only allow the dominant undertaking to present an objective justification for its conduct. The latter requires a demonstration that the conduct is objectively necessary or that it is counterbalanced by economic efficiency justification, and cannot be satisfied through arguing that no anticompetitive effects in fact occurred (as Intel sought to do by adducing evidence that its competitor had flourished despite the allegedly abusive rebates).[148]

In so doing, the ECJ will have to take into account the scope for Type 1 errors which may result from the orthodox approach and the scope for Type 2 errors were a more flexible approach to be adopted and the administrability of any method proposed. The GC, in its judgment, seemed implicitly to assume that Type 2 errors are the most to be feared and that the risk of Type 1 errors is low in rebates cases as exclusivity conditions undermine the principle of undistorted system of competition. It is noticeable, however, that, in contrast to *Post Danmark I*, the GC made no reference to the welfare of consumers, other than when stating the conditions for the application of objective justification and in reiterating that there is no need to prove direct damage to consumers or a causal connection between such damage and the practices at issue to establish an abuse.[149]

---

welfare approach), despite its previous record on a more effects based approach to Article 101, Case C-501/06 P, *GlaxoSmithKline*, cit.

147 See e.g. Case C-10/89 *CL-Sucal v HAG GF AF (Hag II)* [1990] ECR I-3711. In the USA, the Supreme Court has been willing to reconsider its previous rulings where necessary to make antitrust a rational enterprise, for example, where there is widespread agreement that the previous position is inappropriate or where the theoretical underpinnings of those decisions have been called into question; see e.g. *Leegin Creative Leather Prod Inc v PSKS Inc 551 US* 877 (2007).

148 The GC's riposte was that it may have done even better in the absence of the rebates, Case T-286/09 *Intel*, cit., para. 186. This argument is impossible to rebut.

149 *Ibid.*, para. 105.

It has to be accepted, however, that the likelihood of the ECJ departing from the approach set out in long-standing case-law seems extremely remote. Indeed, although the rebates at issue in *Post Danmark II* were not the "second" category of loyalty rebates, the ECJ did, in paragraph 27 of its judgment in this case, refer to the "settled case law that a loyalty rebate, which by offering customers financial advantages tends to prevent them from obtaining all or most of their requirement from competing manufacturers, amounts to an abuse within the meaning of [Article 102]". If the ECJ does therefore follow its previous case-law it could temper the strictness of the rule against loyalty rebates in two ways. First, by recognising that no abuse will be found where no appreciable effect on the market can be demonstrated. A de minimis doctrine in respect of Article 102 was, however, explicitly rejected by the CJ in Post Danmark II.[150] Indeed such a recognition may have come close to accepting that the assumption of anticompetitive effects is not warranted and that some assessment of the amount of the rebate, the duration of the contract and/or the number of contracts concluded is required. Second, given that there is no EU decision or judgment upholding an objective justification or efficiency defence it could provide greater guidance as to how the objective justification condition can be satisfied. In particular, it would seem important for direction to be provided as to how the assumption of foreclosure and elimination of competition can be offset especially given that no theory of harm is articulated and given the obligation on the dominant firm to establish efficiencies that counteract the negative effects[151] and that its conduct will not eliminate effective competition by removing all or most existing sources of actual or potential competition.[152]

The question of how loyalty rebates are to be assessed under Article 102 is now in the hands of the ECJ. In considering its broader impact for the modernisation process a crucial issue will be the *tenor*, rather than simply the outcome, of the ECJ's ruling. Judgments which are more receptive of an analysis requiring some examination of anticompetitive effects and the

150 *Ibid.*, para. 116 ("In addition, the possible smallness of the parts of the market which are concerned by the practices at issue is not a relevant argument. Where the course of conduct under consideration is that of an undertaking occupying a dominant position on a market where for this reason the structure of competition has already been weakened, any further weakening of the structure of competition may constitute an abuse of a dominant position (*Hoffmann-La Roche* ..., paragraph 123). The Court of Justice has therefore rejected the application of an 'appreciable effect' criterion or a *de minimis* threshold for the purposes of applying Article [102] (Opinion of Advocate General Mazák in Case C-549/10 P *Tomra*, paragraph 73 ...") and Case C-23/14 Post Danmark II, cit, paras. 72-74, see Whish, R., cit.

151 And that those gains have been, or are likely to have been, brought about by the conduct and the conduct is necessary for the achievement of the efficiency gains.

152 See Case C-209/10 *Post Danmark I*, cit., para. 42.

importance of the impact of the conduct on consumers, as well as competitors, may allay the fears of those who view the GC's judgment in *Intel* as a stumbling block to modernisation which is out of line with other more recent judgments of the ECJ.

In the meantime the Commission has indicated that although it will, in its decisions relating to exclusivity rebate schemes, apply the test set out by the GC in *Intel*, it remains committed to an effects-based approach; in setting its priorities, therefore it will continue to consider the likely anticompetitive effects of loyalty rebates and their magnitude of anticompetitive harm.[153] Unless, therefore, the ECJ seeks to limit the discretion of the Commission to prioritise its cases on the basis of the objectives set out in its *Guidance Paper*, the Commission is likely to be cautious about prioritising rebates cases in the future. This might provide little comfort, however, to dominant firms fearful of action by a national competition authority or private litigant, based on the law as most recently set out by the GC in *Intel*.

Bibliography

Allan, B., "Article 82: A Commentary on DG Competition's Discussion Paper", *Competition Policy International* 2 (1) (2006).

Areeda P.; Turner, D. F., "Predatory Pricing and Related Practices Under Section 2 of the Sherman Act", *Harv L Rev* 88 (1975).

Areeda, P. E.; Hovenkamp, H., *Antitrust Law*. 2nd ed. Aspen: Aspen Law & C Business, 2002.

Arnull, A., "Owning up to fallibility: Precedent and the Court of Justice", *CMLRev* 30 (1993).

Bork, R. H., *The Antitrust Paradox: A Policy at War with Itself.* N.Y.: Basic Books, 1978, reprinted with a new Introduction and Epilogue, 1993.

Carlton, D. W., "Should 'Price Squeeze' be a Recognized Form of Anticompetitive Conduct", *Journal of Competition Law and Economics* 4 (2008).

Gerber, D., *Law and Competition in Twentieth Century Europe: Protecting Prometheus*. Oxford: Clarendon Press, 1998.

Hovenkamp, H., *Antitrust Enterprise*, pp. 161 and 172; Carlton, D. W., "Should 'Price Squeeze' be a Recognized form of Anticompetitive Conduct?", *Journal of Competition Law and Economics* 4 (2) (2008).

Hovenkamp, H. J.; Hovenkamp, E. N., "The Viability of Antitrust Price Squeeze Claims", *University of Iowa Legal Studies Research Paper*, 08–33 (2009).

Ibáñez Colomo, P., "*Intel* and Article 102 TFEU Case Law: Making Sense of a Perpetual Controversy", LSE, *Law, Society and Economy Working Papers* 29 (2014).

[153] Speech of A. Italianer, "The Object of Effects", CRA Annual Brussels Conference – Economic Developments in Competition Policy. Brussels, 10 December 2014. See also Case COMP/40220, *Qualcomm*.

Italianer, A., "The Object of Effects" (Speech) CRA Annual Brussels Conference – Economic Developments in Competition Policy. Brussels, 10 December 2014.

Jacobson, J., "A Note on Loyalty Rebates", *The Antitrust Source*, June 2010.

Jones, A.; Sufrin, B., "The European Way – reflections on the *Intel* judgment", *Competition Law & Policy Debate* 1 (1) (2015), p. 32.

Kaplow, L., "Rules Versus Standards: An Economic Analysis" (1992–1993) 42 Duke LJ 556.

Krattenmaker, T. G.; Salop, S. C., "Anticompetitive Exclusion: Raising Rivals' Costs to Achieve Power Over Price", *Yale LJ* 96 (1986), p. 209.

Kroes, N., "Preliminary Thoughts on Policy Review of Article 82", Speech at the Fordham Corporate Law Institute New York, 23 September 2005.

Lande, R. H., "Should Predatory Pricing Rules Immunize Exclusionary Discounts", *Utah Law Review* 2006.

Lowe, P., "Consumer Welfare and Efficiency – New Guiding Principles of Competition Policy?" (Speech) 27 March 2007.

McGee, J., "Predatory Pricing Cutting: The Standard Oil (NJ) Case", *Journal of Law and Economics* (1958).

Monti, M., "Fighting Cartels Why and How? Why should we be concerned with cartels and collusive behaviour?", 3rd Nordic Competition Policy Conference, 11–12 September 2000.

Peeperkorn, L., "Conditional pricing: Why the General Court is wrong in Intel and what the Court of Justice can do to rebalance the assessment of rebates", *Concurrences Journal* 1 (2015).

Posner, R. A., *Antitrust Law*. 2nd ed. Chicago: Chicago University Press, 2001.

Ridyard, D., "Interpreting the As-Efficient Competitor Test in Abuse of Dominance Cases", *CompLRev* 10 (2) (2014).

Salop, S. C., "Exclusionary Conduct, Effect on Consumers, and the Flawed Profit-Sacrifice Standard", *Antitrust LJ* 73 (2006).

Strader, J. M., "*Post Danmark's* Recoupment Test", *Comp L Rev* 10 (2) (2014).

"Symposium: Intel", *Competition Law & Policy Debate* 1 (1) (2015).

Venit, J., "Case T-286/09, *Intel v Commission – the Judgment of the General Court:* All Steps Backward and No Steps Forward", *European Competition Journal* 10 (2014).

Vickers, J., "Abuse of market power" Speech to the 31st annual conference of the European Association of Research in Industrial Economics, Berlin, 3 September 2004.

Whish, R., Editorial, "*Intel v Commission*: Keep Calm and Carry on!", *Journal of European Competition Law & Practice* [2014].

Wils, W., "The Judgment of the EU General Court in Intel and the So-Called 'More Economic Approach' to Abuse of Dominance", *World Competition: Law and Economics Review* 37 (4) (2014), forthcoming.

Wright, J. D., "Simple but Wrong or Complex but More Accurate? The Case for an Exclusive Dealing-Based Approach to Evaluating Loyalty Discounts", 3 June 2013.

Zenger, H., "*Intel* and the future of Article 102", *CRA Competition Memo* June 2014.

Exclusionary abuses: refusal to license intellectual property rights

Rosa GREAVES[1] AND Svetlana NASIBYAN[2]

1. Introduction

Intellectual property rights (patents, trade-marks and copyright) are private rights granted by sovereign states in the public interest. There are various justifications put forward in order to explain the need for the existence of intellectual property rights. John Locke's writings about property are probably the most commonly used as, according to him, "every man has a 'property' in his own 'person'. [...] The 'labour' of his body and the 'work' of his hands, we may say are properly his. Whatsoever, then, he removed out of the state that Nature has provided and left it in, he hath mixed his labour with it, and joined to it something that is his own, and thereby makes it his property. [...] For this 'labour' being the unquestionable property of the labourer, no man but he can have a right to what that is once joined to, at least where there is enough, and as good left in the common for others".[3] In applying this to the ownership of intellectual property rights, it follows that "property rights in intangible creations operate as *reward* for the author's intellectual *labour*".[4]

Intellectual property rights are exclusionary rights by their very nature given that the owners of intellectual property may exercise their rights so as to prevent other market operators from either manufacturing products protected by a patent they own, by applying identical or similar marks to their registered trade-marks to identical or similar goods, or by reproducing material protected by a copyright they claim. Thus intellectual property rights cause concerns to the European Commission (the Commission)

---

1 Professor of European Commercial Law, Universities of Glasgow and Oslo. Professor of Law, School of Law, Glasgow University.

2 PhD candidate, School of Law, University of Glasgow; LLM in International Competition Law and Policy.

3 Locke, J., *The Second Treatise on Government* (1690). Indianapolis: Hackett Publishing, 1980, para. 26.

4 Aplin, T.; Davis, J., *Intellectual Property Law: Text, Cases and Materials*. 2nd ed. Oxford: Oxford University Press, 2013, p. 6.

when acting as a competition authority as the exercise of these rights may lead to competition being adversely affected on the internal market. This is particularly so when the owner of intellectual property rights holds a dominant position within the meaning of Article 102 of the Treaty on the Functioning of the European Union (TFEU). The law applicable to the relationship between intellectual property rights and Article 102 TFEU has been clarified by several important Commission decisions and judgments from the European courts which attempted to provide a fair balance between, on one hand, the property rights of market operators and, on the other, the importance of maintaining a competitive market and avoiding barriers to entry or expansion. Nevertheless, problems still remain to be determined as to the extent to which intellectual property owners, holding dominant positions within the meaning of Article 102 TFEU, are free to set the level of royalties without being found to have abused their dominant positions.[5]

This paper will not consider in detail the extent to which the level of royalties can be freely set by a dominant holder of an intellectual property right. The paper will examine how the balance between the exercise of property rights and the maintenance of a competitive market has been achieved by first explaining under what circumstances the owner of an intellectual property right may be considered to hold a dominant position within the meaning of Article 102 TFEU. This will be followed by a review of the relevant case law of the Court of Justice of the European Union (CJEU) and of the General Court (GC) in order to determine when the exercise/exploitation of an intellectual property right by an owner, who holds a dominant position, will be considered an abuse within the scope of Article 102 TFEU. A brief consideration of the position under US antitrust law will be included by way of comparison. A few concluding observations will complete the paper.

2. When are intellectual property right owners in a dominant position within the meaning of Article 102?

Intellectual property law provides different types of protection depending on the type of property that is granted. Therefore, each intellectual property owner will have different rights attached to the ownership. There are only two features which the owners of various intellectual

---

5 Commission Decision of 27 February 2008, COMP/C-3/37.792 (Microsoft royalties) and Case C-170/13, *Huawei v ZTE*, currently before the CJEU on a preliminary reference from a German national court. The Opinion of Advocate General Wathelet was delivered on 20 November 2014 and the CJEU ruling is expected in the first six months of 2015.

property rights have in common. First, the subject matter of the right is intangible property as it lies in the invention, information, computer code, or a research. Secondly, intellectual property ownership grants the owner either a monopoly over a product protected by the right or a certain degree of market power. This second common feature is the most problematic for the application of EU competition rules as *per se* monopoly, in certain circumstances, can adversely affect the EU internal market. However, having a legal monopoly over a product rests at the core of the property right granted by national law. Similarly, an undertaking's market power can be further strengthened by the ownership of intellectual property to the point that they will be considered to be in a dominant position within the meaning of Article 102 TFEU.

EU competition law is clear that a mere possession of intellectual property rights does not automatically attach a "dominance label" on the undertaking.[6] Nevertheless, the ownership of intellectual property is a relevant and appropriate factor in assessing the economic power that an undertaking holds in a defined relevant market. In particular, intellectual property rights may contribute to the findings of barriers to entry[7] in which case the ownership of intellectual property may be considered an obstacle for competitors to enter a market.[8] The fact that an intellectual property right could be treated as a barrier to entry is not surprising given the exclusionary nature of the rights. However, the significant consideration is whether competition law should automatically treat an intellectual

---

6 Case 24/67, *Parke Davis v Probel* [1968] ECR 55; Case C-241-242/91, *P, RTE & ITP v Commission (Magill)* [1995] ECR I-743.

7 Please note that the Commission does not list intellectual property rights as an example of barriers to entry. According to the Commission, "legal barriers, such as tariffs and quotas, or [...] advantages specifically enjoyed by the dominant undertakings, such as economies of scale and scope, privileged access to essential inputs or natural resources, important technologies or an essential distribution and sales network" are the most common examples of barriers to entry. The Commission Guidance on its enforcement priorities in applying Article [102 TFEU] to abusive exclusionary conduct by dominant undertakings, [2009] OJ C 45/2, para. 17.

8 Case 22/78, *Hugin Kassaregister AB and Hugin Cash Registers Ltd v EC Commission* [1979] ECR 1869; Case C-333/94 *P, Tetra Pak International SA v Commission* [1996] ECR I-5951. See also the Commission Decision in *Intel* (COMP/C-3/37.990) where the Commission noted the extensive history of patent infringement litigation initiated by AMD and Intel; therefore, highlighting "the significant intellectual property-related barriers" (para. 858). The decision was appealed to the General Court where it confirmed the Commission's position that intellectual property, among others, created barriers to entry and provided Intel with a dominant position. Case T-286/09 *Intel v Commission* [2014] ECR II-547 (paras. 25-26). The judgment is currently on appeal to the CJEU as Case C-413/14P.

property right as a barrier to entry. The CJEU case law has addressed the relationship between intellectual property law and competition law.

As already stated above, the general rule is that a mere possession of intellectual property does not amount to a possession of dominant position but the settled practice of the Commission and the European courts can pose danger to holders of intellectual property. In order to fall within the scope of Article 102 TFEU, the Commission has to prove that a dominant position exists in the relevant market. The definition of the relevant market can be a complicated process where both the characteristics of a product and economic tools are used in order to define it.[9] The Commission tends to define a relevant market very narrowly and the European courts usually confirm the Commission's finding. The most prominent examples of a narrowly defined relevant market are *United Brands*[10] (banana market), *Hilti*[11] (nails for use with nail-guns), *Tetra Pak II*[12] (cartons for use with filling machines), *Hugin*[13] (cash registers market), *Volvo*[14] and *Renault*[15] (spare parts market), *Commercial Solvents*[16] (aminabutanol market). Therefore, it is clear that the approach the Commission and the European Courts take to the definition of the relevant market is very specific and narrow. This can and probably does pose a danger to intellectual property owners as a specific product protected by an intellectual property right can be determined to be the relevant product market for the purposes of a competition investigation. In *Magill*,[17] for instance, the Commission narrowed the relevant product market to the listings of the weekly TV programmes and TV guides in which they were published. In making this assessment, the Commission in *Magill* took into account the fact that the listings constituted the essential raw material for any guide and that each guide with individual programmes was not interchangeable with one another.[18] The narrower the market, the more likely intellectual property owners (or many other undertakings) will be considered to be in a dominant position within the meaning of Article 102 TFEU.

---

9 Commission Notice on the definition of relevant market for the purposes of [EU] competition law, OJ 1997 C372/5.

10 Case 27/76, *United Brands v Commission* [1978] ECR 207.

11 Case C-53/92, *P Hilti AG v EC Commission* [1994] ECR I-667.

12 *Tetra Pak International SA v Commission*, cit.

13 *Hugin Kassaregister AB and Hugin Cash Registers Ltd v Commission*, cit.

14 Case 238/87, *AB Volvo v Erik Veng* [1988] ECR 6211.

15 Case 53/87, *CICCRA and Maxicar v Renault* [1988] ECR 6039.

16 Cases 6 and 7/73, *Instituto Chemioterapico Italiano Spa and Commercial Solvents Corp v Commission* [1974] ECR 223.

17 *Magill TV Guide v ITP, BBC and RTE* [1989] OJ L078/43.

18 *Ibid.*, para. 20.

3. When is the exercise of an IP right likely to be considered an abuse within the meaning of Article 102?

An intellectual property owner has a legal right to dispose of his property in the way it considers to be most appropriate. As the analysis of the relevant case law shows, the main argument in favour of the protection of the owner's rights is to promote their incentive to innovate. Innovation is at the heart of many types of intellectual property, particularly patent, design rights and copyright. Thus, to require the owner to license compulsorily their intellectual property rights to another could stifle the incentive to innovate and to invest in research and development to the detriment of consumers and society.

By way of example, Article 102 TFEU contains a list of abusive conduct that may be applied to the exploitation of intellectual property rights, *albeit*, none of them expressly provide so. Thus, there are several scenarios when the exploitation (exercise) of intellectual property rights could be considered an abuse of dominance under Article 102 TFEU. To date these situations have arisen in the context of a refusal to license a copyright. The considerably short history of the application of EU competition law to refusal to license copyright shows that, in exceptional circumstances, such a refusal can result in a limitation of production[19] or technical development[20] in violation of Article 102(b) TFEU. The exceptional circumstances test which was introduced in *Magill*[21] and later clarified in the *IMS Health*[22] ruling demonstrates an attempt to create a fine balance between competition law and intellectual property law.

In the case of *Microsoft*[23] the GC slightly expanded the exceptional circumstances test thereby, introducing a lower threshold (from the perspective of intellectual property owners) for the test to be satisfied.

*3.1 The pre-*Magill *case law*

The first time the CJEU considered the application of Article 102 to the refusal to license intellectual property rights was in *Volvo*,[24] an

19 See, *RTE & ITP v Commission (Magill)*, cit.

20 Case T-201/04 *Microsoft v Commission* [2007] ECR II-3601.

21 *RTE & ITP v Commission (Magill)*, cit.

22 Case C-418/01, *IMS Health GmbH & Co OHG v NDC Health GmbH & Co KG* [2004] ECR I-5039.

23 Case T-201/04, *Microsoft v Commission*, cit.

24 *AB Volvo v Erik Veng*, cit. At the same time, the CJEU received a case with the similar question in *CICCRA and Maxicar v Renault*, cit.

Article 267 reference from a national court. In *Volvo*,[25] the CJEU was asked to interpret Article 102 where the owner of a design right in car parts refused to license a design right to a third party. The third party required a license in order to manufacture and sell spare parts for Volvo cars. The Court ruled that "a refusal to grant such a licence cannot in itself constitute an abuse of a dominant position. [...] the exercise of an exclusive right by the proprietor of a registered design [...] may be prohibited by Article [102] if it involves, on the part of an undertaking holding a dominant position, certain abusive conduct."[26] The CJEU did also provide a set of examples of behaviour which the Court considered to be abusive conduct.[27] Nevertheless, the ruling was clear that the very subject-matter of a design right will be respected by EU competition law. Although this ruling was made in relation to a design right, the principle upon which it was based can be applied to other categories of intellectual property.

3.2 Exceptional circumstances test

The seminal case on refusal to license intellectual property rights is *Magill*,[28] when the GC, in a direct action challenging a Commission Decision, had to decide whether a refusal to license a copyright amounted to an abuse within the meaning of Article 102 TFEU. In this case the television companies, the owners of the intellectual property right (copyright), challenged the Commission Decision, which required them to license their copyright in order not to infringe Article 102 TFEU. *Magill* concerned copyright protection over information in television programme listings. RTE, ITP and BBC had a policy where the dissemination of their programme listings were provided free of charge to daily and periodical newspapers but consistently refused to license to any other party. The compilations of their television programme listings were protected by copyright law in the UK and Northern Ireland.[29] There was no comprehensive weekly television guide on the market; therefore, each company published its own television guide. Magill TV Guide Ltd (Magill) attempted to publish a comprehensive television guide in Ireland and Northern Ireland but the broadcasting companies obtained an injunction to prevent

---

25 *AB Volvo v Erik Veng*, cit.

26 *AB Volvo v Erik Veng*, cit., paras. 8-9 (emphasis added).

27 E.g., "arbitrary refusal to supply the spare parts, the fixing of prices for spare parts at an unfair level" were the examples provided by the CJEU in *AB Volvo v Erik Veng, cit.*, para. 9.

28 *RTE & ITP v Commission (Magill)*, cit.

29 Unlike other EU Member States, UK law grants copyright protection over listings, such as weekly TV guides, where labour and effort has been put into the compilation of the information. See the Copyright, Design and Patent Act 1988.

the publication and refused a copyright licence. Magill complained to the Commission[30] arguing that the refusal amounted to an abuse of a dominant position and therefore an infringement of Article 102 TFEU.

The CJEU confirmed that a mere ownership of an intellectual property right does not make an undertaking dominant for the purposes of Article 102 TFEU.[31] However, since the broadcasting companies were the only source of the information contained in the television guides, they held a *de facto* monopoly over it; therefore, being in a position to prevent effective competition on the (weekly) television guides market.[32] These were the main grounds for establishing a dominant position.

In dealing with the abuse of the said dominant position, the CJEU relied on the *Volvo*[33] holding that a refusal to grant a licence forms part of author's rights and a refusal to license cannot in itself constitute abuse of dominance.[34] However, still relying on the ruling in *Volvo*, the Court stated that "the exercise of an exclusive right by the proprietor may, in *exceptional circumstances*, involve abusive conduct."[35] According to the CJEU, the broadcasting companies were the only source of the required information, which was an indispensable raw material for the comprehensive television guide.[36] Therefore, the refusal to grant a licence over the information prevented the appearance of a new product for which there was a potential consumer demand. The CJEU found that the prevention of a new product entering the market was an infringement of Article 102(b) TFEU. The broadcasting companies could not objectively justify the refusal to license the copyright. Lastly, the broadcasting companies reserved to themselves the secondary market of weekly television guides by excluding all competition on that market.

The GC then applied the *Magill* test in *Tierce Ladbroke.*[37] Tierce Ladbroke SA (Ladbroke) runs a betting business company which involves the placing of bets on horse races run abroad. In 1990, Ladbroke lodged complaint with the Commission arguing that the *sociétés de courses*, a French organisation, refused to provide it with the French sound and pictures for its betting outlets in Belgium in contravention of Article 102 TFEU. The Commission rejected the complaint arguing, *inter alia*, that

30 *Magill TV Guide v ITP, BBC and RTE* [1989] OJ L078/43.

31 *RTE & ITP v Commission (Magill)*, cit., para. 46.

32 *RTE & ITP v Commission (Magill)*, cit., para. 47.

33 *AB Volvo v Erik Veng*, cit.

34 *RTE & ITP v Commission (Magill)*, cit., para. 49.

35 *RTE & ITP v Commission (Magill)*, cit., para. 50 (emphasis added).

36 *RTE & ITP v Commission (Magill)*, cit., paras. 52-56.

37 Case T-504/93, *Tierce Ladbroke SA v EC Commission* [1997] ECR-II 923.

Ladbroke failed to prove that the *sociétés de courses* held a joint dominant position and distinguished *Magill* on the facts holding that the refusal did not prevent the appearance of a new product. Ladbroke appealed the Commission Decision to the GC.

The GC upheld the Commission decision holding that, *inter alia*, Ladbroke could not rely on *Magill* as the facts were not analogous.[38] Unlike *Magill*, where the refusal to license prevented Magill from entering the market in comprehensive weekly television guides, Ladbroke was present in the main betting market while the *sociétés de courses* was not. Therefore, their refusal could not amount to creating restrictions to competition in the Belgian market. Furthermore, the GC held that all the requirements set out in *Magill*[39] before a refusal to license can be considered to be an abuse within the meaning of Article 102 TFEU were not present.[40] Unfortunately, in *Magill* the CJEU did not consider whether the exceptional circumstances test's requirements were severable, cumulative or exhaustive. This issue had to be clarified by the CJEU some years later in *IMS Health*.[41]

The *IMS Health* case arose from the complaint of National Data Corporation Health Information Services (NDC) who claimed that Intercontinental Marketing Services Health Inc. (IMS Health) had refused to license its 1860 brick structure which was indispensable for the supply of regional sales data to pharmaceutical companies. The 1860 brick structure was a system which represented regional pharmaceutical sales data in Germany. Its main purpose was to breakdown Germany into small geographical areas and the information received was analysed and compiled into sales reports which were then used by the pharmaceutical companies. When IMS Health's competitors attempted to develop a different brick structure, they were prevented by IMS Health's copyright which led to an injunction being granted by a German court to prevent such attempts. The competitors complained to the Commission arguing that without the 1860 brick structure, they could not provide services to the pharmaceutical companies. At the request of the complainant, the Commission issued an Interim Measures Decision requiring IMS Health to grant licences on demand.[42]

In order to adopt an interim measure decision, the Commission had to consider the likelihood of IMS Health's conduct amounting to an infringement of Article 102 TFEU. In this investigation one approach that

---

38 *Ibid.*, para. 130.

39 I.e. the exceptional circumstances test.

40 *Tierce Ladbroke SA v EC Commission*, cit., para. 131.

41 *IMS Health GmbH & Co OHG v NDC Health GmbH & Co KG*, cit.

42 COMP D3/38.044, OJ 2002 L59/18.

the Commission could have adopted was to have considered whether the 1860 brick structure was an essential facility[43] to which access was being denied by the refusal to license a copyright. Although IMS Health argued on the basis that the test for an essential facility[44] is whether it is impossible for a competitor to duplicate the products in question,[45] the Commission restricted itself to the language of the CJEU case law, concluding that there were "exceptional circumstances" to establish a prima facie case that the refusal to license the intellectual property right itself[46] may be an abuse within the meaning of Article 102 TFEU.

At the same time IMS Health started infringement proceedings against NDC before the German courts, where the key issue turned on whether a refusal to license amounted to an infringement of Article 102 TFEU. The German court referred to the CJEU the question as to when such a refusal amounted to an abuse of a dominant position. The Court confirmed the position in *Volvo* and *Magill* that an intellectual property owner has the exclusive right to refuse a licence, though in exceptional circumstances the refusal to license would amount to the abuse of dominant position within the meaning of Article 102 TFEU.[47]

Relying on the *Oscar Bronner*'s[48] summary of *Magill*, the Court stated that "in order for the refusal by an undertaking which owns a copyright

43 Glossary of terms used in EU competition policy (prepared by DG for Competition, Brussels, July 2002), the essential facility doctrine (EFD) is defined as "a facility or infrastructure which is necessary for [...] competitors to carry on their business" and which "is impossible or extremely difficult to duplicate". The EFD originated in the US in *United States v Terminal R.R. Assn.*, 224 US 383, 32 S.Ct. 507 (1912). The EFD has never been officially recognised by the EU courts but the Commission applied the doctrine for the first time in *Sealink/B&I Holyhead:* Interim Measures [1992] 5 CMLR 255. In that decision, the Commission held that Article 102 is breached if a dominant undertaking "both owns and controls and itself uses an essential facility [...], and which refuses its competitors access to that facility or grants access to competitors only on terms less favourable than those which it gives its own services, thereby placing the competitors at a competitive disadvantage" (para. 64). The CJEU set out limitations on the EFD in Case C-7/97, *Oscar Bronner GmbH & Co. KG v Mediaprint and Others* [1998] ECR I-7791. According to the CJEU, the refusal to grant access to a facility must eliminate all competition on a relevant market; no objective justification is available; a facility must be indispensable for the competitors' ability to carry out their business; and no actual or potential substitute in existence (para. 41).

44 Please note that IMS Health did not consider the 1860 brick structure to be an essential facility because there was no secondary market with stifled competition involved. *IMS Health GmbH & Co OHG v NDC Health GmbH & Co KG*, cit., para. 183.

45 *NDC Health/IMS Health*: Interim Measures [2002] OJ L59/18, para. 126.

46 *Ibid.*, at paras. 180-184.

47 *IMS Health GmbH & Co OHG v NDC Health GmbH & Co KG*, cit., paras. 34-35.

48 *Oscar Bronner GmbH & Co. KG v Mediaprint and Others*, cit.

to give access to a product or service indispensable for carrying on a particular business to be treated as abusive, it is sufficient that three *cumulative* conditions be satisfied, namely, that that refusal is preventing the emergence of a new product for which there is a potential consumers demand, that it is unjustified and such as to exclude any competition on a secondary market."[49] Thus, in *IMS* the CJEU made it clear that the requirements of the exceptional circumstances test are cumulative. Furthermore, the Court, citing *Oscar Bronner*, stated that two stages of production need to be identified in order to assess whether the refusal to grant a licence would constitute an abuse. The upstream market (the market of origin of the actual product) and the downstream market (the market where the product from the upstream market is used) should be both present and interconnected, as "the upstream product is indispensable in as much as for supply of the downstream product."[50] However, the CJEU added that "it is sufficient that a potential market or even hypothetical market can be identified. Such is the case where the products or services are indispensable in order to carry on a particular business and where there is an actual demand for them on the part of undertakings which seek to carry on the business for which they are indispensable".[51]

The introduction of a hypothetical market into the exceptional circumstances test was not welcomed as "the criterion of a secondary market would be meaningless, as it would be met in all or almost all cases".[52]

In relation to the "new product" requirement, the CJEU held that the refusal to license will be an abuse "only where the undertaking which requested the licence does not intend to limit itself essentially to duplicating the goods or services already offered on the secondary market by the owner of the copyright, but intends to produce new goods or services not offered by the owner of the right and for which there is a potential consumer demand".[53] The Court left some room for a debate as to the precise nature of products' newness and it was suggested that "perhaps, a minor change to an existing product is not enough; there must be a new kind of product".[54] However, the CJEU explicitly denied the duplica-

---

49 *IMS Health GmbH & Co OHG v NDC Health GmbH & Co KG*, cit., para. 38 (emphasis added).

50 *IMS Health GmbH & Co OHG v NDC Health GmbH & Co KG*, cit., para. 45.

51 *IMS Health GmbH & Co OHG v NDC Health GmbH & Co KG*, cit., para. 44.

52 Killick, J., "IMS and Microsoft Judged in the Cold Light of IMS", *Comp L. Rev.*, 1 (2) (2004), pp. 27-28.

53 *IMS Health GmbH & Co OHG v NDC Health GmbH & Co KG*, cit., para. 49.

54 Korah, V., *Intellectual Property Rights and the EC Competition Rules*. Oxford and Portland, Oregon: Hart Publishing, 2006, p. 145.

tion of products was sufficient to meet the exceptional circumstances test. Thus the ruling has been interpreted by some commentators as reconciliation between intellectual property and competition laws "based on their mutual interest in innovation".[55]

Lastly, the CJEU left to the national courts to decide the facts and which considerations could qualify as the objective justification for the purposes of the exceptional circumstances test. The decision in *Microsoft*,[56] discussed below, provides more detailed information as to what constitutes an "objective justification" for the application of the exceptional circumstances test.

3.3 The Microsoft *extension*

Microsoft[57] is a case where the GC took the opportunity to "extend" the exceptional circumstances test. The Commission received a complaint from Sun Microsystems (Sun) against Microsoft Corporation (Microsoft) on the grounds of Microsoft's refusal to supply its interoperability information over which Microsoft had a copyright. Sun, in particular, complained that Microsoft refused to disclose interface information which was necessary for Sun and other companies to create workgroup server operating systems (WGOS) in order to operate with Microsoft's desktop and server operating systems. Microsoft's market position was calculated to be a near worldwide monopoly, i.e. its dominant position was not in dispute. In fact, the GC commented that "it is settled case law that [Article 102] covers not only practices which may prejudice consumers directly but also those which indirectly prejudice them by impairing an effective competitive structure [...] Microsoft impaired the effective competitive structure on the work group server operating systems market by acquiring a significant market share on that market".[58] This statement could be interpreted as meaning that Microsoft's very presence on a market was enough to impair the effective competition; whereas, the impairment of effective competition is considered to be an infringement of Article 102 TFEU. Such an interpretation may be considered as contrary to the judgment in *Michelin* where it was held that being dominant is not "a recrimination but simply means that, irrespective of the reasons for which it has such a dominant position, the undertaking concerned has a special responsibility not to

[55] Anderman, S. D.; Kallaugher, J., *Technology Transfer and The New EU Competition Rules: Intellectual Property Licensing After Modernisation*. New York: Oxford University Press, 2006, p. 286.

[56] *Microsoft v Commission*, cit.

[57] *Microsoft v Commission*, cit.

[58] *Microsoft v Commission*, cit., para. 664.

allow its conduct to impair genuine undistorted competition on the common market".[59] The GC seems to go further and suggest that Microsoft was violating Article 102 TFEU by simply being dominant.

The GC confirmed the Magill/IMS test provides that the "new product" requirement was only mentioned in the cases which concerned the refusal to license intellectual property rights[60] and that "the appearance of a new product [...] falls to be considered under Article [102(b)]".[61] It is correct that when the CJEU, in *Magill*,[62] applied Article 102(b) TFEU to the refusal to license a copyright, the Court referred to the limitation of production as the most relevant type of abusive conduct in these circumstances. This enabled the GC, in *Microsoft*, to hold that "the circumstances relating to the appearance of a new product [...] cannot be the only parameter which determines whether a refusal to license an intellectual property right is capable of causing prejudice to consumers [...] such prejudice may arise where there is a limitation not only of production or markets, but also of technical development".[63] The limitation of technical development is one of the examples of abuses listed under Article 102(b) TFEU. The GC's opinion was based on the assumption that consumers would be harmed by being locked in a homogenous Windows solution.[64] The Court added that "the limitation of technical development" is not going to encourage third parties to clone the intellectual property owner's product; rather, they would introduce more developed products.[65] This reasoning does not include the fact that since the intellectual property owner's competitors are not the ones who invest in the research and development (R&D) they would compete with the intellectual property holders on price.[66]

The judgment also provided that it was not necessary "to demonstrate that all competition on the market would be eliminated. What matters, for the purpose of establishing an infringement of [Article 102], is that the refusal at issue is liable to, or is likely to, eliminate all effective competition on the market".[67]

---

59 Case 322/81, *Nederlandsche Banden-Industrie Michelin v Commission* [1983] ECR 3461, para. 57.

60 *Microsoft v Commission*, cit., para. 334.

61 *Microsoft v Commission*, cit., para. 643.

62 *RTE & ITP v Commission (Magill)*, cit.

63 *Microsoft v Commission*, cit., para. 647.

64 *Microsoft v Commission*, cit., para. 650.

65 *Microsoft v Commission*, cit., para. 658.

66 Howarth, D., McMahon, K., "Windows has performed an illegal operation: The Court of First Instance's judgment in Microsoft v Commission", *ECLR* 117 (2008), p. 124.

67 *Microsoft v Commission*, cit., para. 563.

In relation to an objective justification, the GC held that according to settled case law "if the mere fact of holding intellectual property rights could in itself constitute objective justification for the refusal to grant a licence, the exception established by the case law could never apply. In other words, a refusal to license an intellectual property right could never be considered to constitute an infringement of [Article 102].[68] Microsoft tried to justify the conduct by arguing that a compulsory licensing would affect the incentive to innovate. The Commission's response to this argument was that "on balance, the possible negative impact of an order to supply on Microsoft's incentives to innovate is outweighed by its positive impact on the level of innovation of the whole industry (including Microsoft)".[69] The GC confirmed the Commission's balancing test and added that it should be considered together with the Commission's proposition that "the need to protect Microsoft's incentives to innovate cannot constitute an objective justification that would offset the exceptional circumstances identified".[70]

The position of the GC and of the Commission on the validity of the "incentives to innovate" justification is understandable. The justification for refusing to license may be reasonable for owners of intellectual property but the overuse of this justification by those that hold a dominant position could undermine the application of Article 102 TFEU to anticompetitive practices. On the other hand, such a straightforward dismissal of the incentives to innovate justification contradicts the general acceptance of the important role innovation plays for the market growth. The Commission itself acknowledged the importance of innovation as it "constitutes an essential and dynamic component of an open and competitive market economy. Intellectual property rights promote dynamic competition by encouraging undertakings to invest in developing new and improved products and processes. So does competition by putting pressure on undertakings to innovate. Therefore, both intellectual property rights and competition are necessary to promote innovation and ensure a competitive exploitation thereof".[71] Therefore, the GC and the Commission's refusal to accept Microsoft's incentives to innovate justification could be understood that, in this particularly case, competition failed to promote innovation.

The decision in *Microsoft*[72] is to-date the most important case the GC had to consider in the context of the application of Article 102 TFEU

68 Case T-201/04, *Microsoft v Commission*, cit., para. 690.

69 The Commission Decision on *Microsoft* (COMP/C-3/37.792), para. 784.

70 *Microsoft v Commission*, cit., para. 707.

71 Guidelines in the application of Article 101 of the Treaty on the Functioning of the European Union to Technology Transfer Agreements (2014/C 89/03), para. 7.

72 *Microsoft v Commission*, cit.

to a refusal to license an intellectual property right. In March 2012, the Commission opened a formal investigation to investigate whether MathWorks Inc.[73] stifled competition by allegedly refusing to provide a competitor with end-user software licences and interoperability information.[74] The Commission confirmed that, as in *Microsoft*, the software interoperability was at the heart of the investigation. In September 2014, the Commission announced that it had decided to close the antitrust proceedings against MathWorks after undertaking a formal antitrust investigation.[75]

3.4 Standard-Essential Patents and charging excessive royalties

A recent development that is causing concern is the practice of some owners of intellectual property rights of charging excessive royalties when required by a competition authority or by a judgment of the CJEU or by agreement to license their intellectual property right. The situation may arise in one of two ways. First, the owner of the intellectual property right may be compelled to license in order to remedy an infringement of Article 102 TFEU. This was the situation in the seminal case of *Microsoft*.[76] The other situation arises where intellectual property owners, normally the owners of patents, agree with standardisation organisations that they will grant to any third party a licence on fair, reasonable and non-discriminatory terms (FRAND) where they are owners of a standard-essential patent. However, when a licence is sought from owners of standard-essential patents, the latter set excessive royalties which arguably amounts to excessive pricing which is expressly listed as an example of an abuse within the scope of Article 102 TFEU. When the third party fails to take a licence but continues to produce parts or products protected by standard-essential patents, the owners of the patents oppose the infringement by seeking injunctions under national law to prevent the unlicensed use of their property.[77] The issues raised in these situations are complex and require reconciliation between intellectual property and competition laws.

---

[73] MathWorks' software products are widely applied in the designing and simulating control systems which are used, e.g., in anti-lock braking systems for cars.

[74] EU Commission Press Release: Commission opens proceedings against MathWorks. Can be accessed at: http://europa.eu/rapid/press-release_IP-12-208_en.htm?locale=en.

[75] 39840 The MathWorks at: http://ec.europa.eu/competition/elojade/isef/case_details.cfm?proc_code=1_39840.

[76] *Microsoft v Commission*, cit.

[77] For discussion of this issue see A. Jones, *Standard-essential patents: FRAND commitments, injunctions and the smartphone wars* (2014) at http://papers.ssrn.com/sol3/papers.cfm?abstract_id=2394495.

Although the Commission has had opportunities to consider these issues[78] the CJEU is expected to finally clarify the extent to which EU competition law will be applied to these situations. A preliminary reference to the CJEU has been made by the Landgericht Düsseldorf in *Huawei v ZTE.*[79] The ruling is eagerly awaited. The CJEU has been asked to answer several questions which should clarify under what circumstances, if any, seeking an injunction from a national court to prohibit infringements or charging excessive royalties by the owner of a standard-essential patent is an abuse of a dominant position within the meaning of Article 102 TFEU. Advocate General Wathelet, in his Opinion delivered in November 2014,[80] focussed primarily on whether seeking an injunction in the factual circumstances of the reference was an abuse. The Advocate General struggled to reconcile the right of owners to protect their property by seeking injunctions against infringers[81] with their commitments to a standardisation organisation to grant licences on FRAND terms. He expressly conceded that he was proposing a "middle path" as a solution to the dilemma.[82] He admitted that restricting the right of the owners of intellectual property rights to bring such actions necessarily "constitutes a significant limitation of intellectual property rights" but also stressed that the right to intellectual property is not an absolute right.[83] Thus, he proposed "clearly defined circumstances"[84] when the right will necessarily be curtailed in the general interest. In cases where intellectual property right owners commit to license their rights should the standard protected

---

78 In 2014, the Commission adopted a Decision holding that when Motorola Mobility sought and enforced an injunction against Apple before a German Court on the grounds of a standard essential patent, it constituted an abuse of dominant position under Article 102 TFEU (Case AT.39985-Motorola – Enforcement of GPRS standard essential patents, Commission Decision of 29 April 2014 (IP 14/489). See also Press Release: http://europa.eu/rapid/press-release_IP-14-489_en.htm; On the same day, the Commission accepted legally binding commitments by Samsung Electronics that Samsung will not seek injunctions before courts in Europe on the grounds of its standard essential patents. See Case AT.39939-Samsung – Enforcement of UMTS standard essential patents, Commission Decision of 29 April 2014 (IP 14/490). See Press Release: http://europa.eu/rapid/press-release_IP-14-490_en.htm?locale=en.

79 Case C-170/13 *Huawei Technologies Co. Ltd v ZTE Corp., ZTE Deutschland GmbH.*

80 Http://curia.europa.eu/juris/documents.jsf?num=C-170/13.

81 Since Case 15/74 *Centrafarm BV and Adriaan de Peijper v Sterling* [1974] ECR 1147 at para. 9 p. 1162 the right to oppose infringements has been considered part of the "specific subject-matter" of a patent, and thus a matter for the national law that governs the existence of the intellectual property right.

82 The Opinion, cit., para. 52.

83 *Ibid.*, paras. 62 and 63.

84 *Ibid.*, para. 62.

by their patents be adopted, then a sort of "licence of right"[85] arises following the incorporation of the patent into a standard. The Advocate General concluded that, in these circumstances, it would be an abuse of a dominant position to bring an action for an injunction where the infringers have shown themselves to be objectively ready and willing to conclude a licensing agreement. Wathelet then proceeded to impose a number of obligations on both the owners and the infringers in order to secure a degree of transparency, fairness and proportionality between them. As far as the level of royalties was concerned, he left the matter for the national court to establish the appropriateness of the level of royalty sought by the owners.

Although it is unlikely the Court would resort to the essential facility doctrine to conclude that such owners are abusing their dominant position by charging excessive royalties, the Court may find it necessary to adopt another set of "exceptional circumstances" to balance the rights of owners and the interests of a competitive market.

4. The position under US Antitrust law

The position under US antitrust law is simpler than under EU competition law. US antitrust law takes the position that no conflict exists between antitrust law and intellectual property law as they both are complementary in nature due to the shared interest in the promotion of innovation.[86] Such an approach can be supported further by the argument that for the refusal to license intellectual property rights to violate s. 2 of the Sherman Act "there must be clear evidence that the exercise of the right facilitates monopolisation that extends beyond the scope of the IPR itself".[87] The same principle, which has already been discussed above, applies in the EU, i.e. the refusal to license an intellectual property right is not unlawful if it is done within the permitted boundaries of the law. The refusal to license patents is at the heart of the relationship between intellectual property and US antitrust laws. In *Eastman Kodak*, the Supreme Court held that the "power gained through some natural or legal advantage such as patent, copyright, or business acumen can give rise to liability" if "a seller exploits his dominant position in one market to expand empire into the next".[88] In other words, patent protection does not grant a monopolist with a total immunity from antitrust application, especially when the

85 *Ibid.*, para. 65.

86 *Atari Games Corp. v Nintendo of Am., Inc.*, 897 F.2d 1572, 1576 (Fed. Cir. 1990).

87 Hovenkamp, H.; Janis, M. D.; Lemley, M. A., "Unilateral Refusals to License", *Journal of Competition Law and Economics* 1 (2006), p. 20.

88 (90-1029), 504. US. 451 (1992), at No. 29.

said firm is trying to leverage its monopoly into the secondary market. *Kodak*[89] confirmed that approach and added that a right to refuse a licence could be regarded as "a presumptively valid business justification for any immediate harm to consumers"[90] but "nonetheless, this presumption is rebuttable".[91] The Ninth Circuit concluded that a dominant firm has a duty to sell its patented parts and to license its copyright protected software to its competitors. In *Xerox*,[92] however, the Federal Circuit took a different view and declined to follow *Kodak*. The Court rejected the logic of the Ninth Circuit's conclusion on the presumptively valid business justification for consumer harm on the basis that the pre-textual required "an evaluation of the patentee's subjective motivation for refusing to sell or license its patented products for pretext".[93] It can be seen that US antitrust law, like EU competition law, does not have an extensive history on the relationship between competition law and intellectual property law. Both recognise the importance innovation plays for market growth and development. Both also recognise the importance of competition law as a means of encouraging businesses to innovate. Therefore, both have to ensure that the promotion of innovation (in this context) does not lead to intellectual property owners using their intellectual property in an anti-competitive manner, i.e. against their competitors.

US antitrust authorities also have the same concerns in relation to the standard-essential patents' enforcement as the European Commission.[94] In July 2013, the US Federal Trade Commission announced that Google Inc. agreed to amend some of its business practices in order to end its involvement in the unfair licensing on its standard-essential patents for cellular, video codec, and wireless local-area-network (LAN) standards.[95] Google agreed to honour its previous commitments to allow its competitors an

89 *Image Technical Services, Inc. v Eastman Kodak Co.*, 125 F.3d 1195 (9th Cir. 1997).

90 *Ibid.*, at 1218 (para. 104).

91 *Ibid.*, at 1219 (para. 111).

92 *In Re Independent Service Organizations Antitrust Litigation*, 203 F.3d 1322 (Fed. Cir. 2000).

93 *Ibid.*, para. 16.

94 For more information on the brief comparison between the EU and US on the treatment of the FRAND encumbered SEPs see Edith Ramirez addressing the 8th Annual Global Antitrust Enforcement Symposium on the topic "Standard-Essential Patents and Licensing: An Antitrust Enforcement Perspective" (Georgetown University Law Center, Washington, DC, September 10, 2014). See https://www.ftc.gov/system/files/documents/public_statements/582451/140915georgetownlaw.pdf.

95 See https://www.ftc.gov/news-events/press-releases/2013/07/ftc-finalizes-settlement-google-motorola-mobility-case for all the relevant documents.

access to its patents on FRAND terms and conditions.[96] In January 2013, the US Department of Justice and the US Patent & Trademark Office published a joint statement dealing with remedies in relation to FRAND-encumbered standard essential patents.[97] In 2014, the US Department of Justice spoke about the progress and achievements in respect of remedies for FRAND-encumbered standard-essential patents.[98] Antitrust authorities of both the US and EU do recognise the importance of having efficient remedies in place for FRAND-encumbered standard-essential patents.

5. Concluding Observations

Intellectual property rights are exclusionary in nature. The rights conferred on the owners may be described as either rewards for achievement or incentives to innovate. Owners of intellectual property are granted, *inter alia*, the right to exclude competitors from access to their property by refusing to licence their rights and the right to set a high level of royalties for licensing those rights. These practices are not normally considered to be anticompetitive within the meaning of EU competition law. However, in situations where the holders of the rights are in a dominant position within the meaning of Article 102 TFEU, then the owners do not necessarily enjoy such freedom of action. The balance between intellectual property and competition law is struck in favour of competition law. In the case of a refusal to license the CJEU has developed the "exceptional circumstances" *Magill* test which, although not welcomed by all, has been clarified and extended in *IMS* and *Microsoft*, and is now generally accepted.

The importance of having a well-balanced test should not be underestimated. Both competition law and intellectual property should promote innovation. In this respect, innovation plays an inseparable part in market growth. For such reasons, incentives to innovate used to be commonly cited by intellectual property holders as an objective justification for their refusal to license. After the decision in *Microsoft*, it seems to be unlikely

---

96 See Press Release: https://www.ftc.gov/news-events/press-releases/2013/07/ftc-finalizes-settlement-google-motorola-mobility-case. An interesting point was made by the court in *Apple Inc. v Motorola Inc.*, 869 F. Supp. 2d 901, 914 (N.D. Ill. 2012) where the court held that if a company committed itself to license on FRAND terms, then the patent holder commits itself to license a patent to "anyone willing to pay a FRAND royalty and thus implicitly acknowledged that a royalty is adequate compensation for a license to use that patent".

97 See: http://www.uspto.gov/about/offices/ogc/Final_DOJ-PTO_Policy_Statement_on_FRAND_SEPs_1-8-13.pdf.

98 "A year in the life of the Joint DOJ-PTO Policy Statement on Remedies for FRAND encumbered Standards-Essential Patents". See: http://www.justice.gov/atr/public/speeches/304638.pdf.

that incentives to innovate would ever succeed as a valid justification for the purposes of the test. This might leave intellectual property holders without realistic defences and, therefore, denied the possibility to satisfy the exceptional circumstances test. Further consideration by the European courts is clearly needed.

It is highly likely that the CJEU will devise a set of requirements in order to reconcile the right of owners of intellectual property in setting the level of royalties with the obligation of owners of standard-essential patents to reach agreement at a level compatible with FRAND.

Bibliography

A. Jones, *Standard-essential patents: FRAND commitments, injunctions and the smartphone wars* (2014). Available at: http://papers.ssrn.com/sol3/papers.cfm?abstract_id=2394495.

"A year in the life of the Joint DOJ-PTO Policy Statement on Remedies for FRAND encumbered Standards-Essential Patents". Available at: http://www.justice.gov/atr/public/speeches/304638.pdf.

Anderman, S. D.; Kallaugher, J., *Technology Transfer and The New EU Competition Rules: Intellectual Property Licensing After Modernisation*. New York: Oxford University Press, 2006.

Aplin, T.; Davis, J., *Intellectual Property Law: Text, Cases and Materials*. 2nd ed. Oxford: Oxford University Press, 2013.

Hovenkamp, H.; Janis, M. D.; Lemley, M. A., "Unilateral Refusals to License", *Journal of Competition Law and Economics* 1 (2006).

Howarth, D., McMahon, K., "Windows has performed an illegal operation: The Court of First Instance's judgment in Microsoft v Commission", *ECLR* 117 (2008).

Killick, J., "IMS and Microsoft Judged in the Cold Light of IMS", *Comp L. Rev.*, 1 (2) (2004).

Korah, V., *Intellectual Property Rights and the EC Competition Rules*. Oxford and Portland, Oregon: Hart Publishing, 2006.

Locke, J., *The Second Treatise on Government* (1690). Indianapolis: Hackett Publishing, 1980.

Ramirez, E., "Standard-Essential Patents and Licensing: An Antitrust Enforcement Perspective", 8th Annual Global Antitrust Enforcement Symposium (Georgetown University Law Center, Washington, DC, September 10, 2014). Available at: https://www.ftc.gov/system/files/documents/public_statements/582451/140915georgetownlaw.pdf.

Remedies and Article 102 TFEU

Recent public enforcement experience

Rita Leandro VASCONCELOS[1]

1. Introduction

The public enforcement consequences that an undertaking may face when breaching Article 102 of the Treaty on the Functioning of the European Union (TFEU) are essentially of two kinds: substitutionary remedies[2] (e.g. fines and periodic penalty payments), and structural or behavioural remedies.[3]

Each kind pursues different competition policy objectives and choosing to apply one or the other will depend on the objectives that the Commission wishes to attain. Fines are mostly used for punishment and deterrence, whereas remedies are used to restore competition to affected markets.

Remedies have only been referred to explicitly in legislation after the enactment of Regulation 1/2003[4] and its use by the Commission has been rather scarce. The limited remedial experience at European level and the choices made by the Commission as to the design of the remedies and the procedure leading to their imposition or acceptance begs the question of Whether the Commission's recent practice has been pursued coherently.

---

1 Associate lawyer of Cuatrecasas, Gonçalves Pereira Law Firm; Phd Student, Católica Porto Law School, Catholic University of Portugal.

2 See Economides, N.; Lianos, I., "The Quest for Appropriate Remedies in the EC Microsoft Cases: A Comparative Appraisal", in *Microsoft on Trial: Legal and Economic Analysis of a Transatlantic Antitrust Case.* Oxford: Edward Elgar Publishing, 2010, p. 431.

3 In this article we will refer to remedy as a structural or behavioural remedial measure.

4 Council Regulation 1/2003/EC of 16 December 2002 on the implementation of the rules on competition law laid down in Articles 81 and 82 of the Treaty (OJ L 1/1, 04.01.2003).

2. The emergence of structural and behavioural remedies

Prior to 2004, Regulation 17[5] did not specifically address the Commission's powers to impose remedies for breach of Article 102 TFEU in addition to fines. The early case law of the Court of Justice of the European Union (CJEU) did not elaborate on these concepts either and the expression "cease the breach" was used not only to declare the incompatibility of a certain conduct with EU competition law but also to support the positive and negative courses of action eventually imposed by the Commission on the undertakings. It was in *Commercial Solvents*[6] that the CJEU acknowledged a wide interpretation of Article 3 (1) of Regulation 17 including the possibility for the Commission to impose a certain positive conduct. This position was endorsed in *AKZO*[7] and in *Magill.*[8]

The concept of remedies was developed by the General Court (GC) in *Microsoft.*[9] The GC distinguished between the Commission's decisions aimed at imposing an obligation to cease and desist, where the infringing undertaking must take every measure necessary to comply with that order, and the decisions aimed at imposing remedial measures, which must be taken by the breaching undertakings without delay; otherwise, a penalty may be applied. It was the *Microsoft* case, both in its EU and US dimensions, that flagged up the need to build a coherent theory of remedies[10] regarding the need to intervene, the choice of the remedy and its adequacy to bring the infringement to an end and to restore competition.

Articles 7 and 9, together with Recitals 12 and 13 of Regulation 1/2003 provide the Commission with the possibility to impose remedies or accept voluntary implementation thereof, in order

---

5 Regulation No. 17. First Regulation implementing Articles 85 and 86 of the Treaty (OJ 13/204, 21.02.1962).

6 Joined cases 6 and 7-73, *Istituto Chemioterapico Italiano S.p.A. and Commercial Solvents Corporation v Commission*, [1974] ECR 223 paras. 45-46.

7 Case C-62/86, *AKZO Chemie BV v Commission*, [1991] ECR I-3359 paras. 155-157.

8 Case T-76/89, *Independent Television Publications Ltd v Commission*, ECR [1991] II-575 para. 70.

9 Case T-201/04, *Microsoft v Commission*, [2007] ECR II-3601 para 1256.

10 Lianos, I., "Is the Availability of 'Appropriate' Remedies a Limit to Competition Law Liability under Article 102? The Mischiefs of 'Discrecionary Remedialism' in Competition Law", in Etro, F.; Kokkoris, I. (eds.), *Competition Law and the Enforcement of Article 82*. Oxford: Oxford University Press, 2010, pp. 165-202. On the case, see Pais, S. O., *Entre Inovação e Concorrência – Em defesa de um modelo europeu*. Porto: Universidade Católica Editora, 2011, p. 577.

to restore competition in the market. Article 7 of Regulation 1/2003 allows the Commission to:

> impose any behavioural or structural remedies which are proportionate to the infringement committed and necessary to bring the infringement effectively to an end. Structural remedies can only be imposed either where there is no equally effective behavioural remedy or where an equally effective behavioural remedy would be more burdensome for the undertaking concerned than the structural remedy.

Recital 12 adds that

> changes to the structure of an undertaking as it existed before the infringement was committed would only be proportionate where there is a substantial risk of a lasting or repeated infringement that derives from the very structure of the undertaking.

According to Article 9 and Recital 13, the Commission may accept commitments offered by the undertakings concerned in order to terminate the proceedings that meet its concerns[11] – remedies – and make them binding.

As to the competition policy objectives targeted by the use of different sanctions, remedies serve the purpose of restoring competition in affected markets[12] and changing the undertakings' incentives in order to avoid repetition of the breach.[13] These contrast with the competition policy objectives underlying the fines, which are mainly punishment and deterrence.[14] Other objectives, debatable or not, may be present in public enforcement

---

[11] Wils, W., "The Use of Settlements in Public Antitrust Enforcement: Objectives and Principles", Ehlermann, C.-D.; Marquis, M. (eds.), *European Competition Law Annual 2008: Antitrust Settlements under EC Competition Law*. N.Y.: Hart Publishing, 2010, p. 30.

[12] To restore competition does not mean to reach perfect competition. See Economides, N.; Lianos, I., *op. cit.*, p. 396.

[13] See Hellström, P.; Maier-Rigaud, F.; Bulst, F., "Remedies in European Antitrust Law", *Antitrust Law Journal* 76 (2009), p. 43. See also Melamed, A., "Afterword: The Purposes of Antitrust Remedies", *Antitrust Law Journal* 76 (2009), p. 364, and OCDE "Remedies and Sanctions for Abuse of Market Dominance", *OECD Policy Brief* (December 2008), p. 2.

[14] Komninos, A., "Private enforcement in the EU with emphasis on damages actions", in Lianos, I.; Geradin, D. (eds.), *Handbook on European Competition Law: Enforcement and Procedure*. Oxford: Edward Elgar Publishing, 2013, pp. 230-232, and Komninos, A., *EC Private Antitrust Enforcement, Decentralised Application of EC Competition Law by National Courts*. Oxford and Portland – Oregon: Hart Publishing, 2008, p. 7.

decisions, such as regulatory aims,[15] construction of the internal market[16] or clarification of the content of the prohibitions.[17-18]

The sanction that has been used more often by the Commission in abuse of dominance cases is beyond any doubt the fine. In this regard, the *Intel* case is noteworthy. The Commission imposed a fine of €1.06 billion on the undertaking for fidelity rebates that allegedly excluded competitors.[19] On the contrary, the Commission's practice after Regulation 1/2003 regarding structural or behavioural remedies in Article 102 cases is still being built.[20]

3. Types of remedies and principles governing their choice

Remedies are generally of two kinds: structural and behavioural. The former represent a change in the structure of the dominant undertaking removing the incentives to behave in an anticompetitive way (by divesting a subsidiary or certain assets) whereas the latter are commitments as to the undertaking's conduct in the future (prohibition to discriminate between customers, for example).[21] Since abuses of dominance are essentially behavioural breaches, it is only natural that the most popular remedies used are behavioural.[22] Quasi-structural remedies are an in-between category. These remedies would include, for instance, obligations to provide access or to expand capacity in energy cases.[23]

---

15 Ibañez Colomo, P., "On the application of Competition Law as regulation: elements for a theory", *Yearbook of European Law* 29 (2010), pp. 209-292.

16 Gerard, D., "Public enforcement: the ECN – network antitrust enforcement in the European Union", in Lianos, I.; Geradin, D. (eds.), *Handbook on European Competition Law: Enforcement and Procedure*. Oxford: Edward Elgar Publishing, 2013, p. 191.

17 O'Donoghue, R.; Padilla, A., *The Law and Economics of Article 102 TFUE.* 2nd ed. Oxford and Portland – Oregon: Hart Publishing, 2013, p. 883.

18 It is debatable whether public enforcement pursues any compensatory objectives, since these are mainly present in private enforcement claims. However, it is clear that in a wider perspective, competition law remedies also target victims' compensation. See Pitofsky, R., "Antitrust at the Turn of the Twenty-First Century: The Matter of Remedies", *Georgetown Law Journal* 91 (2002), pp. 169, 170.

19 COMP/C-3/37.990, *Intel* (2009). Upheld by the judgement of the GC on Case T-286/09, *Intel Corp v Commission*, not yet reported.

20 Lianos, I., "Competition Law Remedies in Europe", in Lianos, I.; Geradin, D. (eds.), *Handbook on European Competition Law: Enforcement and Procedure*. Edward Elgar Publishing, 2013, p. 362.

21 De la Mano, N.; Nazzini, R.; Zenger, H., "Article 102", in Faull, J.; Nikpay A. (eds.), *The EU Law of Competition.* 3rd ed. Oxford: Oxford University Press, 2014, p. 339.

22 O'Donoghue, R.; Padilla, A., *op. cit.*, p. 880.

23 Alexiadis, P.; Sependa, E., "Structural remedies under European union antitrust rules", *Structural remedies: A unique antitrust tool, Concurrences* 2 (2013), p. 21.

It is possible to distinguish between remedies that aim at exploitative conduct (such as discriminatory conditions) and exclusionary abuses and within the latter to distinguish between input foreclosure (where a competitor is harmed as a client, margin squeeze, refusal to deal) and customer foreclosure abuses (where the conduct is only indirectly aimed at the competitor, such as predatory pricing, exclusionary rebates and tying).[24] To remedy exploitative abuses an adjustment to customer contracts may be a necessary measure.[25] To remedy input foreclosure cases it may be necessary to take positive action to establish the conditions of the commercial relationship between the infringing undertaking and the victim of the abuse.[26]

Other possible classifications of remedies distinguish between positive and negative conduct,[27] price-related and nonprice-related, ex-ante and ex-post (according to the type of procedure, commitments infringement declaration).[28]

As stated above, remedies pursue a strong restorative objective and must therefore be specifically designed to address particular competition concerns. Additionally, remedies are prospective in nature, which implies a prognosis assessment. Given this context, when dealing with the choice of (a certain) remedy for a case, the Commission's action must abide by certain principles.

Firstly, remedies must be proportionate. The proportionality principle acts as a limit to the Commission's powers and is set forth in Article 7(1) of Regulation 1/2003. In fact, remedies will have a direct impact on the undertakings' rights and property, which will be restricted by the Commission's action.[29] Structural remedies clash with the undertakings' property rights while behavioural remedies directly affect the undertakings' economic freedom and business autonomy. Therefore, the burden imposed on the undertakings cannot exceed what is necessary to reach

24 Hjelmeng, E., "Competition law remedies: striving for coherence or finding new ways?", *Common Market Law Review*, 50 (2013), p. 1016.

25 Hjelmeng, E., *op. cit.*, p. 1015.

26 *Idem*, p. 1016.

27 Frese, M., *Sanctions in EU Competition Law: Principles and Practice*, (2012) (available at http://dare.uva.nl/document/459139), p. 182.

28 Gongedo, P., "Separazione Funzionale o Strutturale nelle Industrie Regolate? I Vincitori Non Puniscono; Possibilmente Cooperano (e Innovano)", in Ghidini, G.; Liboneti, B.; Marcheti P. (eds.), *Concorrenza e Mercato: Rassegna degli Orientamenti dell'Autorità Garante*. Milano: Giuffrè Editore, 2008, p. 383.

29 Andreangeli, A., "The public enforcement of Articles 101 and 102 TFEU under Council Regulation 1/2003: due process considerations", in Lianos, I.; Geradin, D. (eds.), *Handbook on European Competition Law: Enforcement and Procedure*. Oxford: Edward Elgar Publishing, 2013, pp. 142 and 163.

the objective of restoring competition to the market and must be adequate to the attainment of such an objective. Where there is more than one possible solution, the Commission should choose the least burdensome.[30] In this regard remedies should be closely linked to a theory of harm[31] and are often a good test of the theory of harm's soundness and of the need to intervene.[32] Proportionality is thus a balancing exercise between the intrusiveness of the remedy and the importance of addressing the infringement.[33]

This is also the position of the CJEU. In *Commercial Solvents*, the CJEU stated that the Commission's power to declare that an infringement is brought to an end "*must be applied in relation to the infringement which has been established.*"[34] In *Microsoft*, the GC has clearly applied the proportionality principle to the imposition of remedies[35] stating that

> the Commission does not have unlimited discretion when formulating remedies to be imposed on undertakings for the purpose of putting an end to an infringement. In the context of the application of Article 3 of Regulation No. 17, the principle of proportionality requires that the burdens imposed on undertakings in order to bring an infringement to an end do not exceed what is appropriate and necessary to attain the objective sought, namely re-establishment of compliance with the rules infringed.

The proportionality of remedies may vary according to the procedure. In Article 9 decisions the proportionality principle is more limited than in Article 7 decisions and is fulfilled when the Commission verifies that the undertaking did not offer a less onerous commitment, but does not impose the obligation on the Commission to look actively for the less onerous solution.[36] Therefore, the potential scope of the remedies is wider in Article 9 decisions than in Article 7 decisions.[37]

---

30 Economides, N.; Lianos, I., "A Critical Appraisal of Remedies in the EU Microsoft Cases", *Columbia Business Law Review* 2 (2010), p. 413.

31 Lianos, I., "Competition Law Remedies in Europe", *op. cit.*, p. 386.

32 O'Donoghue, R.; Padilla, A., *op. cit.*, p. 927.

33 O'Donoghue, R.; Padilla, A., *op. cit.*, p. 886. See, generally, Case C-331/88, *The Queen v Minister of Agriculture, Fisheries and Food and Secretary of State for Health, ex parte: Fedesa and others* [1990] ECR I-4032, para. 13.

34 *Commercial Solvents, cit.*, para. 45.

35 *Microsoft, cit.*, para. 1216 and para. 1276, quoting *Magill, cit.*, para. 93. See also Joined cases C-241/91P and C-242/91 P, *Radio Telefis Éireann and Independent Television Publications (RTE and ITV) v Commission* [1995] ECR I-743, para. 93.

36 Case C-441/07 P, *Commission v Alrosa Company Ltd.* [2010] ECR I-5949.

37 Hjelmeng, E., *op. cit.*, pp. 1007-1037.

Secondly, structural remedies are subsidiary in relation to behavioural ones. This rule is enshrined in Recital 12 of Regulation 1/2003, leading some authors to state that there is a presumption that structural remedies are disproportionate in nature, and that they are only proportionate when there is no suitable behavioural alternative.[38] In our view, although structural remedies may be theoretically proportionate, it is certainly difficult to meet an adequate proportionality standard to impose structural remedies under Article 7.

Thirdly, remedies should be clear and precise.[39] Otherwise, the undertakings' legal certainty would be impaired.

Effectiveness and direct enforceability also play an important role. Remedies should effectively terminate the infringement and should not be excessively difficult to monitor.[40] This is particularly important when the Commission chooses between a fine that can be accompanied by a cease and desist order, aimed at terminating the infringement in cases where the conduct found to be an abuse has not ended by the time the decision is taken, and a structural or behavioural remedy. Fines and cease and desist orders are easier to impose and to monitor. On the contrary, given that remedies are prospective in nature they become more difficult to design and, where they are not limited to a specific course of action (such as the divestment of an activity), harder to monitor.

4. Commission's recent decisional practice

The decisional practice of the Commission reveals that this institution is willing to intervene, imposing or accepting remedies in order to solve several types of abuse of dominant position cases (exclusionary conduct, such as access problems of network foreclosure, input foreclosure, customer foreclosure or access to standard essential patents (SEPs), exploitative conduct and market partitioning cases). However, since remedies are imposed or accepted where the infringement derives from the very structure of the undertaking, it is not surprising that an analysis of the Commission's most recent practice reveals that it mainly exercises its remedial power to solve access problems. Also, remedies have been mostly used in connection with Article 9 decisions and in markets subject to at least some degree of regulation. It was in the energy sector that the Commission used structural remedies for the first time, but some

---

38 O'Donoghue, R.; Padilla, A., *op. cit.*, p. 887.

39 Hellström *et al.*, *op. cit.*, pp. 49-51.

40 De Smijter, E.; Sinclair, A., "The Enforcement System under Regulation 1/2003", in Faull, J.; Nikpay, A. (eds.), *The EU Law of Competition.* 3rd ed. Oxford: Oxford University Press, 2014, p. 123.

remedies accepted or imposed in communications and IT markets have been close to structural.

In the foreclosure cases of *RWE*[41] and *ENI*[42] the Commission accepted no less than structural remedies. The Commission was concerned with the undertakings' possible network foreclosure due to capacity hoarding, and margin squeeze. The Commission found that the vertically integrated undertakings had an inherent conflict of interest in controlling both the transmission and the supply of gas. Divestiture allowed for the removal of such an incentive to benefit their downstream companies. The remedies were effective and proportionate in the Commission's view, not only because the undertakings had not committed to less onerous ones, but also due to the potential harm to the large number of customers connected to their networks. In *GDF* gas foreclosure and *E.ON* gas foreclosure,[43] where long-term capacity reservations were at stake, the Commission accepted behavioural remedies of capacity releasing. The difference between the two sets of cases that justified the choice for structural v. behavioural remedies was that in the latter the incentive to abuse a dominant position did not stem from the very structure of the undertaking. In fact, the capacity reservation was made by the downstream arm of the undertaking[44] and not the upstream one controlling the transmission network.

However, in the *Deutsche Bahn* cases[45] the approach was not exactly the same. The Commission feared a potential margin squeeze created by the pricing system of the vertically integrated group for traction current to railway undertakings on the markets for the provision of rail freight and long distance passenger transport services. The company undertook to implement a new pricing system for traction current with separate supply prices for electricity and separate grid access fees. At the same time the undertaking committed to offer third-party access to its traction current network to enable competing providers to emerge. This was a case where, notwithstanding the vertical integration, the Commission accepted behavioural remedies. These remedies, however, did not fall short of intrusiveness (in fact, third-party access is more consistent with a case of essential facilities than of margin squeeze).

---

41 Case COMP/39.402 *RWE gas foreclosure* (2009).

42 Case COMP/39.315 *ENI* (2010).

43 Case COMP/39.316 *GDF gas foreclosure* (2009) and Case COMP/39.317 *E.ON gas foreclosure* (2010).

44 Gauer, C.; Kjølbye, L. "Energy", in Faull, J.; Nikpay, A. (eds.), *The EU Law of Competition.* 3rd ed. Oxford: Oxford University Press, 2014, p. 1630.

45 Cases AT.39.678/AT.39.731 *Deutsche Bahn I/II* (2013).

These cases seem to contrast with the *CEZ* case,[46] where although there was no vertical integration, the Commission did not settle for less than a structural remedy. *CEZ* was allegedly reserving capacity on the electricity grid, which it did not control, with a view to preventing competing entry in the generation market (since a generator could not start producing without securing transmission capacity). The undertaking's commitment was to divest generation assets in order to compensate for having prevented or at least significantly delayed the emergence of a generation competitor. Again, this remedy has got far-reaching consequences and divestiture is probably more suited for cases where there are vertical integration issues.

In tying cases, such as *Microsoft I*, the Commission ordered the undertaking to market a windows version free of Internet Media Player.[47] In *Microsoft II* (tying), the undertaking agreed in an Article 9 decision to introduce a "Browser Choice Screen" allowing consumers to choose freely from a randomly selected set of web browsers at the start-up of their PC[48] (must-carry remedy). In *Rio Tinto Alcan*[49] the Commission expressed its concerns regarding a contractual tying in the aluminium production market. The undertaking committed, for a period of five years, to remove the tying clauses from the relevant agreements and to introduce an objective and non-discriminatory process for selecting qualified competing suppliers who would be provided with the relevant technical specifications and *Rio Tinto Alcan*'s licensees would be able to choose among them. Although these cases cannot be characterised as structural remedies, they do limit the undertaking's commercial freedom to decide how to market its products. In *Microsoft II*, the Commission has probably gone a step too far while accepting the must-carry obligation. In fact, this kind of remedy is more suited for essential facilities cases.[50]

The issue of long-term electricity contracts in France[51] was a case of customer foreclosure whereby, in the Commission's view, the scope, duration, and exclusive nature of *EDF*'s supply contracts could prevent other electricity suppliers from entering the French electricity market. Among other remedies *EDF* undertook to release an average of 65% of the electricity that it had contracted with large customers every year. Again, the

---

46 Case COMP/39.727 *CEZ* (2013).

47 Case COMP/C-3/37.792 *Microsoft* (2004). The undertaking was also commanded to supply interoperability information in order to meet another Commission's finding.

48 Case COMP/39.530, *Microsoft* (2009).

49 Case COMP/39.230, *Rio Tinto Alcan* (2012).

50 Economides, N.; Lianos, I., *op. cit.*, p. 445.

51 Case COMP/39.386, *Long term contracts in France* (2010).

remedy seems to go beyond simply mirroring the abuse, which would be not to impose exclusivity.

In market partitioning cases such as *Swedish interconnectors*,[52] the Commission expressed its concerns that the undertaking was abusing a dominant position by curtailing export capacity for Swedish interconnectors when it anticipated internal congestion within the Swedish transmission system, thereby discriminating between different network users and segmenting the internal market. In an Article 9 decision, the undertaking committed to reorganizing the market by subdividing the transmission system into two or more bidding zones in order to limit congestion, as well as to invest in new capacity. Once more, the remedies were close to structural and it is very debatable whether the Commission may impose its own view of the investment needs on the undertakings.

Exploitative abuses were also covered by the Commission's remedial action. The most notorious cases are *German electricity wholesale market* and *German electricity balancing market*.[53] The Commission was concerned that *E.ON*, a vertically integrated undertaking, was engaging in a strategy of withholding electricity capacity and favouring its less efficient downstream affiliate companies and passing on the extra costs to the final consumer. *E.ON* undertook to divest generation capacity and its transmission system business. These were the first cases closed with structural remedies.

In other decisions the remedies were more traditional, in the sense that they were closer to the theory of the abuse. These are the cases, for example, of *De Beers v Alrosa*,[54] where *De Beers* committed to the Commission to terminating its supply relationship with *Alrosa* whereby the latter was to sell a large portion of its rough diamond production exclusively to the former, *IBM*,[55] where the undertaking committed to supply spare parts to undertakings providing maintenance services, and *Rambus*,[56] where an obligation to license on FRAND-terms was agreed, in order for the undertaking to free itself of the Commission's concerns for patent ambush and inflated royalties. More recently, in *Samsung*[57] and *Motorola*[58] cases, the outcome was similar. The Commission was concerned that the undertak-

52 Case COMP/39.351, *Swedish Interconnectors* (2010).

53 Cases COMP/39.388 and COMP/39.389, *German electricity wholesale market* and *German electricity balancing market* (2008).

54 Case COMP/38.381, *De Beers v Alrosa* (2006), upheld in the CJEU *Alrosa* case.

55 Case COMP/39.692, *IBM Maintenance Services* (2011).

56 Case COMP/38.636, *Rambus* (2009).

57 Case AT.39939, *Samsung, enforcement of UMTS standard essential patents* (2014).

58 Case AT.39985, *Motorola, enforcement of GPRS standard essential patents* (2014).

ings were seeking interlocutory and permanent injunctions against Apple before the courts of several Member States on the basis of its Universal Mobile Telecommunications System ("UMTS") standard essential patents ("SEP") which they had previously committed to license on fair, reasonable and non-discriminatory ("FRAND") terms. SEPs are standards that implementers of technologies, such as UMTS, cannot avoid using in their standard-compliant products. *Samsung* agreed not to seek injunctions on the basis of its Mobile SEPs against any potential licensee willing to enter on a license agreement on FRAND terms. *Motorola* did not commit, but in an Article 7 decision the Commission imposed a cease and desist order.[59]

The latest highest profile case is the Commission's ongoing investigations into *Google* search activities for alleged discrimination against competing search engines.[60] *Google* offered two sets of commitments, in 2013 and 2014, but the Commission has eventually declined the commitments and sent the undertaking a statement of objections in 2015. The possibility of the Commission accepting Google's commitments was being criticised in two different ways. On the one hand, the criticism was directed at the absence of an explicit theory of harm. On the other hand, this case being novel, a commitments decision would not allow the development of competition law in this regard. It remains to be seen how the case will be closed.

5. Taking stock of the Commission's practice

The Commission's practice has evolved throughout the years. Firstly, there was a shift from simply ordering the termination of the infringement to remedies that actively promote competition, notably by facilitating market entry.[61] The majority of remedies that have been imposed or accepted have fallen short of true divestiture, but many are nearly quasi-structural remedies, like the access-related commitments and commitments to expand capacity.[62]

Secondly, there seems to be an over use of Article 9 decisions when compared to Article 7 decisions. This has the disadvantage of not allowing

59 The commission did not impose a fine, inter alia, given the novelty of the case. This is an interesting combination of Article 7 and Article 9 decisions, which may help to clarify the law, Whish, R.; Bailey, D., Competition Law, 8th ed. Oxford: Oxford University Press, 2015

60 Commission's press release of 15 April 2015 (http://europa.eu/rapid/press-release_IP-15-4780_en.htm).

61 Hjelmeng, E., *op. cit.*, p. 1027.

62 Alexiadis, P.; Sependa, E., *op. cit.*, p. 21.

for the construction of a sound decisional practice, because those decisions are not based on a finding of an infringement but rather on addressing the Commission's concerns. Nevertheless, it does have the advantage of allowing swifter solutions, involving the undertakings at stake, which may serve to reach remedies that are easier to implement and to reduce litigation.

Thirdly, and related to the last point, the acceptance of stringent remedies in commitment decisions, especially due to the more lenient proportionality test to which they are subject, is in some cases not based on a clear theory of harm, which begs the questions whether the remedies would be acceptable in an Article 7 decision and whether the undertakings have merely accepted those commitments in order to terminate the proceedings.[63] In this regard, the *CEZ* case brings about another issue, the undertaking accepted structural remedies, which should only be proportionate where there is a substantial risk of a lasting or repeated infringement that derives from the very structure of the undertaking. However, in this case the undertaking was not vertically integrated and one can hardly state that it was an infringement derived from its very structure. Some authors defend the Commission's position, stating that these commitments would have met the Article 7 standards since Recital 12 cannot be interpreted as limiting the imposition of structural remedies to breaches deriving from the structure of the undertakings only and therefore that they are not reserved to cases where the undertaking is vertically integrated.[64] In this regard, these authors draw a distinction between divestiture of an entire business unit and divestiture of some of the undertaking's assets. In the latter case the remedy is proportionate even where the undertaking is not vertically integrated.[65] In our view, since under Article 102 it is not forbidden to hold a dominant position[66], it does seem difficult to defend such wide powers for the Commission, especially because structural remedies are by nature difficult to reconcile with the proportionality

63 O'Donoghue, R.; Padilla, J., *op. cit.*, p. 914. Schweitzer, H., "Commitment Decisions under Article 9 of Regulation 1/2003: The Developing EC Practice an Case Law", in Ehlermann, C.-D.; Marquis, M. (eds.), *European Competition Law Annual 2008: Antitrust Settlements under EC Competition Law*. Oxford: Hart Publishing, 2010, p. 559.

64 Gauer, C.; Kjølbye, L., *op. cit.*, pp. 1633 and 1634.

65 *Idem*.

66 Nazzini, R., *The Foundations of European Union Competition Law: The Object and Principles of Article 102*. Oxford: Oxford University Press, 2011, p. 279.

principle[67] Also, such powers should not serve as mere economic policy or regulatory instruments, giving the Commission an interventionist role.[68]

Fourthly, the strongest remedies imposed or agreed have occurred in regulated sectors[69] and have aimed especially at facilitating market access, thus going much further than simply mirroring the abuse. The energy cases are the best example. These followed the Commission's sector specific inquiry in 2005,[70] where it identified access issues. The far-reaching remedies were thus used to overcome the shortcomings of the liberalisation process.[71] It is debatable whether this can happen in different markets. Also, in regulated markets one can question whether the Commission may impose remedies that go further than the obligations that the Commission itself imposes through its Directives.[72] Another issue is to evaluate the proportionality of the remedies in light of Recital 12 in the context of the fact that regulatory reforms may change the likelihood of repetition of the infringement.[73]

As to the sectors which are more prone to remedies, one may notice a difference between the commitments in the telecoms, IT, media and those in energy. While the latter are more directed to introduce competition to the market, fostering liberalisation,[74] the former need to be quick and address a specific competition concern swiftly, due to the constant evolving nature of those markets.

Finally, although great care must be taken with the imposition or acceptance of far-reaching remedies, it is to be seen whether this tool may prove to be important for the restorative purpose of competition enforcement, notably by promoting competition and market entry in a way that would not be possible to achieve with a mere cease and desist order.[75] In

---

67 Hjelmeng, E., *op. cit.,* p. 1013.

68 Ojha, L., "Les Mesures Correctives et Sanctions de l'Abus de Position Dominante: Une Perspective Comparée", *Bulletin CEDIDAC* 59 (2012) p. 4.

69 Alexiadis, P.; Sependa, E., *op. cit.*, p. 21.

70 *Idem*, p. 23.

71 Talus, K., "Just What is the Scope of the Essential Facilities Doctrine in the Energy Sector?: Third Party Access-Friendly Interpretation in the EU v. Contractual Freedom in the US", *Common Market Law Review* 48 (5) (2011) p. 1595. Scholz, U.; Purps, S., "The Application of EC Competition Law in the Energy Sector", *Journal of European Competition Law & Practice* 1 (1) (2010) p. 51.

72 Gauer, C.; Kjølbye, L., *op. cit.*, p. 1632. This occurred in the RWE and ENI cases.

73 Gauer, C.; Kjølbye, L., *op. cit.*, p. 1632.

74 Bellis, J. F., "Article 102 TFEU: The Case for a Remedial Enforcement Model along the Lines of Section 5 of the Federal Trade Commission Act", *Concurrences* 1 (2013), p. 59.

75 Hjelmeng, E., *op. cit.*, p. 1022.

this regard, it is only natural that the Commission chooses to use Article 9 decisions when aiming at more stringent remedies. Public enforcement consistency is needed and should be measured in terms of proportionality. Is it necessary to impose a remedy? Has the right remedy been chosen? Was it adequate to bring the infringement to an end?

Bibliography

Alexiadis, P.; Sependa, E., "Structural remedies under European union antitrust rules", *Structural remedies: A unique antitrust tool*, *Concurrences* 2 (2013).

Andreangeli, A., "The public enforcement of Articles 101 and 102 TFEU under Council Regulation 1/2003: due process considerations", in Lianos, I.; Geradin, D. (eds.), *Handbook on European Competition Law: Enforcement and Procedure*. Oxford: Edward Elgar Publishing, 2013.

Bellis, J. F., "Article 102 TFEU: The Case for a Remedial Enforcement Model along the Lines of Section 5 of the Federal Trade Commission Act", *Concurrences* 1 (2013).

De la Mano, N.; Nazzini, R.; Zenger, H., "Article 102", in Faull, J.; Nikpay A. (eds.), *The EU Law of Competition*. 3rd ed. Oxford: Oxford University Press, 2014.

De Smijter, E.; Sinclair, A., "The Enforcement System under Regulation 1/2003", in Faull, J.; Nikpay, A. (eds.), *The EU Law of Competition*. 3rd ed. Oxford: Oxford University Press, 2014.

Economides, N.; Lianos, I., "A Critical Appraisal of Remedies in the EU Microsoft Cases", *Columbia Business Law Review* 2 (2010).

Economides, N.; Lianos, I., "The Quest for Appropriate Remedies in the EC Microsoft Cases: A Comparative Appraisal", in *Microsoft on Trial: Legal and Economic Analysis of a Transatlantic Antitrust Case*. Oxford: Edward Elgar Publishing, 2010.

Frese, M., *Sanctions in EU Competition Law: Principles and Practice*, (2012) (available at http://dare.uva.nl/document/459139).

Gauer, C.; Kjølbye, L., "Energy" in Faull, J.; Nikpay, A. (eds.), *The EU Law of Competition*. 3rd ed. Oxford: Oxford University Press, 2014.

Gerard, D., "Public enforcement: the ECN – network antitrust enforcement in the European Union", in Lianos, I.; Geradin, D. (eds.), *Handbook on European Competition Law: Enforcement and Procedure*. Oxford: Edward Elgar Publishing, 2013.

Gongedo, P., "Separazione Funzionale o Strutturale nelle Industrie Regolate? I Vincitori Non Puniscono; Possibilmente Cooperano (e Innovano)", in Ghidini, G.; Liboneti, B.; Marcheti, P. (eds.), *Concorrenza e Mercato: Rassegna degli Orientamenti dell'Autorità Garante*. Milano: Giuffrè Editore, 2008.

Hellström, P.; Maier-Rigaud, F.; Bulst, F., "Remedies in European Antitrust Law", *Antitrust Law Journal* 76 (2009).

Hjelmeng, E., "Competition law remedies: striving for coherence or finding new ways?", *Common Market Law Review*, 50 (2013).

Ibañez Colomo, P., "On the application of Competition Law as regulation: elements for a theory", *Yearbook of European Law* 29 (2010).

Komninos, A., "Private enforcement in the EU with emphasis on damages actions", in Lianos, I.; Geradin, D. (eds.), *Handbook on European Competition Law: Enforcement and Procedure*. Oxford: Edward Elgar Publishing, 2013.

Komninos, A., *EC Private Antitrust Enforcement, Decentralised Application of EC Competition Law by National Courts*. Oxford and Portland – Oregon: Hart Publishing, 2008.

Lianos, I., "Competition Law Remedies in Europe", in Lianos, I.; Geradin, D. (eds.), *Handbook on European Competition Law: Enforcement and Procedure*. Edward Elgar Publishing, 2013.

Lianos, I., "Is the Availability of 'Appropriate' Remedies a Limit to Competition Law Liability under Article 102? The Mischiefs of 'Discrecionary Remedialism' in Competition Law", in Etro, F.; Kokkoris, I. (eds.), *Competition Law and the Enforcement of Article 82*. Oxford: Oxford University Press, 2010.

Melamed, A., "Afterword: The Purposes of Antitrust Remedies", *Antitrust Law Journal* 76 (2009).

Nazzini, R., *The Foundations of European Union Competition Law: The Object and Principles of Article 102*. Oxford: Oxford University Press, 2011.

O'Donoghue, R.; Padilla, A., *The Law and Economics of Article 102 TFUE*. 2nd ed. Oxford and Portland – Oregon: Hart Publishing, 2013.

Ojha, L., "Les Mesures Correctives et Sanctions de l'Abus de Position Dominante: Une Perspective Comparée", *Bulletin CEDIDAC* 59 (2012).

Pais, S. O., *Entre Inovação e Concorrência – Em defesa de um modelo europeu*. Porto: Universidade Católica Editora, 2011.

Scholz, U.; Purps, S., "The Application of EC Competition Law in the Energy Sector", *Journal of European Competition Law & Practice* 1 (1) (2010).

Schweitzer, H., "Commitment Decisions under Article 9 of Regulation 1/2003: The Developing EC Practice an Case Law", in Ehlermann, C.-D.; Marquis, M. (eds.), *European Competition Law Annual 2008: Antitrust Settlements under EC Competition Law*. Oxford: Hart Publishing, 2010.

Pitofsky, R., "Antitrust at the Turn of the Twenty-First Century: The Matter of Remedies", *Georgetown Law Journal* 91 (2002).

Talus, K., "Just What is the Scope of the Essential Facilities Doctrine in the Energy Sector?: Third Party Access-Friendly Interpretation in the EU v. Contractual Freedom in the US", *Common Market Law Review* 48 (5) (2011).

Whish, R.; Bailey, D., *Competition Law*. 8th ed. Oxford: Oxford University Press, 2015.

Wils, W., "The Use of Settlements in Public Antitrust Enforcement: Objectives and Principles", Ehlermann, C.-D.; Marquis, M. (eds.), *European Competition Law Annual 2008: Antitrust Settlements under EC Competition Law*. N.Y.: Hart Publishing, 2010.

Part III

State Aid: new regulations

The evolution of the “effects on trade” and “distortion of competition” requirements under the EU State aid regime

Manuel Fontaine CAMPOS[1]

Introduction

The EU Court of Justice considers since *Altmark* that the effects of an aid consisting in the distortion or threat of distortion of competition and disturbance of trade between Member States are part of the State aid concept, under Article 107(1) of the TFEU. A State that wishes to grant aid will only be subject to the requirement of notification to the European Commission and to the obligation of non-implementation of the aid (pending a Commission decision) provided that the aid fulfils those requirements. Recently, a commentator considered that “the most fundamental defect in the Commission’s State aid practice is that when it finds that a measure is selective, it assumes almost automatically that it distorts competition, although this assumption is not justified”.[2] To realize the extent to which such situations may happen it is necessary to determine the exact content of those requirements. That is the object of this paper.

1. The meaning of “effects on trade” and “distortion of competition” according to the text and legislative context of Article 107(1)

The Treaty establishing the European Coal and Steel Community did not condition the ban of subsidies and State aid to effects on trade and distortion of competition. The aid was prohibited – Article 4(c) – without the need to demonstrate the production of any effects.[3] In the EEC Treaty,

---

1 Dean of Católica Porto Law School, Catholic University of Portugal; Assistant Professor, Católica Porto Law School; Researcher at Católica Research Centre for the Future of Law.

2 See Lang, J. T., “EU State Aid Rules – The Need for Substantive Reform”, *EStAL* 3 (2014), p. 453.

3 See European Court of Justice (ECJ), case 30/59, *De Gezamenlijke*, pp. 39-40, and Advocate General (A. G.) Lagrange, case 30/59, *De Gezamenlijke*. This was later

now renamed Treaty on the Functioning the European Union (TFEU), the incompatibility of the aid with the common market was expressly conditioned to cumulative verification of effects on trade between Member States and distortion of competition.

Why were these two requirements added? The comparison between the ECSC and the TFEU systems of State aid control reveals that the latter is much more open to State aids than the former. Contrary to the ECSC, Article 107 TFEU does not strike all aid with the "prohibition and abolition" sanction. First, it distinguishes aid that is compatible from aid deemed incompatible with the internal market. The difference between incompatible aid and aid compatible *per se* (which is not classified as "State aid") lies in the production, or not, of certain effects: affectation of trade and distortion of competition. Thus, in relation to the ECSC regime, the introduction of the mentioned requirements served to extend the scope of State aids permitted *per se*: those who do not affect trade between Member States or do not distort or threaten to distort competition.

On the other hand, even the preliminary incompatibility of State aid as a result of application of Article 107(1) does not necessarily involve its prohibition. It only means that the Commission is obliged to conduct a thorough investigation (Article 108(2)), which aims at verifying whether any of the exceptions laid down in Article 107(2) and (3) are applicable. If they are, that means that the aid, after all, is or may be considered compatible with the common market and that, therefore, the aid should be authorized. This is an important point if we want to understand the interpretation by the Court of Justice of the requirements which are here under scrutiny.[4]

The following question is to know why the aid that does not meet the two requirements of distortion of trade and competition should not be considered State aid. Some useful elements can be drawn from the textual

restated by the Court of First Instance (CFI): "In contrast to Article [107(1) TFEU], that prohibition is general and unconditional. Consequently, the aid covered by the ECSC Treaty is deemed incompatible with the common market without there being any need to establish or even to consider whether there is, in actual fact, any interference with the conditions of competition or it is liable to occur" – CFI, case T-158/96, *Acciaierie di Bolzano*, para. 113.

4 The difference between incompatible aid and aid deemed compatible with the common market is that, while both produce the mentioned undesirable effects, in the case of the latter, the objectives pursued justify the authorisation by the European Commission. Thus, the fact that the fulfilment of Article 107(1) requirements does not lead to the immediate prohibition of the aid but only to a comparison between negative and desired objectives, in accordance with Article 107(3) may explain why the Commission and the Court, as we shall see, interpreted those requirements quite broadly and facilitated its filling.

meaning of Article 107 and from a systematic comparison among articles of the TFEU.

As to the requirement of *effects on trade between Member States* it is apparent from the text of Article 107(1) that trade taking place within each Member State is not covered, but only those exchanges classically referred to as imports and exports. However, given that these designations apply to trade in goods, it must be questioned whether other types of cross-border economic relationships are also covered. There seems to be no basis in the Treaty for restricting the application of Article 107 to trade in merchandises. On the contrary: the "incompatibility" referred to in paragraph 1 is with the "internal market". Since Article 26(2) TFEU provides that the "internal market shall comprise an area without internal frontiers in which the free movement of goods, *persons, services and capital* is ensured", other types of trade disturbance seem relevant, as long as trade is of a cross-border nature.[5]

On the other hand, the wording of Article 107(1) and the comparison with other rules of the TFEU may be misleading. Thus, the expression "in so far as it affects trade between Member States" seems to require a concrete verification of those effects. A comparison with the terms of other requirements contained in the legal hypotheses of Article 107 and of other Articles also leads to this conclusion. Article 107(1) requires that the aid "distorts

---

5 Both the ECJ and the CFI considered that Article 107(1) applies to other types of cross-border trade besides trade in goods. Thus they considered that trade had been affected when the aid was granted to undertakings whose main activity was the provision of air transport services – see CFI, case T-214/95, *Vlaamse Gewest* –, road transport – ECJ, case C-280/00, *Altmark* –, shipping – ECJ, case C-15/98 and C-105/99, *Sardegna Lines* –, as well as financial services – ECJ, case C-222/04, *Cassa di Risparmio di Firenze*. Calvo Caravaca, A. L.; Carrascosa Gonzalez, J., *Mercado Único y Libre Competencia en la Unión Europea*. Editorial Colex, 2003, p. 690, argue in favour of the application of State aid rules, whatever the economic activity. If the concept of affectation of trade seems to cover the flow of goods, services and eventually capital (Baudenbacher, C., *A Brief Guide to European State Aid Law*. London, The Hague, Boston: Kluwer Law International, 1997, p. 26, refers to "payments"), could the same be said of the flow of people, whether they concern workers or the exercise of the right of establishment? Regarding the latter, it seems relevant to look at Article 50(2), (h), TFEU, which provides that the European Parliament and the Council should ensure, by means of directives, "that the conditions of establishment are not distorted by aids granted by Member States". It seems therefore that the Treaty considers that State aids may distort the conditions for exercising the right of establishment. As we will see, the ECJ seems to consider in its judgments that the disturbance of the exercise of the right of establishment by a foreign company is an "effect on trade". In the case of workers it seems strange to describe travel to other Member States as "trade", although it concerns the exercise of an economic activity. Anyway, there is no case law on this matter, and that could be an indicator that, in practice, it was never considered that disturbances of the flow of workers between States constitute an "effect on trade".

or threatens to distort competition". Articles 101 and 102 rule on actions of undertakings "likely to affect trade between Member States". The difference regarding the "effects on trade" requirement of Article 107/1, which does not speak of threat or susceptibility, is remarkable. Thus it would seem that effects on trade should be specifically checked.[6]

That interpretation, however, would be wrong, because it would be irreconcilable with the State aid control system established by Article 108. Under this system, Article 107(1) can only be referring to *predictable* effects on trade. According to Article 108(3), any plans to grant or alter aid must be notified to the European Commission so that it can decide whether they are incompatible with the common market. Only after a positive decision on that matter can the "new aid" be granted. The essential aspect of this control is that it is of a preventive nature, before the aid is granted. This has the following consequence: since the Commission is the only entity that can assess the aid and decide on its incompatibility and since this activity is undertaken, as a rule, before the aid is granted, then the requirement of "effects on trade" cannot refer to effects verified as a result of that grant. Thus, this requirement can only be interpreted as referring to a forecast, a prediction, made by the Commission.[7]

Looking now at the requirement of *distortion or threat of distortion of competition*, both the wording of Article 107 and what has just been said regarding the functioning of the State aid control system are enough

6 The first commentators of the EEC Treaty adopted this interpretation: see Wohlfahrt, E.; Everling, U.; Gläsner, H.; Sprung, R., "Die Europäische Wirtschaftsgemeinschaft. Kommentar", *Zeitschrift für ausländisches öffentliches Recht und Völkerrecht* 21 (1961), Article 92, note 5, and Leanza, U., "Commento all'articolo 92 del Trattato", in *Commentario CEE*, Vol. II. Milano: Giuffrè Editore, 1965, p. 722. Accordingly, see A. G., Reischl, case 52/76, *Benedetti/Munari*, p. 191, which defended the need to present statistics showing the disturbance of trade by the aid. Defending the opposite position, which came to be adopted by the ECJ, see Scheuing, D., *Les Aides Financières Publiques aux Entreprises Privées en Droit Français et Européen*. Paris: Berger-Levrault, 1974, p. 281, and Waelbroeck, M.; Frignani, A., *Commentaire J. Megret – Le Droit de la CEE – 4 – Concurrence*. 2nd ed. Bruxelles: Éditions de l'Université de Bruxelles, 1997, p. 356. Noting the opposition between the text of Article 107(1), especially if compared with the text of Articles 101 and 102, and the interpretation adopted by the ECJ, see Ballarino, T.; Bellodi, L., *Gli Aiuti di Stato nel Diritto Comunitario*. Napoli: Editoriale Scientifica, 1997, p. 70, and Morais, L., *Direito da Concorrência – Perspetivas do seu Ensino*. Coimbra: Almedina, 2009, p. 281.

7 Accordingly, see CFI, case T-298/97, *Alzetta Mauro*, paras. 76-77. The classic argument of the Court to relieve the Commission of the duty to check concrete effects on trade refers to unlawful aid: when aid is implemented without notification to the Commission, although the analysis of the actual disturbance of trade would be possible, this would favour defaulting States in relation to those which notified the aid on time. See ECJ, case C-301/87, *France/Commission*, para. 33, and case C-75/97, *Maribel*, para. 48.

to demonstrate that the Commission must only predict the occurrence of such a distortion, without having to demonstrate the concrete verification. As to the content of the requirement, Article 107(1) makes clear what is to *distort* competition: favouring certain undertakings or the production of certain goods. It is because the undertakings which receive the aid are favoured in relation to competitors that competition ceases to be "real". Notice that this is a concept of distortion of competition different from that which the Court has developed in relation to Articles 101 and 102. As some authors rightly say, while Articles 101 and 102 intend to protect competition, Article 107(1) aims at the protection of competitors.[8]

In conclusion, for an aid to be incompatible with the common market there must be a predictable change in cross-border trade flows,[9] whether they relate to goods, services or capital, and, eventually, the establishment of undertakings. It should be equally predictable that recipient companies are favoured in the face of competitors, that is, that they become impaired in their ability to compete with them. This being said, there is still a number of questions which the Court had the opportunity to answer through an extensive case law, which will be analysed below.

2. The case law of the European Court of Justice regarding the requirements of "effects on trade" and "distortion of competition"

The interpretation made by the ECJ of the requirements was from the very beginning quite extensive. In *Italy vs. Commission*, Advocate General Werner asked the question of whether the distortion of competition and the effects on trade should be proved using data or if the Commission could assume the occurrence of those effects if there was

---

8 See Bellis, J. F., "Les critères de la distorsion de concurrence et de l'effet sur le commerce interétatique", in Dony, M.; Smits, C. (eds.), *Aides d'Etat*. Bruxelles: Éditions de l'Université de Bruxelles, 2005, pp. 97-98, and Ebner, M.; Gambaro, E., "The Notion of State Aid", in Santa Maria, A., *Competition and State Aid – An Analysis of the EC Practice*, Kluwer Law International, 2007, p. 32. Cruz Vilaça, J. L., "Material and Geographical Selectivity in State Aid – Recent Developments. A Personal View", *European State Aid Law Quarterly* 4 (2009), pp. 447-448, criticizes this position, arguing that the criteria of distortion of competition in Articles 101, 102 and 107 should be interpreted uniformly.

9 Plender, R., "Definition of Aid", in Biondi, A.; Eeckhout, P.; Flynn, J., *The Law of State Aid in the European Union*. Oxford: Oxford University Press, 2004, p. 31, refers to a "propensity" of aid to affect trade.

trade with other Member States and competitors in those States.[10] Both the Advocate General and the Court supported the latter position:

> "the *natural* consequence of the grant of an aid to an industry in a Member State must be to increase that industry's competitiveness vis-à-vis its competitors in other Member States"[11] and, consequently, "*necessarily* affects trade between the Member States".[12]

Similarly, in the exemplary case *Philip Morris*, the Court followed the opinion of Advocate General Capotorti,[13] and considered that if aid alleviates the costs of an increase of the company's production capacity, this puts it into a competitive advantage in relation to competitors; and that, where aid strengthens the position of an undertaking compared with other undertakings competing in intra-Community trade, this trade is *necessarily* affected, as long as the company in question is geared to international trade. The Court did not find it necessary for the Commission to characterize the relevant market nor to analyse the structure of the market to verify how the aid affects competition.[14]

Thus, it could be concluded that, whenever planned aid fulfils other requirements of the State aid concept, one could presume the production of effects on trade and the distortion of competition.[15] The Commission seems to have taken that view: there were cases in which, after finding that the planned aid fulfilled the elements of advantage, selectivity and

---

10 The test using that data would not involve the demonstration of the actual effects of the aid, given the preventive nature of the Commission's control, as mentioned. To perform this test the Commission would have to resort to an economic model that would allow a forecast of the impact on competition and trade of the granting of aid, as is true of Article 101 TFEU.

11 A. G. Warner, case 173/73, *Italy/Commission*, p. 728.

12 ECJ, case 173/73, *Italy v Commission*, para. 19.

13 See A. G. Capotorti, case 730/79, *Philip Morris*, pp. 2696-2698. The Advocate General had followed the Commission's position: any aid in favour of the production of a good that is traded between Member States necessarily affects trade; also, it necessarily distorts competition, safe exceptional circumstances, such as the inexistence of competitors in the common market producing like or similar products.

14 See ECJ, case 730/79, *Philip Morris*, paras. 9, 11 and 12. The ECJ thus concluded that the distortion of competition test should not be understood in the same way under Article 107 and Article 101. Similarly, see CFI, case T-92/00 e T-103/00, *Territorio Histórico de Álava*, paras. 222-223.

15 Supporting this view, regarding the distortion of competition test, see Scheuing, D., cit., 1974, p. 280. Also, the Advocates General line of thought, in the 1970s and 1980s, was that the criteria of effects on trade and distortion of competition should be interpreted broadly: besides Advocates General Warner and Capotorti, see A. G. Darmon, case 248/84, *Germany/Commission*, para. 4, Slynn, A. G. Gordon, case 67/85, *Van der Kooy*, p. 219, and A. G. Lenz, case 62/87, *Glaverbel*, paras. 16-17.

state origin, it affirmed without substantiating the elements of effects on trade and distortion of competition. However, in the *Leeuwarder* case, the Court annulled a Commission decision declaring State aid incompatible with the common market, invoking that the Commission's conclusion that the aid affected trade between Member States and distorted competition was not sufficiently substantiated. It follows from this judgment that the Commission should, to predict a distortion of competition, check for competing companies ("situation of the relevant market") and indicate the market share of the company that will receive assistance. As to effects on trade, the Commission should check the pattern of trade between Member States and detail the company's exports.[16] Thus, although a presumption of affectation of trade and distortion of competition was not recognized, it cannot be said that evidence of fulfilment of these requirements was very difficult. Anyway, the ECJ subsequently facilitated this filing even further.

Thus, in *Germany vs Commission*, the ECJ understood that when regional (or even sectoral) aid programmes are concerned, the Commission still has to establish the existence of competitors and trade between Member States in potentially covered markets. However, it is no longer required to detail the market shares and exports of the beneficiary companies (which is quite understandable, as these are not determined). Those elements are replaced by a consideration of the amounts or percentage of aid, of the nature of the supported investments and other terms of the programme.[17]

The fact that the intensity or amount of aid was taken into account, in the case of regional or sectoral aid, could raise the suggestion that, if such intensity or amount were minor, the aid would not affect competition and trade (*de minimis* aid). Likewise would concur the requests made by the ECJ to the Commission to specify, when individual aid is concerned, the market share and the importance of exports of the beneficiary company.

16 See ECJ, case 296/82, *Leeuwarder Papierwarenfabriek*, para. 24. An example of the application of these guidelines of the Court by the Commission is the *Deufil* case – ECJ, 310/85, *Deufil*, p. 901.

17 See ECJ, case 248/84, *Germany/Commission*, para. 18. Similarly, see ECJ, case C-75/97, *Maribel*, para. 48, and case C-310/99, *Italy/Commission*, para. 89. Later, in the judgment of the *Açores* tax scheme, the ECJ went even further, considering that, given the aid's characteristics (reductions of the enterprises income tax in the Portuguese autonomous region of Azores), the Commission was right to conclude that "since those reductions apply to all economic sectors in the Azores, [...] at least some of the undertakings concerned carry on economic activities involving such trade and, therefore, trade between Member States is likely to be affected" – ECJ, case C-88/03, *Açores*, para. 91. In this case, the Commission did not even have to prove the existence of competitors and trade between Member States.

If competition and trade could be affected, whatever the amount of aid, its intensity, the market share and the importance of the beneficiary's exports, what would be the use of those elements? However, Advocate General Lenz rejected that argument in the case *Glaverbel.*[18] This was confirmed by the Court in the case *Tubemeuse*:

> "the relatively small amount of aid or the relatively small size of the undertaking which receives it does not as such exclude the possibility that intra-Community trade might be affected".[19]

On the other hand, the constant reference by the ECJ to the fact that the Commission needed to specify exports made by recipients of aid could create the impression that only when an exporter was at stake would there be "effects on trade". The Court readily denied this claim, stating that such trade disturbance could occur:

> "where that undertaking competes with products coming from other Member States, even if it does not itself export its products. [...] Where a Member State grants aid to an undertaking, domestic production may for that reason be maintained or increased with the result that [...] undertakings established in other Member States have less chance of exporting their products to the market in that Member State".[20]

Thus, trade flows whose allocation is concerned are not only exports of the Member State granting the aid to other Member States but also imports from these States.

The evolution of the case law in cases *Tubemeuse* and *France/ Commission* led Advocate General Van Gerven to conclude that the requirement of the production of effects in intra-Community trade is satisfied whenever the recipient company operates in a (foreign or domestic)

---

[18] A. G. Lenz, 62/87, *Glaverbel*, paras. 16-17. According to the Advocate General, the disparity of interpretation between Article 107 and Article 101 (where a *de minimis* distortion of competition is not considered relevant) stems from the fact that actions of States should be subject to a more demanding analysis than actions of companies. Also relevant is the fact that paragraph 3 of Article 107 provides a more extensive range of exceptions than Article 101(3). Advocate General Capotorti had already considered that while agreements between undertakings do not necessarily have the purpose or effect of restricting competition, State aid necessarily has. Also, the fact that Article 107 is directed at States and not businesses justifies a more stringent treatment of their intervention, not only because it has a greater dimension, but because governments have a tendency to try to escape the prohibition of granting aids – see A. G. Capotorti, case 730/79, *Philip Morris*, p. 2699.

[19] ECJ, case C-142/87, *Tubemeuse*, para. 43. Similarly, on the distortion of competition, see CFI, case T-214/95, *Vlaamse Gewest*, para. 46: "Where the benefit is limited, competition is distorted to a lesser extent, but it is still distorted".

[20] ECJ, case 102/87, *France v Commission*, para. 19.

market where there is real competition between producers located in different Member States. Also, given the advanced state of integration of national markets, this requirement would only be left unfilled when the recipient undertaking operates in a product market for which, due to high transport costs or other circumstances, there is no international trade.[21] Put another way, this requirement would be reduced to the distortion of competition test (understood as referring to the competition with companies from other Member States and not to competition with likewise domestic companies). Therefore, the requirements that have been analysed would be filled when the aid is awarded to a company that has competitors from other Member States. This was apparently confirmed by the Court in numerous occasions:

> "where an undertaking operates in a sector in which [...] producers from various Member States compete, any aid which it may receive from the public authorities is liable to affect trade between the Member States and impair competition, inasmuch as its continuing presence on the market prevents competitors from increasing their market share and reduces their chances of increasing exports".[22]

Taking this into account the (few) cases where the grant of aid would not entail effects on trade and distortion of competition would be situations where the recipient company operates in markets where there are no competing producers from other Member States. That would happen, either because that product was not internationally traded (Advocate General Van Gerven) or because of the absence in the common market of products like or similar to the subsidized product (Advocate General Capotorti). However, even such exceptions came to be considered too broad, given the subsequent decisions of the Court of Justice and the CFI. In fact, the *coup de grâce* in the relevance of the requirements at stake, especially in the affectation of trade, was given in the cited case *Tubemeuse*. The Court held that the fact that an undertaking exported most of its production to third countries did not exclude that competition was distorted, given the interdependence between the markets in which Community undertakings operate. Indeed, as Advocate General Tesauro said, such aid could allow the assisted firm to practice in the Community market prices substantially lower than otherwise.[23] The CFI in case *AITEC* considered that, although there was no trade between Member States at the time of payment of the

---

21 See A. G. van Gerven, case C-303/88, *Italy v Commission*, para. 19.

22 ECJ, case C-305/89, *Italy v Commission*, para. 26. Similarly, see ECJ, case C-278/92, *Spain/Commission*, paras. 40-42, case C-75/97, *Maribel*, para. 51, and case C-156/98, *Germany/Commission*, para. 32.

23 See A. G. Tesauro, case C-142/87, *Tubemeuse*, para. 27, and ECJ, *ibid.*, paras. 32, 35.

grant to the undertaking, the Commission, taking into account that "even then, the orientation of Greek exports cement for certain other Member States of the Community was foreseeable", was required to examine "the foreseeable effects" of the aid on competition and intra-EU trade.[24]

Thus, the criteria of effects on trade and distortion of competition have to be subject to a dynamic analysis, projecting foreseeable trends into the future.[25] In fact, intra-EU trade is affected, although exports are made to countries outside the EU, because the recipient company will attain a more solid competitive position and, predictably, will then direct its exports to other Member States. So, consequently, the above mentioned exceptions must still be considered too broad: aid will not affect trade nor distort competition only in those situations where the aided company does not operate *nor is expected to operate* in any market where there are competitors from other Member States, because it does not exist *nor is expected to come into existence* international trade of that product in the markets where the company is involved, or because products like or similar to the subsidized product do not exist in the common market *nor are they expected to come into existence*. Putting it into the affirmative, aid distorts competition and affects trade only when it is granted to a company which operates *or that predictably will operate* in a market where there are, or *are expected to come into existence*, competing producers from other Member States.

That this is the logical conclusion of the cases cited was quickly confirmed by the CFI, which cited approvingly the Commission's argument, according to which the fact that the aided company was the only with presence in a given market was

> "irrelevant to the Commission's assessment: the aid received will in any event reduce the *chances* of competitors, actual or potential, who wish to penetrate the market in that particular route and will thus distort competition to that extent at least. Nor is there *anything to prevent* VLM from making use of the assistance to launch operations on other routes".[26]

But the *predictability* that was required by previous case law appeared now turned into a mere *possibility*.[27] And if aid distorts com-

24 See CFI, case T-447/93, *AITEC*, paras. 139-140, and case T-298/97, *Alzetta Mauro*, para. 80.

25 See A. G. Tesauro, case C-142/87, *Tubemeuse*, para. 29.

26 CFI, case T-214/95, *Vlaamse Gewest*, para. 44.

27 Ehlermann, C.-D.; Vallery, A., "Giving Meaning to the Condition of Effect on Trade: The Court's Judgement in Xunta de Galicia, a Missed Opportunity?", *EStAL* 4 (2005), p. 712, remarked this change of words in the case law of the Court, although, in fact, that resulted already from the ECJ ruling in *France vs. Commission* – see ECJ,

petition and affects trade when it is granted to a company which operates or which *may come to operate* in a market where there are or there will *possibly be* competing producers from other Member States, the distance separating this from the recognition of a real presumption becomes truly tenuous. Only in cases where the aided company operates in a market where it is *impossible* that there will be competitors from other Member States and it is *impossible* that the aided company will operate in a market with competitors will there be no effects on trade and distortion of competition.

A further development of the EU courts' case law resulted from the CFI judgment in the case *Territorio Histórico de Alava*:

> "even if a large part of [the recipient company's] production is intended for non-member countries, [the recipient company] is in direct competition with other companies established in the Community as regards exports to those countries".[28]

Thus, the problem no longer lies in the fact that aid to export to third state markets leads to an increased competitiveness of the company in the EU market, but on the fact that the increased competitiveness is found in the very foreign markets. Consequently, it is enough that aid be awarded to a company producing tradable goods, even if they are not traded with other Member States, so long as there is trade with third countries (and provided there is at least one competitor from another Member State)[29] for competition to be distorted and trade affected.[30]

---

case 102/87, para. 19 – and in other cases: see ECJ, case C-303/88, *Italy/Commission*, para. 27, case C-278/92, *Spain/Commission*, para. 17, case C-75/97, *Maribel*, para. 47, and case C-280/00, *Altmark*, paras. 77-78. This case law always refers to the reduction of chances (i.e., possibilities) of companies established in other Member States to export their products to the market of the granting Member State.

28 CFI, case T-127/99, T-129/99 and case T-148/99, *Territorio Histórico de Álava*, para. 214.

29 Stressing this requirement, see Scheuing, D., cit., 1974, p. 282, and Winter, J., "State Aids (Articles 92 and 93)", in *Discipline Communautaire et Politiques Economiques Nationales – Community Order and National Economic Policies*. Deventer: Kluwer Law and Taxation Publishers, 1984, p. 449. More recently and similarly, see Ballarino, T.; Bellodi, L., cit., 1997, p. 73, Bellis, J. F., cit., 2005, pp. 99-100, and Ebner, M.; Gambaro, E., cit., 2007, p. 32.

30 The Court seems to have receded slightly in the *Wam* case, which concerned aid to commercial expansion in third countries. The aid was granted to a company operating in a liberalized market in the EU which had competitors in other Member States. Nevertheless, the ECJ considered that, given that the amount of aid was very low, the Commission had not sufficiently motivated the production of a disturbance on trade and competition – see ECJ, case C-494/06 P, *Wam*, para. 62.

Regarding the requirement of the presence of a competitor, could there be any situation where the aided company operates in a market where it is impossible that there will be competitors from other Member States? In fact, this happens in economic sectors that have not yet been liberalized.[31] In the case *Sardegna Lines*, the ECJ annulled a Commission decision for failure to state reasons because it did not "take into account, in that respect, the fact that, until 1 January 1999, island cabotage in the Mediterranean *was excluded from the liberalisation of maritime transport services* within Member States".[32]

Inversely, in the case *Italy vs. Commission*, the ECJ said that: "the fact that an economic sector has been the subject of *liberalisation* at Community level will suffice to indicate the real or potential effect of the aid on competition and its effect on trade between Member States".[33] As we can see, the situations covered by the requirements of distortion of trade and competition spread continuously in the EU Courts case law, towards the recognition of a presumption of the verification of those requirements, in cases involving the granting of aid. Advocates General Jacobs and Maduro expressly use the term presumption.[34] In fact, EU courts, following the Commissions' enduring opinion, concluded there are aids which, by their nature, generate a real presumption of competition distortion: operating aids.[35] These are aids "intended to relieve an undertaking of the expenses which it would itself normally have had to bear in its day-to-day management or its usual activities".[36] Operating aids cannot even be considered compatible in the light of the paragraph 3, c) exception of Article 107: according to the case law, it should always be considered that they alter the conditions of EU trade to an extent contrary to the common interest.[37] Nevertheless, it seems that if operating aid

31 See Dony, M.; Renard, F.; Smits, C., *Contrôle des aides d'Etat.* 3rd ed. Bruxelles: Institut d'Études Européennes, Éditions de l'Université de Bruxelles, 2007, p. 72.

32 ECJ, case C-15/98, *Sardegna Lines*, para. 69.

33 ECJ, case C-66/02, *Italy/Commission*, para. 116.

34 See A. G. Jacobs, case C-113/00, *Spain/Commission*, para. 24, and A. G. Maduro, case C-237/04, *Enirisorse*, para. 36. Similarly, see Ballarino, T.; Bellodi, L., cit., 1997, pp. 73-75, and Baudenbacher, C., cit., p. 26, which speak about a rebuttable presumption; Evans, A., *European Community Law of State Aid.* Oxford: Clarendon Press, 1997, pp. 77, 94; Martins, M., *Auxílios de Estado no Direito Comunitário.* Cascais: Princípia, 2002, p. 86; Tesauro, G., *Diritto Comunitario.* 3rd ed. CEDAM, 2003, pp. 746-749; Bellis, J. F., cit., 2005, pp. 99-100; and Ebner, M.; Gambaro, E., cit., 2007, pp. 32, 35.

35 See CFI, case T-459/93, *Siemens*, para. 48, case T-214/95, *Vlaamse Gewest*, para. 43, and case T-55/99, *CETM*, para. 83.

36 CFI, case T-459/93, *Siemens*, para. 48.

37 See ECJ, C-86/89, *Italy v Commission*, No. 18, and CFI, T-459/93, *Siemens*, No. 76-78.

is granted to an enterprise that works in a non-liberalized sector there will be no presumption of competition distortion, since the market is by definition closed to competition. In fact, there will be no "State aid" and Article 107(3)(c) is not even applicable.

Besides the mentioned cases of aids granted to undertakings operating in non-liberalised sectors, could there be other instances where the aided company operates in a market where it is impossible that it will have competitors from other Member States?

One could put the hypothesis that this could occur also when the recipient undertaking operates in a market of non-internationally-tradable products, i.e. products that are unlikely to be subject to cross-border trade (one could think of many services, like restaurants, hairdressers, taxis, etc.). This would be consistent with the fact that EU Courts often ask the Commission the demonstration of the existence of intra-EU trade (and of competitors from other Member States) to conclude that there was a disturbance of trade and competition. The existence of trade would show that the product at stake is internationally tradable.[38] The practice of the Commission to consider that certain aid granted to strictly local activities, though it could distort competition at the regional level, does not affect trade between Member States[39] could be construed as applying the idea that, if the goods or services produced by the beneficiary company are not internationally tradable, trading conditions are not affected.[40] This hypothesis would give a useful content to the "effects on trade" criteria. Therefore, the requirements of affectation of trade and dis-

38 The judgment of the ECJ in *Spain vs. Commission*, case C-351/98, para. 58, also seemed to demonstrate this thesis: "the statement of reasons [by the Commission], is sufficient to explain the effect of the Plan on competition and trade between Member States since the Plan [...] relates to services the supply of which is liberalised between the Member States *and those services are by nature liable to be the subject of inter-State supplies*". Thus, in order to satisfy the distortion of trade and competition criteria, it would seem sufficient that the aided company operates in a liberalized market and produces internationally tradable goods or services. One could think that, if any of those requisites was not completed, there would be no distortion of trade or competition.

39 See, in this regard, the Commission's decisions regarding aids to a leisure pool in Dorsten (Decision 258/2000, 21/12/2000, OJ 2001 C 172, p. 16) and to a Dutch marina (Decision of 29/10/2003, OJ 2004 L 034, p. 63, paras. 55-56), in which it found that "even if some distortion of (local) competition is not excluded, the support (if any) has no effect on trade", since "it can not reasonably be expected that this support will lead ship owners from other Member States to use the marinas concerned for mooring (be it fixed or daily) rather than a marina in another Member State".

40 Expressing some perplexities regarding these Commission's decisions, see Arhold, C., "The Case Law of the European Court of Justice and the Court of First Instance on State Aids in 2004/2005", *European State Aid Law Review* 2 (2005), pp. 192-193.

tortion of competition would end up reduced, respectively, to the determination that the goods or services produced by the beneficiary company are internationally tradable and that the market in cause is or had been liberalized.[41] Of course, this hypothesis is based on the presupposition that the State aid control system aims at protecting competitors located in other Member States. Only if the products made by the aided company are internationally tradable could competitors get hurt, either by increased subsidized imports into their domestic markets or by reduced exports into the aided company's domestic market. But what if those competitors wish to exercise the right of establishment in the domestic market of the subsidized company? In that case, even if the products at stake are not internationally tradable, they normally are at the local, regional or national level. Therefore, State aid to an undertaking which produces non-internationally-tradable goods may very well harm foreign competitors who wish to create an establishment in that State's territory.

If one considers that the criterion of "effects on trade" was thought of to distinguish cases in which foreign companies are hindered from those in which only national undertakings are, for the purpose of subjecting to the assessment of the Commission only the first cases, we may be forced to conclude that, since foreign companies may be adversely affected in the exercise of their right of establishment, trade should be considered affected. The ECJ seems to have taken this stance in the case *Eventech*, were the market at stake involved a non-internationally-tradable service: the provision of cab rides in London. The ECJ, after saying that "the condition that the aid must be capable of affecting trade between Member States does not depend on the local or regional character of the transport services supplied" affirmed that, as a result of State aid, "the opportunities for undertakings established in other Member States to penetrate the market in that Member State are thereby reduced".[42] What this means, of course, is that the "effects on trade" and "distortion of competition" criteria are reduced to checking the existence of a liberalized market and of at least one competitor in another Member State, since even aid to producers of non-tradable products can be considered as potentially affecting commercial exchanges.

41 We defended this position, albeit with caution, in Fontaine, M., *O controlo da concessão de ajudas públicas na União Europeia e na Organização Mundial do Comércio*, Universidade Católica Portuguesa, 2011, pp. 434, 439.

42 See ECJ, case C-518/13, *Eventech*, paras. 67, 69. The ECJ had already adopted a similar position in *Altmark* – see ECJ, case C-280/00, paras. 77-79. Similarly, see European Commission, *Draft Commission Notice on the notion of State aid pursuant to Article 107(1) TFEU*, 2014, p. 48.

There is, however, at least one aspect in the European Courts' case law which, together with the exception of non-liberalized markets, has evolved against the general trend to recognize a presumption of distortion of trade and competition: the recognition of the existence of *de minimis* aid and the consideration of aids granted to activities with "purely local" impact. The Commission described certain types of aid (with the exception of those granted in certain sectors), of an amount of less than €200,000 in three years, as *de minimis* aid, and exempted them from the notification requirement, arguing that they did not have an appreciable effect on trade and competition between Member States.[43] The Court accepted this, despite it seemed to counter its above mentioned case-law, considering it an exercise of "discretion that [the Commission] has to assess the possible economic effects of aid measures".[44] This openness of the Court led Advocate General Jacobs to defend the possibility, beyond the situations already specified in the Commission regulations, that:

> in economic sectors with little competition in intra-Community trade (e.g. car repairs, taxis, restaurants or sectors with prohibitive transport costs) aid of a relatively small amount granted to small undertakings operating on essentially local markets might not affect trade between Member States.[45]

The Commission, likewise, sustains that "due to their specific circumstances, certain activities have a purely local impact and consequently do not affect trade between Member States"[46] and followed that policy in various cases. It remains to be seen if the ECJ will consider that policy compatible with a correct interpretation of Article 107(1).

Conclusion

In conclusion, one can say that what results from the EU courts case law is that the production of effects on trade and the distortion of competition are a normal consequence of the granting of aid which fulfils the other requisites of Article 107 (1). This will not happen, however: (1) if the aided

---

43 See Commission Regulation 1407/2013. The fundamental reason for the move was the need for administrative simplification and to focus scarce resources of the Commission in the analysis of the most important cases.

44 ECJ, case C-351/98, *Spain/Commission*, paras. 52-53, and case C-113/00, *Spain/ Commission*, para. 34.

45 Jacobs, A.-G., case C-113/00, *Spain v Commission*, para. 25.

46 European Commission, cit., 2014, p. 49. Common features of such decisions would be that: "(a) the aid does not lead to demand or investments being attracted to the region concerned and does not create obstacles to the establishment of undertakings from other Member States; (b) the goods or services produced by the beneficiary are purely local or have a geographically limited attraction zone; (c) there is at most a marginal effect on the markets and on consumers in neighbouring Member States".

company operates only in a non-liberalized market; or (2) if there are no competitors established within the EU; or (3) if aid is *de minimis*; or (4) if the aided company's activity is purely local.

As is obvious, these cases refer to a small share of all State aid situations. This makes the State aid system subject to criticisms like the one made by John T. Lang: "If the Commission would limit its investigations to situations in which there is a significant distortion of competition, it would be concentrating on the cases that should be given priority, and it would avoid a large and unnecessary workload".[47] Whether the criticism is just is another matter, but it is true that the requirements of trade and competition distortion are often presumed and almost never exert a selection function.

Bibliography

Arhold, C., "The Case Law of the European Court of Justice and the Court of First Instance on State Aids in 2004/2005", *European State Aid Law Review* 2 (2005).

Ballarino, T.; Bellodi, L., *Gli Aiuti di Stato nel Diritto Comunitario*. Napoli: Editoriale Scientifica, 1997.

Baudenbacher, C., *A Brief Guide to European State Aid Law*. London, The Hague, Boston: Kluwer Law International, 1997.

Bellis, J. F., "Les critères de la distorsion de concurrence et de l'effet sur le commerce interétatique", in Dony, M.; Smits, C. (eds.), *Aides d'Etat*. Bruxelles: Éditions de l'Université de Bruxelles, 2005.

Calvo Caravaca, A. L.; Carrascosa Gonzalez, J., *Mercado Único y Libre Competencia en la Unión Europea*. Editorial Colex, 2003.

Cruz Vilaça, J. L., "Material and Geographical Selectivity in State Aid – Recent Developments. A Personal View", *European State Aid Law Quarterly* 4 (2009).

Dony, M.; Renard, F.; Smits, C., *Contrôle des aides d'Etat*. 3rd ed. Bruxelles: Institut d'Études Européennes, Éditions de l'Université de Bruxelles, 2007.

Ebner, M.; Gambaro, E., "The Notion of State Aid", in Santa Maria, A., *Competition and State Aid – An Analysis of the EC Practice*. Kluwer Law International, 2007.

Ehlermann, C.-D.; Vallery, A., "Giving Meaning to the Condition of Effect on Trade: The Court's Judgement in Xunta de Galicia, a Missed Opportunity?", *EStAL* 4 (2005).

Evans, A., *European Community Law of State Aid*. Oxford: Clarendon Press, 1997.

Fontaine, M., *O controlo da concessão das ajudas públicas na União Europeia e na Organização Mundial do Comércio,* Universidade Católica Portuguesa, 2011.

[47] See Lang, J. T., cit., p. 453.

Lang, J. T., "EU State Aid Rules – The Need for Substantive Reform", *EStAL* 3 (2014).

Leanza, U., "Commento all'articolo 92 del Trattato", in *Commentario CEE*, Vol. II. Milano: Giuffrè Editore, 1965.

Martins, M., *Auxílios de Estado no Direito Comunitário*. Cascais: Princípia, 2002.

Morais, L., *Direito da Concorrência – Perspetivas do seu Ensino*. Coimbra: Almedina, 2009.

Plender, R., "Definition of Aid", in Biondi, A.; Eeckhout, P.; Flynn, J., *The Law of State Aid in the European Union*. Oxford: Oxford University Press, 2004.

Scheuing, D., *Les Aides Financières Publiques aux Entreprises Privées en Droit Français et Européen*. Paris: Berger-Levrault, 1974.

Tesauro, G., *Diritto Comunitario*. 3rd ed. CEDAM, 2003.

Waelbroeck, M.; Frignani, A., *Commentaire J. Megret – Le Droit de la CEE – 4 – Concurrence*. 2nd ed. Bruxelles: Éditions de l'Université de Bruxelles, 1997.

Winter, J., "State Aids (Articles 92 and 93)", in *Discipline Communautaire et Politiques Economiques Nationales – Community Order and National Economic Policies*. Deventer: Kluwer Law and Taxation Publishers, 1984.

Wohlfahrt, E.; Everling, U.; Gläsner, H.; Sprung, R., "Die Europäische Wirtschaftsgemeinschaft. Kommentar", *Zeitschrift für ausländisches öffentliches Recht und Völkerrecht* 21 (1961).

The hard side of soft power – the Portuguese Competition Authority recommendation to the Government on stranded costs in the electricity sector

Mariana TAVARES[1]

1. Introduction

Member States provide for varying degrees of State aid for industries operating within their territory to help achieve a wide variety of policy objectives, such as to reduce regional disparities within a country, to promote research and development and innovation activities, or to promote a high level of environmental protection.[2] This may be considered, with certain limits, to be generally beneficial to the economy by providing a stronger productive base.[3] However, sometimes benefits are less obvious and can impair the development of the internal market by distorting competition.[4]

At the High Level Forum of Member States, which took place in December 2014, Margrethe Vestager, European Commissioner for Competition, mentioned in her speech that "too much state aid is still badly designed and hinders growth. By preventing inefficient companies from leaving the market or awarding tax breaks to multinationals, it disadvantages the young, innovative companies that could revolutionise our economy. By providing conditions that the private sector cannot match, it crowds

---

1 Head of cabinet of the President of the Portuguese Competition Authority; Invited Professor, Católica Global School of Law.

2 Commission staff working document, *Common methodology for State aid evaluation*, Brussels, 28.05.2014, SWD(2014) 179 final, p. 3.

3 *Eleventh Report on Competition Policy*, 1981, p. 179.

4 See e.g. State aid action plan, 07.06.2005, COM(2005)107 final where the Commission states "State aid should only be used when it is an appropriate instrument for meeting a well-defined objective, when it creates the right incentive, is proportionate and when it distorts competition to the least possible extent. For that reason, appreciating the compatibility of State aid is fundamentally about balancing the negative effects on competition with its positive effects in terms of common interest."

out private investment. By benefiting domestic companies over rivals in other Member States, it fragments the single market, the cornerstone of our prosperity."[5] Commissioner Vestager then challenged the "Member States as well as the Commission, to work together in partnership to make every euro of taxpayers' money count"[6] in order "to promote good aid, while stamping out bad aid and ensure transparency of where the money go."[7]

An important filed where the intervention of the Commission and the Member States may be complementary is State aid evaluation and limitation of negative effects of an aid in competition. In 2012, the Commission set out an ambitious State aid reform programme in the Communication on State aid modernisation.[8] State aid evaluation is a cornerstone feature of the reform package and is intended to contribute to a better understanding of the actual impact State aid has on the markets.[9]

In this context, National Competition Authorities may be particularly well placed to monitor the evolution of State aids and their impact in competition and contribute to State aid evaluation. The PCA's recommendation to the Government on stranded costs in the electricity sector illustrates well how the action of a national competition authority, even if in the form of a non-binding opinion – a soft power instrument – can complement the action of the European Commission and limit the negative impact of a State aid in competition.

In 2004, following the notification by the Portuguese Government, the European Commission considered compatible with the internal market a State aid scheme for stranded costs compensation for EDP, a leading company in the energy sector and owner of hydropower plants, with the duration of 10 years.[10] Following this decision, the Portuguese Government enacted Decree-Law 240/2004, of 27 December 2004, which implemented the mechanism of stranded costs compensation. In 2013 the Portuguese Competition Authority (PCA) issued a recommendation to the Portuguese Government advising the re-examination of the

5 Speech at High Level Forum of Member States by Margrethe Vestager, 18 December 2014, available at http://ec.europa.eu/commission/2014-2019/vestager/announcements/speech-high-level-forum-member-States-margrethe-vestager-commissioner-competition-18-december-2014_en.

6 *Idem.*

7 *Idem.*

8 Communication from the Commission to the European parliament, the Council, the European Economic and Social Committee and the Committee of the Regions, Brussels, 08.05.2012, COM(2012) 209 final.

9 Occasional discussion papers by the Competition Directorate-General of the European Commission – Competition policy brief, Issue 7, June 2014.

10 Case N 161/2004, C(2004) 3468fin, 22.09.2004.

stranded costs' compensation mechanism in order to reduce the impact on competition of the State aid. This recommendation followed a declaration by the European Commission, in 2013, that it had no information available as to the implementation of the State aid allowing to conclude that the aid has been misused or otherwise become no longer compatible with the internal market. Other national Competition authorities have used their soft power in matter of State aid previously approved by the European Commission in order to limit its effects on competition, sometimes even by recommending the non-implementation of the aid. Such was the case, for example, of the Spanish competition authority regarding the draft law on the national electrical sector, notably the provisions regarding an aid to indigenous coal power plants.

This article covers the topic related to the Commission's decision regarding the compensation scheme of stranded costs in the Portuguese electricity sector (part I), the recommendation of the Portuguese Competition Authority to the Government on the compensation scheme of stranded costs (part II), the complementarity of the action by the national competition authority and by the European Commission in matter of the evaluation of the impact of a State aid in competition (part III), followed by conclusions.

2. Compensation of Stranded Costs in the Portuguese Electricity Sector – State Aid No. 161/2004

In April 2004, in the context of the electricity market liberalization, triggered by Directive 2003/54/EC of the European Parliament and of the Council of 26 June 2003,[11] the Portuguese Government notified to the Commission its plans to abolish the long term power purchase agreements (PPAs) and replaced them by compensation payments for stranded costs (CMEC compensation scheme) to be financed by a tariff paid by the consumers charged on the energy bill.

The Portuguese electricity industry was then mostly organized on a single-buyer framework whereby all generators sold their energy through the PPAs. An important amount of the electricity produced in Portugal at the time was not sold directly in the market. It was purchased by the publicly owned electricity operator, "REN"– Rede Elétrica Nacional, under the PPAs. REN purchased a guaranteed amount of electricity from the three electricity suppliers at a guaranteed price that covered a series of investment costs.[12]

---

[11] OJ L 176, 15.07.2003, p. 37.

[12] *Portuguese experience in the creation of an Iberian electricity wholesale market: lessons learned from the regional integration of a small country on a wider market*, Contribution from Portugal to the Session II. Electricity Market in Latin

The Portuguese Government notified a draft decree-law to the Commission establishing a compensation scheme of stranded costs – the CMEC compensation scheme – a top up payment to generators to preserve the revenue levels set up in the extinct PPAs.

By decision of 22 September 2004[13] the Commission decided not to raise objections to the CMEC compensation scheme notified by the Portuguese Government. In application of the Communication relating to the methodology for analysing State aid linked to stranded costs,[14] the Commission concluded that the CMEC stranded costs mechanism was compatible with the internal market, pursuant to Article 107 (3) c) of the Treaty on the Functioning of the European Union (TFEU), then Article 87 (3) (c) of the Treaty Establishing the European Community (TEC).

The Commission considered that, in the case at stake, stranded costs arise because old power plants built prior to liberalization would not be sufficiently efficient to face a competitive electricity market. The Commission recognized that the investment in those power plants would cause real losses after liberalisation and concluded that in the absence of any type of compensation, these losses would jeopardise the availability of the undertaking concerned. It considered that the CMEC compensation scheme was a State aid under Article 107 (1) TFEU but that it was compatible with the internal market, pursuant to Article 107 (3) (c) TFEU, i.e. "aid to facilitate the development of certain economic activities or of certain economic areas, where such aid does not adversely affect trading conditions to an extent contrary to the common interest."

The methodology of analysis used by the Commission was similar to the methodology used in previous decisions regarding stranded costs[15] as it reflects economic costs that correspond to the actual sums invested.[16] The Commission analysed the costs categories that were communicated by the Portuguese authorities to be covered by the compensations where a power plant's income is insufficient to cover them and concluded that the compensations would not exceed what is necessary to repay the shortfall

America: Regional integration and competition issues, of the OECD Latin American Competition Forum, Montevideo 16-17 September 2014. Available at: http://www.oecd.org/officialdocuments/publicdisplaydocumentpdf/?cote=DAF/COMP/LACF(2014)20&docLanguage=En.

13 N 161/2004, cit.

14 Adopted by the Commission on 26.07.2001. Commission letter SG (2001) D/290869 of 06.08.2001.

15 See State aid NN 49/99 – Spain, OJ C 268, 22.9.2001, p. 7, and State aid N 133/01 – Greece, OJ C 9 15.01.2003, p. 6.

16 *Idem*, pp. 5-8.

in investment costs repayment over the asset's lifetime, including where necessary a reasonable profit margin.

The computation of the maximum value of the compensations was based on a number of economic assumptions, including, in particular, a base market price equal to the price that would be offered by a new entrant using a combined cycle gas turbine. If the actual market price is lower than the latter, it will only be taken into account for the calculation of the compensation. According to the Commission, the mode of computation of the stranded costs took account of the actual evolution of electricity prices. The periodical adjustment in compensations will take account of the difference between the foreseen electricity price that is used for the purpose of computing the maximum amount of compensations and the actual electricity price, following the Commission's decision.[17] On 27 December 2004, the Portuguese Government enacted Decree-Law 240/2004, of 27 November, establishing the CMEC compensation scheme, covering 34 power plants, of which 27 were hydropower plants.

The introduction of the CMEC compensation scheme was implemented at the same time as the Iberian Electricity Market (MIBEL) which started on 1 July 2007.[18] Since then, till 2011, €1,496.5 million have been paid to EDP under CMEC compensation scheme.[19]

3. The PCA recommendation to the Government concerning the Stranded Costs to the Portuguese electricity sector

Following information regarding the functioning of the secondary reserve power provision sent by the Energy Services Regulatory Authority (ERSE), the PCA decided to open an investigation to analyse the effects of the CMEC in competition.[20]

---

17 European Commission Press Release, IP/04/1123, 22 September 2004.

18 State Aid SA.35429 (2013/C) (ex 2012/Cp) _ Extension of use of public water resource for hydro electricity generation. Invitation to submit comments pursuant to Article 108(2) of the Treaty on the Functioning of the European Union. (2014/C 117/06), para. 15.

19 In Spain, the country that integrates MIBEL with Portugal, no type of CMEC compensation scheme exists since 2006. In 1997, in the context of the liberalization of the Spanish electricity market, an analogous mechanism had been introduced – the CTC (Costes de Transición a la Competencia – Cost to the transmission to competition), in order to compensate the stranded cost they were also subject to compensation before liberalization. The CTC compensation scheme should have been in place for 10 years, 31 December 2007. However, it was abolished before by Royal Decree 7/2006.

20 *PCA's Recommendation to the Government on stranded costs in the electricity sector*, of 25th November 2013, paras. 1 to 3, Portuguese version available at: http://

Under Article 65 of the Portuguese Competition Act[21] an "[a]id for undertakings granted by the State or any other public body should not restrict, distort or affect competition in the domestic market, as a whole or in a substantial part of it, and to a significant extent." Under the same provision the Portuguese Competition Authority can analyse any aid or projected aid and formulate to the Government or any other public body a recommendation for eliminating any negative impact on competition resulting from the aid, and the recommendations must be made public at the PCA website.[22]

In November 2013, the PCA enacted a recommendation to the Government advising on the modification of the CMEC revision mechanism in a way that ex-post profits should be calculated optimizing both production and balancing services limiting, therefore, the negative impact on competition.[23] The recommendation followed an investigation by the PCA to the provision of electricity balancing services which concluded that the provision of electricity balancing services in Portugal remains highly concentrated. The historical operator – EDP – has a clearly identifiable dominant position.[24] CMEC power plant participation in secondary reserves auctions was much lower when compared to the market based plants. Lower CMEC power plant revenues from secondary reserves services led to increasing CMEC compensations born by consumers.

PCA investigation also concluded that entry barriers remained high and that the fall in demand originated by the economic crisis has made new entries unlikely in the medium term. Demand for balancing services is highly inelastic, as they play a crucial role of balancing in security of supply. The PCA investigation concluded that unilateral conduct combined with the incentives provided by stranded costs compensations has led to important competition distortions in secondary reserves power

www.concorrencia.pt/vPT/Estudos_e_Publicacoes/Recomendacoes_e_Pareceres/Documents/Recomendacao_2013_01.pdf.

21 Law 19/2012, of 8 May 2012.

22 The new Competition Act, Law 19/2012, of 8 May, reinforced the powers to the PCA in State aid matters allowing for ex officio action by the PCA (Article 65 (2)). Under the 2003 competition act, Law 18/2003, of 11 June, the PCA could only analyse a State aid and made recommendations only if it had been requested to analyse a measure by any interested party (Article 13 (2)).

23 *PCA's Recommendation to the Government on stranded costs in the electricity sector*, cit., para. 41.

24 *Portuguese experience in the creation of an Iberian electricity wholesale market: lessons learned from the regional integration of a small country on a wider market*, cit., para. 32.

provision. The CPA then recommended to the Government modifying the CMEC revision mechanism so as to prevent such type of behaviour.

Following the PCA recommendation, by April 2014 the Government published a set of corrective measures[25] in order to address the PCA's recommendation and the concerns presented by ERSE related with price increases since 2012 in secondary reserves provision, which include new CMEC adjustment calculations criteria for secondary reserves, a price cap on secondary reserves provision, and an independent audit on the risk of overcompensation and the amount of past overcompensations.

4. State aid evaluation and limitation to the negative impact in competition – a field for complementarity action by the national competition authorities and the European Commission

Evaluation contributes to better informed decision-making, is a beneficial learning process for all parties involved, facilitates transparency and accountability, and helps allocate scarce resources more efficiently.[26] In this context, National Competition Authorities may be particularly well placed to monitor the evolution of State aids in national territory and their impact in competition and contribute to limit the impact in competition of a State aid.

The 2014's PCA recommendation to the Government on stranded costs in the electricity sector is a good example of this. This case is particularly interesting as the Commission had been called to re-analyse the compatibility of CMEC compensation scheme and decided not to take action. On 18 September 2012, a group of private citizens filed a complaint to the Commission against alleged illegal State aid granted by Portugal to EDP among which the CMEC compensation scheme on which the Commission raised no objection in its decision of 22 September 2004. Grounded on a short sentence,[27] the Commission concluded that "the information available as to implementation of the mechanism does not allow concluding at this stage that the aid has been misused or otherwise become no longer compatible with the internal market."[28] Nevertheless,

---

25 Order No. 4694/2014, of 1st April, *Official Journal of the Portuguese Republic*, 2nd Series, No. 64 of 1st April 2014.

26 Occasional discussion papers by the Competition Directorate-General of the European Commission – Competition policy brief, Issue 7, *cit.*

27 State Aid SA.35429 (2013/C) (ex 2012/Cp), cit.

28 In contrast, the European Commission, as part of the Memorandum of understanding on specific economic policy conditionality concerning Portugal – Memorandum of understanding on specific economic policy conditionality signed between the Portuguese

the PCA, on the grounds of its power to formulate to the Government recommendation for eliminating any negative impact on competition resulting from the aid,[29] formulated recommendations, that were implemented by the Government, to reduce the impact of CMEC State aid scheme in competition.

The conclusion of the Commission that it has no information allowing it to consider that the CMEC compensation scheme had been misused or otherwise become no longer compatible with the internal market contrasts with measures regarding the energy sector that had been established in the Memorandum of Understanding on specific economic and competition policy conditionality for granting financial assistance to Portugal, to which the Commission was a signing party, that stressed the need to reduce the amount of compensation paid under the CMEC compensation scheme in order to foster competition in the national energy sector.

In May 2011 the Portuguese Government reached an agreement with the European Commission, the European Central Bank and the International Monetary Fund regarding a Memorandum of Understanding on specific economic policy conditionality for granting financial assistance to Portugal (MoU).[30] The MoU laid down quite an extensive programme of economic and fiscal commitments to be implemented by Portugal, specifying detailed criteria.[31] Within the topic on framework

Government, the European Commission, the European Central Bank and the International Monetary Fund, 17 May 2011 – considered necessary for the Portuguese Government to "[t]ake measures in order to limit the additional cost associated with the production of electricity under the ordinary regime, in particular through renegotiation or downward revision of the guaranteed compensation mechanism (CMEC) paid to producers under the ordinary regime and the remaining long-term power-purchase agreements (PPAs)" (point 5.6). Such measures were included on the part of the MoU referring to the energy market that established the following objectives for the measures established: "to complete the liberalisation of the electricity and gas markets; ensure that the reduction of the energy dependence and the promotion of renewable energies is made in a way that limits the additional costs associated with the production of electricity under the ordinary and special (co-generation and renewables) regimes; ensure consistency of the overall energy policy, reviewing existing instruments. Continue promoting competition in energy markets and to further integrate the Iberian market for electricity and gas (MIBEL and MIBGAS)".

29 Article 65 Law 19/20012.

30 Memorandum of Understanding between Portugal and the EC, the ECB and the IMF on specific economic policy conditionality for granting financial assistance to Portugal, 17 May 2011.

31 These fiscal and economic commitments covered several topics: fiscal policy; financial sector regulation and supervision; fiscal-structural measures; labour market and education; goods and services markets; housing market; and framework conditions.

conditions, the MoU devoted an entire section to competition, public procurement and the business environment in Portugal, with the aim of: (i) ensuring a level playing field and minimising rent-seeking behaviour by strengthening competition and sector regulators; (ii) eliminating special rights of the State in private companies (golden shares); (iii) reducing administrative burdens on companies; (iv) ensuring fair public procurement processes; and (v) improving effectiveness of existing instruments dealing with export promotion and access to finance and supporting the reallocation of resources towards the tradable sector. The MoU put forth several measures, some structural in nature, with the aim of increasing the level of competition in many different industries. Many of those measures follow previous recommendations issued by the PCA, as is the case with the energy sector, telecoms, postal services and regulated professions, among other sectors of economic activity.[32]

In what concerns the energy market, the MoU included several measures aiming at: (i) completing the liberalisation of the electricity and gas markets; (ii) ensuring that the reduction of the energy dependence and the promotion of renewable energies is made in a way that limits the additional costs associated with the production of electricity under the ordinary and special (co-generation and renewables) regimes; (iii) ensuring consistency of the overall energy policy and reviewing existing instruments. Moreover, the government ought to continue promoting competition in energy markets and to further integrate the Iberian market for electricity and gas (MIBEL and MIBGAS).

The MoU also contemplated measures regarding the CMEC compensation scheme in order to limit the additional cost associated with the production of electricity under the ordinary regime, in particular through renegotiation or downward revision of the guaranteed compensation mechanism.

The measures regarding the reduction of the CMEC compensation scheme established by the MoU raises some questions to the Commission's analysis of the CMEC under State aid framework. The CMEC State aid scheme had been authorised by the Commission on the grounds of Article 107 (3) (c) (then Article 87 (3) (c) TEC) as allowing the development of an economic activity. Under this provision the Commission may authorise "aid to facilitate the development of certain economic activities or of certain economic areas, where such aid does not adversely affect trading conditions to an extent contrary to the common interest." The

[32] For more details on the MoU see Tavares, M.; Gata, J. E., "The Memorandum of Understanding on specific economic and competition policy conditionality for granting financial assistance: Portuguese point of view", *e-Competitions* 37518.

Commission has a wide discretion on whether or not to allow aid under article 107 (3) TFEU,[33] on the ground of examination and appraisal of economic facts and circumstances that are often complex and liable to change rapidly.[34] Article 107 (3) (c) enables de Commission to authorize a much wider range of aids than under either Article 107 (3) (a) or (b) and it is the most frequently used discretionary exception. In order for the aid to be accepted it is necessary that it has the effect of facilitating the development rather than merely intending to do so.[35] To fall within Article 107 (3) (c) TFEU an aid "must not affect trading conditions to an extent contrary to the common interest". The beneficial effects of the aid and the development of certain economic activities and regions must be balanced against its adverse effects on trading conditions and the maintenance of undistorted competition.[36] This balance requires that the Commission takes into account all those factors which characterize the measure in question including intensity, nearness to market activity and the method of financing the aid.[37] Also information regarding the situation on the markets in question, in particular the positions of the beneficiary aid and of competing undertakings, must be taken into consideration.

Following a costs analysis, the Commission concluded, in its decision of 2004, that the CMEC compensation scheme would not exceed what is necessary to repay a shortfall in investment cost repaying over the asset's lifetime.[38] In 2013 when called to reanalyse to compatibility of the CMEC compensation scheme with the Treaty the Commission concluded that it had no information allowing it to consider that the CMEC compensation

33 Case 730/79, *Philip Morris v Commission* [1980] ECR 2671, para. 17; cases 62&72/87, *Exécutif Régional Wallon v Commission* [1988] ECR 1573, para. 21; case T-55/99, *CTM v Commission* [2000] ECR II-3207, para. 109; case T-151/99, *Hijos de Andrés Molina SA v Commission* [2002] ECR II-nyr, para. 48.

34 Case C-301/87 *France v Commission* [1990] ECR I-307, para. 15; case C-39/94, *SFEI* [1996] ECR-3547, para. 36; case C-169/95, *Spain v Commission* [1997] ECR I-135, para. 18; case T-67/94, *Ladbroke Racing* [1998] ECR II-1, para. 147.

35 *Vide* AG Slym in *Germany v Commission* [1984] ECR 1501-1502, 169-170.

36 *Vide XIVth Report on Competition Policy* (1984), point 202, expressly endorsed by the Court of First Instance (now General Court) in *British Airways* [1998] ECR II-2405 para. 283. Case 47/69 *France v Commission* [1970] ECR 487, para. 7.

37 E.g. Case 47/69 *France v Commission* [1970] ECR 487, paras. 17-97. In this case the aid to the promotion of research in the textile sector itself was considered by the Commission as being compatible with Article 87 (3) (c) (now Article 107 (3) (c) TFEU) but its method of financing, including a levy on the sale of both domestic and imported textile products, was contrary to the common interest since its importers contributed to the levy without receiving any benefit in return.

38 Commission decision State aid No. 161/2004, cit.

scheme had misused or otherwise become no longer compatible with the internal market.[39]

There seems to be a lack of coherence between the analysis of the Commission under State aid framework, namely its decision of 2013 of not to take action regarding the CMEC compensation scheme for lack of information that the aid had been misused,[40] and the Commission economic policy analysis in the context of the MoU for granting financial aid to Portugal. In the 2004 decision declaring the CMEC compensation scheme compatible with the internal market under Article 107 (1) (c) TFEU, the Commission considered that the State aid was necessary to repay a shortfall in investment costs repayment over the assets lifetime and that in the absence of any type of compensation, the losses would jeopardise the viability of the undertaking concerned. On the other hand, in the MoU the reduction of the amount of compensation paid was considered necessary to foster competition in the electricity sector. Both conclusions seem to be incompatible.

The PCA intervention, in the form of a recommendation to the Government that has been implemented by the latter, showed to be an important mechanism to reduce, if not eliminate, the impact of the negative effects of the CMEC compensation mechanism in competition.

Another example of complementary intervention of a national competition authority is the case of the Spanish Competition Authority (SCA) – Informe INP 103/13 – regarding the draft law on the national electric sector, which included a State aid that had been deemed compatible with the internal market by the Commission,[41] whereby it recommended to the government not to implement an aid due to its impact on competition.

On 12 May 2010, Spain notified to the Commission an aid to public service competition linked to a preferential dispatch mechanism for indigenous coal power plants. Such aid is based on Article 25 of Law 54/1997 of 27 November 1997 on the electricity sector,[42] which stipulates that the Government may establish procedures, compatible with the free market in electricity production, in order to ensure the continued operation of generation units using indigenous sources of primary energy, up to a limit

39 *Vide* above text accompanying notes 557 and 558.

40 *Idem.*

41 *Informe INP 103/13*, available at: http://www.cncompetencia.es/Inicio/GestionDocumental/tabid/76/Default.aspx?EntryId=198973&Command=Core_Download&Method=attachment.

42 *Ley 54/1997, de 27 de noviembre, del Sector Eléctrico.*

of 15% of the total primary energy required to generate sufficient electricity to meet demand on the national market, calculated on an annual basis.[43]

The Commission considered the State aid as compatible with the internal market under Article 106 (2) TFEU. The Commission considered the conditions set forth by the Community Framework for State aid in the form of public service compensation[44] under which public service compensations qualifying as State aid in the meaning of Article 107 TFEU may be declared compatible with the internal market under Article 106 (2) TFEU to be fulfilled. The Commission also mentioned that similar public service compensation schemes, involving coal or other domestic fuels such as brown lignite or peat, have been approved in the past in Austria, Ireland, Slovenia and also Spain.[45]

The Commission considered that "the directive that governs the functioning of the EU electricity market allows Member States to put in place such public service obligations, motivated by reasons of security of energy supply, within a limit of 15% of national electricity consumption. The State support is in line with EU State aid rules on public service compensations because it will not result in over-compensating electricity generators for fulfilling the obligations imposed on them".[46]

The Spanish Competition Authority however, when called to advise[47] on the drafted laws implementing the State aid to indigenous coal power plants, expressed negative opinion and considered that the State aid mechanism has a negative impact on competition and does not have sufficient objective justification for such restriction.

In its report, the SCA, referring to previous opinions expressed on the same matter,[48] expressed its disagreement with the proposed measure considering that it resulted in a strong competitive distortion in the power generation market without sufficient justification of its need to ensure the supply of electricity.[49] Moreover, the SCA also mentioned that regardless

43 State aid No. N178/2010, European Commission decision of 29.09.2010, C(2010)4499, paras. 1 and 8.

44 OJ C 297 of 29.11.2005, p. 4.

45 See decisions N 49/1999, N 34/1999, N 6A/2001 and C 7/2005.

46 Commission Press Release, IP/10/1198, 29 September 2010.

47 The Spanish Competition Authority was consulted pursuing Article 25 (a) of the Law 15/2007, 3 June 2007 (competition act). Its opinion is not binding.

48 The same opinion had been expressed regarding previous drafted laws. See *IPN 33/09 Real Decreto de procedimiento de resolución de restricciones de restricciones por garantía de suministro* and *IPN 44/10 Procedimiento de resolución de restricciones por garantía de suministro 2.*

49 *Informe INP 103/13*, cit., p. 18.

of the compatibility of the measure with the TFEU, some of the negative effects identified in its previous reports have been materialized with the implementation of equivalent measures. In particular, the measure has a negative impact on competition and efficiency in the generation market, with impact on the formation of energy prices on the daily and intraday market.[50]

5. Conclusion

Article 107 (1) TFEU prohibits any aid granted by a Member State or through State resources in any form whatsoever which distorts or threatens to distort competition by favouring certain undertakings or the production of certain goods, in so far as it affects trade between Member States. It establishes the general principle that State aids are incompatible with the internal market. The Treaty also identifies some exception of State aids that are compatible with the internal market[51] and others[52] that, though in principle would be incompatible with the internal market, may be deemed compatible if they promote the common interest.

The Treaty gave the Commission, in cooperation with the Member States, the responsibility to monitor the State aids, and to keep under constant review all systems of aid existing in the Member States.[53] National Competition Authorities may be particularly well placed to monitor the evolution of State aids. National competition authorities do not have the power to declare an aid compatible or incompatible with the internal market, but some may, under their national laws, analyse the impact of an aid in competition and use mechanisms of soft power to limit a negative impact that can prove effective.

The PCA's recommendation on stranded costs in the electricity sector, which was implemented by the Government, serves as a good example of a soft power initiative of a national competition authority that complements the action of the European Commission in limiting the negative impact in competition of a State aid that had been deemed compatible with the internal market by the European Commission.

Even in the absence of binding powers in matter of State aid, the intervention of national competition authorities in the evaluation of the impact in competition of a State aid approved by the Commission has a positive effect as it brings to the market and to national and European authorities

[50] *Idem.*

[51] Article 107 (2) TFEU.

[52] Article 107 (3) TFEU.

[53] Article 108 (1) TFEU.

more information on the effects of the aid in competition increasing, helping the responsibly authorities to limit, if not neutralize, the negative impact in competition of a State aid.

Bibliography

Portuguese experience in the creation of an Iberian electricity wholesale market: lessons learned from the regional integration of a small country on a wider market, Contribution from Portugal to the Session II. Electricity Market in Latin America: Regional integration and competition issues, of the OECD Latin American Competition Forum, Montevideo 16–17 September 2014.

Tavares, M.; Gata, J. E., "The Memorandum of Understanding on specific economic and competition policy conditionality for granting financial assistance: Portuguese point of view", *e-Competitions* 37518.

Competition in the aviation sector: the problem with public financing of airports and airlines

Isabel Fernández TORRES[1]

1. Deregulation of air transport and development of regional airports

It is well known that the process of opening up the aviation sector to free competition has brought with it the imposition of discipline regarding state aid. The implementation of one-time aid for restructuring, called "one time-last time,"[2] has made it possible for airlines to adjust their activity to a legal-economic framework of free competition. However, the strong competition among airlines (due in large part to the eruption of European-scale and low cost airlines on the market) has also stimulated competition among regional airports. This has led to an increase in public involvement in the sector, awarding funding to airports in an ideal position to achieve economic and social cohesion and development in the regions, but also to under-used airports. Thus, small airports may have problems reaching the level of profitability needed to survive (especially those that have fewer than 1 million passengers annually); moreover, operators are unlikely to accept the risk of opening new routes or of starting up in unknown airports that have not yet shown their potential. In these cases, low cost companies negotiate subsidies with political powers, either directly or through airport managers.

In fact, there are several decisions (in response to complaints presented mainly by traditional airlines) that have been adopted by the Commission along these lines. Of note are those concerning the establishment of

---

1 Assistant Professor, Faculty of Law, Complutense, University of Madrid.

2 Mönter, R., "The Commission's state aid policy and airline restructuring: a "one last time" opportunity or never-ending story?", *European Business Law Review*, February 1997, p. 45 ff.

Ryanair in Charleroi,[3] the Paris airports,[4] German regional airports,[5] or the Intermed case,[6] which have marked the basic guidelines developed and, in part accepted, by the Guidelines on airport financing and state start-up aid for airlines that operate in regional airports, dated 9 December 2005,[7] which today have been replaced by others.

However, the use and abuse of public financing in the aviation sector that has taken place in recent years in all EU countries (despite the fact that Member States had failed to communicate to the Commission several cases in which public entities had given subsidies) led the Commission to revise the 2005 Guidelines in 2011, which were passed after being submitted to a public consultation[8] on 20 February 2014.[9] The revised guidelines also take into account the new economic and legal situation with regard to the public financing of airports and airlines. With this reform, the Commission intends to cover deficiencies in the market, establish guidelines that are consistent with policies modernizing state aid, and also avoid wasteful spending of public funds, all of which is in line with

---

3 European Commission Decision 2004/393/EC, of 12 February 2004, concerning advantages granted by the Walloon Region and Brussels South Charleroi Airport to the airline Ryanair in connection with its establishment at Charleroi (*Official Journal of the EU* L 137 of 30.04.2004). See Kristoferitsch, H.; Signes de Mesa, J., "El futuro de las aerolíneas de bajo coste (A propósito de la decisión Charleroi y las Directrices sobre la financiación de aeropuertos y puestas en marcha de nuevas rutas)", *REDE* 20 (2006), pp. 533-554; Petit Lavall, M. V., "Las Directrices 2005 de la Comisión Europea sobre ayudas públicas al sector aéreo tras las Decisiones Ryanair e Intermed", *Derecho de los Negocios* 182 (2005), p. 9 ff.; Fernández Torres, I., "Aeropuertos regionales y libre competencia. En busca de un ansiado equilibrio mediante la aplicación de las directrices de 2005. (Análisis de las decisiones y jurisprudencia comunitarias)", *RCD* 4 (2009), pp. 260-261.

4 Also, CJEU Judgement of 24 October 2002 (*Aéroports de Paris v Commission*, matter C-82/01).

5 Ruling of 19 January 2005 (matter N 644/2002).

6 Ruling of 20 October 2004 (matter C 79/2002).

7 See the European Commission Communication on *Community Guidelines on airport financing and state start-up aid for airlines that operate in regional airports*, of 9 December 2005, 2005/C 312/01 (*Official Journal of the EU* C 312, of 9 December 2005), available at http://eur-lex.europa.eu/legal-content/EN/ALL/?uri=CELEX:52005XC1209(03); and the Opinion of the Committee of the Regions on "*The future of European airports*," of 10 October 2007 (2007/C 305/03, *Official Journal of the EU* of 15 December 2007).

8 Communication from the Draft Guidelines Committee of the EU on state aid for airports and airlines, available at: http://ec.europa.eu/competition/consultations/2013_aviation_guidelines/index_en.html.

9 Guidelines on state aid to airports and airlines of 20 February 2014 (2014/C 99/03), available at http://eur-lex.europa.eu/legal-content/EN/TXT/PDF/?uri=OJ:C:2014:099:FULL&from=EN.

the Communication on modernization of state aid.[10] That is, aid policy should be focused on making aid available to cover deficiencies in the market and to pursue objectives of European interest, as well as on avoiding wasteful spending of public resources.

2. Public financing of airports and airlines: the 2014 Guidelines

2.1 General approach

The Commission believes that airports carry out economic activities that give them the status of a company[11] for the purposes of Article 107 of the Treaty of the Functioning of the EU and, therefore, all of the regulations in this Treaty regarding state aid are applicable.

In accordance with this approach, direct aid that is aimed at covering operating losses (operating aid) is incompatible with the common market, unless these losses arose from the imposition of public service obligations, and the aid is awarded to individual consumers without discrimination due to the origin of the product; or in the case of aid (contributions of capital, loans and financial guarantees) provided to public airlines awarded under special conditions different from market conditions, aid for regional economic development, and the development of certain economic activities that are not governed by the Treaty on the Functioning of the EU (TFEU) and its guidelines, the transfer of public shares in public airlines that are undergoing a privatization process in conditions other than those set out in the Treaty, as well as ancillary and complementary activities in air transportation, which are liable to be considered state aid when their exercise constitutes an exclusive right recognized by an airline.[12] That is, aid aimed at covering the financing deficit for operating costs is prohibited. Thus, the objective of the 2014 Guidelines is to guarantee

10 Communication from the Commission to the European Parliament, Council, the European Economic and Social Committee and the Committee of the Regions on State aid modernization in the EU (SAM), COM(2012) 209 final. Finally completed with Resolution of 17 January 2013, the European Parliament adopted a Resolution on State aid Modernisation.

Available at http://www.europarl.europa.eu/sides/getDoc.do?pubRef=-//EP//TEXT+TA+P7-TA-2013-0026+0+DOC+XML+V0//EN.

11 The previously cited Decision of the Commission and Judgment of 12 December 2000 in the matter of Paris Airports (Matter T-128/98) considers that said activities "consist of allowing the use of airport facilities by airlines and different service agencies, in return for a fee freely fixed by the airport management entity and, on the other hand, they do not form part of the exercise of a task conferred by public law and can be dissociated from the related activities in the exercise of such a task."

12 Mönter, R., *The Commission's state aid policy and airline restructuring*, cit., pp. 45-48.

effective competition in the sector and streamline public financing of infrastructure.

These 2014 Guidelines have been passed in accordance with the goals of the modernization program aimed at providing Member States a regulatory package that protects competition and makes references to the recommendations already set out in the Opinion on State Aid Modernization.[13]

In the framework of the Europe 2020 Strategy,[14] the Commission insists on the importance of sustainable growth in transportation[15] and within this scheme proposes the efficient use of resources, the elimination of unjustified subsidies, and the exercise of free, undistorted competition. This development must be directed by transparency, non-discrimination, and proportionality in the public financing offered to regional airports, as well as protection of the common interest in state aid awarded to airlines.

From this perspective, the 2005 Guidelines attempted to specify the methods for financing airport construction, development and maintenance, as well as expanding channels for obtaining direct aid for aviation operation, including start-up aid for airlines operating in regional airports, without distinguishing between possible beneficiaries according to their legal status (Public Administrations or companies), or whether they belonged to the public or private sector. These criteria are largely maintained in the 2014 Guidelines which, however, do try to restrict aid to the cases explicitly defined therein and limit aid by duration and intensity. We can see the need to create a long-term development policy for regional airports given that (as the Opinion of the Committee of Regions states)[16] the 2005

---

13 On 25 November 2012, the European Economic and Social Committee adopted an opinion on State Aid Modernisation: http://www.eesc.europa.eu/?i=portal.en.int-opinions. 23584.

Likewise on 29 November 2012, the Committee of the Regions adopted an opinion on State Aid Modernisation: http://eur-lex.europa.eu/LexUriServ/LexUriServ.do?uri=OJ:C:2013:017:0025:0029:EN:PDF.

14 Commission Communication of 3 March 2010, "Europe 2020: A strategy for intelligent, sustainable and inclusive growth" COM(2010) 2020 final of 3 March 2010. Available at http://europa.eu/legislation_summaries/employment_and_social_policy/eu2020/em0028_en.htm.

15 See White paper "Roadmap to a Single European Transport Area," Roadmap to a Single European Transport Area: Towards a competitive and resource efficient transport system, COM(2011) 144. Available at http://ec.europa.eu/transport/themes/strategies/2011_white_paper_en.htm.

16 Own-initiative opinion of the Committee of the Regions on the Draft Community guidelines on financing of airports and start-up aid to airlines departing from regional airports (2006/C 31/06), Official Journal of 7/2/2006, http://eur-lex.europa.eu/LexUriServ/LexUriServ.do?uri=OJ:C:2006:031:0023:0024:ES:PDF. Opinion of the European Economic and Social Committee on the "Review of the EU guidelines

Guidelines did not lead to the establishment of national systems that precisely defined conditions for aid, which has led to a certain amount of laxity and impunity. Therefore, as a general criterion, companies must progressively increase their efficiency and decrease their need for financing.

The key criterion for determining the existence of public aid for the purposes of Article 107.1 of the TFEU is the market economy investor principle. In this regard, the Committee of the Regions in its Opinion of 28 November 2013[17] expresses its concern for the consequences that could arise from applying the private investor principle for infrastructures, a sector in which the state plays an irreplaceable role given that the cost of the large investments that need to be made is unsustainable and impossible for the private investor to assume. From this perspective, the Committee believes that it is neither reasonable nor realistic, and could even be detrimental to the general well-being, to rigorously subject the state to this principle without taking into account social, political-regional and sector considerations regarding infrastructure operations. Infrastructures certainly provide a public service.

The concept of private investor is as simple as it is important in that it determines that advantages awarded by public authorities are not subject to the state aid scheme if it can be shown that the state is acting in the same way a private investor would, under market conditions.[18] In other words, and from the perspective of the entity receiving the aid, the principle can be stated as follows: "[an entity] that benefits from an economic advantage that it would not have received under normal market conditions" (matter SFEI v La Poste, C-93/94) or, in the terms of the CJEU Judgment of 10 July 1985, *Belgium v Meura Commission and Bosch*,[19]

---

of 1994 and 2005 on aviation and airports" (additional opinion) (2012/C 299/10), Official Journal of 4 October 2012.

17 https://toad.cor.europa.eu/corwipdetail.aspx?folderpath=COTER-V/043&id=22335.

18 The Courts have also referred to the normal, rational, discerning investor (ICC Judgment of 12 December 1996, Air France/Commission T-358/94, Rec. 1996, p. II-2109, section 110), or prudent (CJEU Judgment of 16 May 2002, France/Commission, C-482/99, Rec. 1999, p. I-4397, section 30), C-305/89, Italy v Commission (Alfa Romeo I), 1991. See Fernández Torres, I., *El caso Charleroi y las Directrices de 2005 a examen tras la Sentencia del TPI de 17 de diciembre de 2008: el problema del inversor privado*, cit., pp. 388-390; Pérez Rivarés, J. A., *Régimen jurídico de las ayudas públicas al transporte aéreo en la Unión Europea*. Barcelona: Bosch, 2011, p. 218.

The Commission thoroughly analyses the principle of the market economy investor in its decisions and, as an example, here we cite a recent decision: Commission Ruling of 21 January 2010 C12/2008 (ex NN74/07), agreement between the Bratislava Airport and Ryanair; matter C38/2008 (ex NN53/2007), financing agreements related to the expansion of Terminal T2 of the Munich airport.

19 Matter 40/85.

if "under normal conditions, a private partner would have provided the capital in question, based on the foreseeable possibilities for profitability, overlooking any social, regional-political or sector considerations." In the consultation aimed at reviewing the 2005 Guidelines which ended in June 2011,[20] detailed questions were presented about what criteria should be taken into consideration to determine if the benefits awarded or the public financing of airport management did or did not constitute state aid. This was largely due to the fact that the General Court of the EU, in its Judgment of 17 December 2008, repealed the Decision of the Commission in the matter Ryanair/Charleroi due to the incorrect application of this principle.[21] The new 2014 Guidelines specify the concept of "market economy investor," stating that the conduct of "a public investor may be compared with that of a private investor guided by prospects of profitability in the longer term, over the lifetime of the investment" (Point 50 of the 2014 Guidelines), and therefore there must be a business plan that shows an analysis conducted before the granting of public financing which demonstrates that the principle is satisfied (Point 51 of the 2014 Directives). Where an airport has public resources at its disposal, aid to an airline using the airport can, in principle, be excluded where the relationship between the airport and that airline satisfies the market economy operator principle. This is usually the case if:

- the price charged for the airport services corresponds to the market price, or
- it can be demonstrated through a previous analysis that the airport/airline arrangement will lead to a positive incremental profit contribution for the airport (Point 53 of the 2014 Directives).

The European Commission deems it essential to classify airports in different categories[22] to propose an itemization of the different levels of

20 See Section C of the questionnaire in the document titled "Review of the Community Guidelines on airport financing and start-up aid to airlines departing from regional airports." http://webcache.googleusercontent.com/search?q=cache:06kR76W5Ug8J:ec.europa.eu/competition/consultations/2011_aviation_guidelines/es.rtf+&cd=1&hl=es&ct=clnk&gl=es&client=safari.

21 See Fernández Torres, I., *El caso Charleroi y las Directrices de 2005 a examen tras la Sentencia del TPI de 17 de diciembre de 2008: el problema del inversor privado*, cit.

22 The European Commission (see Committee of the Regions Report on an Opinion of 2 July 2002 on the capacity of regional airports (CdR/393/2002 fin)) distinguishes the four following categories:

– category A, for "large community airports, with more than 10 million passengers annually;

– category B, made up of "national airports", which includes those airports that have an annual passenger volume of between 5 and 10 million;

competition among airports and the correlating degree of effect on the intra-community market as a result of the awarding of state aid.[23] At the same time, it submits to review all aid from public powers, whether national, regional, or local, which benefits airports (especially regional airports), airport operators, and airlines, including any financial advantage, regardless of its form, unless, in accordance with European case law, this aid were comparable to private investments made according to economic market criteria.

"The Commission considers that arrangements concluded between airlines and an airport can be deemed to satisfy the MEO [market economy operator] test when they incrementally contribute, from an *ex ante* standpoint, to the profitability of the airport. The airport should demonstrate that, when setting up an arrangement with an airline (for example, an individual contract or an overall scheme of airport charges), it is capable of covering all costs stemming from the arrangement, over the duration of the arrangement, with a reasonable profit margin on the basis of sound medium-term prospects" (Point 63 of the 2014 Directives).

These Guidelines are what the European Commission must abide by when evaluating and, as a result, approving or denying public financing for construction, development, operation and maintenance of airport infrastructure and equipment (i.e., runways, terminal buildings, platforms, control towers or ancillary facilities – security, rescue, fire protection, etc.), the provision of airport services (ground handling, fire fighters, security, etc.), the implementation and development of commercial activities and setting up routes to regional airports, in compliance with the provisions of Articles 107 and 108 of the TFEU.[24]

– category C, made up of "large regional airports", which have an annual volume of 1 to 5 million passengers; and, lastly,

– category D, which includes "small regional airports", which have fewer than 1 million passengers a year.

23 As indicated above, a report from the Air Transport Group of the School of Engineering at Cranfield University in the UK carried out at the behest of the Directorate-General for Energy and Transport of the European Commission ("Study on competition between airports and the application of State aid rules" September 2002) reveals that in general, large international airports (hubs) compete amongst themselves in all transport markets, and this competition varies in intensity depending on factors such as congestion and the existence of alternative intermodal transport. Large regional airports generally compete with their counterparts as well as with the large European hubs, while small, isolated airports do not compete with other airports, barring some exceptions.

24 Dony, M.; Smits, C., *Aides d'État*, cit.; Estoa Pérez, A., *El control de las ayudas de Estado*. 1st ed. Madrid: Iustel, 2006; and Dony, M., *Commentaire J. Mégret: contrôle des aides d'Etat – Droit communautaire de la concurrence*. 3rd ed. Bruxelles: Eds. de l'Université de Bruxelles, 2007, Vol. 3, Book No. 2.

2.2 Prohibited aid under the 2014 Guidelines

Taking into account that up until now regional airports have benefited from generalized aid, there will be a gradual transitional period for them to adapt to the new reality (10 years), during which time, exceptionally, some categories of operational aid may be justified under certain conditions. Thus, operational aid awarded to airports shall be considered compatible with the internal market (Art. 107.3 c) TFEU for a transitional period (Point 112, 2014 Guidelines), provided that the following cumulative conditions are fulfilled (Point 79 as regards points 113 to 134 of the 2014 Guidelines):

1) Airport traffic should not exceed 3 million passengers[25] (Point 119 of the 2014 Guidelines);
2) Existence of incentive effect (Point 124 of the 2014 Guidelines);
3) Limitation of aid to minimum necessary and calculation of aid amount (aid amount established as a single quantity for the whole transitional period of up to 10 years, maximum, which is the period in which the necessary model adjustments should be made, Points 125 and following 2014 Guidelines). The amount of aid is established as a set quantity that will cover the operating deficit during the maximum period of 10 years;
4) Airport access;
5) Progressive reduction.

In order to be able to benefit from this aid, airports must work with a business plan or model that guarantees that, after this transitional period, the airport will be able to cover its own costs. That is, at the end of the transitional period, the airport should fully cover its operating costs. As

---

25 In Point 118 of the 2014 Guidelines, the Commission estimates that airport categories and their financial viability can be established as follows:

a) Airports with up to 200,000 passengers per annum may not be able to cover their operating costs to a large extent;
b) Airports with annual passenger traffic between 200,000 and 700,000 passengers may not be able to cover their operating costs to a substantial extent;
c) Airports with annual passenger traffic of 700,000 to 1 million

should in general be able to cover their operating costs to a greater extent;

d) Airports with annual passenger traffic of 1-3 million should, on average, be able to cover the majority of their operating costs;
e) Airports with annual passenger traffic above 3 million are usually profitable at operating level and should be able to cover their operating costs.

Currently, the main European hubs with at least 5 million passengers a year make up 78% of passenger traffic; airports with a passenger volume of 1 to 5 million have 18%, while airports with less than 1 million passengers are only used by 4%.

the aim of the Guidelines is to streamline public expenditure, aid to airports located in the area of influence of a pre-existing airport or an airport not operating at full capacity (or almost) will be considered incompatible.

Airport size based on average annual passenger traffic	**Maximum investment aid intensity**
> 5 million	0% (aid not authorized)
3-5 million	up to 25% (only reimbursable advance)
1-3 million	up to 50%
< 1 million	up to 75%

Airports with annual passenger traffic of up to 700,000 may face increased difficulties in achieving the full cost coverage. Therefore, the Guidelines set out a special scheme for these airports, taking into account that they would have received more aid (Point 130 of the 2014 Guidelines). At the end of the transitional period, this operating aid must cease to be awarded. However, the Committee of the Regions in their last Opinion on the Guidelines, published 15 April 2014, expresses its concern on this point, especially as regards smaller airports which may be forced to close. At the same time, it recognized the need to prevent the duplication of non-profitable airports by avoiding capacity excesses. Furthermore, it believes that the method followed by the Commission to attain its objectives is not appropriate, given that it largely ignores market dynamics and the fact that 80% of an airport's costs are fixed,[26] and therefore not dependent on passenger traffic (infrastructures and security obligations). Therefore, the cost per passenger for a small airport is much greater than a large airport, which distributes the costs among a greater number of passengers. Thus, it is more difficult for a smaller airport to obtain financial balance (with little chance of increasing its size due to the unfavourable conditions of the territory where it is located).[27]

Subsidies for the operation of airport infrastructure are classified as State aid that is incompatible with the common market, unless they are

26 See the document EU Guidelines on State aid to airports and airlines, 2014. Available at http://eur-lex.europa.eu/legal-content/ES/TXT/?uri=uriserv:OJ.C_.2014.114.01.0011.01.SPA.

27 The Committee of the Regions, in its Opinion of 28 November 2013, indicates that the volume of losses for small airports per year (€445 million annually) is not so great when we consider their contribution to GDP, which is €16.2 billion a year and that they provide 265,000 jobs. Therefore, they maintain that operating aid should not be prohibited for these small airports.

public service compensations[28] and fall under the exceptional cases set out in Articles 106.2 and 107.3.a) and c) of the Treaty (points 67–68 of the 2014 Guidelines). In principle, therefore, it is understood that companies must assume their operating costs.

As regards air transportation services, public service obligations should only be conceded according to the conditions set out in Regulation (EC) 1008/2008 of the Parliament and of the Council, of 24 September 2008, on common regulations for operation of air services in EU territory. The 2014 Guidelines state that "such obligations can only be imposed with regard to a specific route or group of routes, and not with regard to any generic route originating from a given airport, city or region. Moreover, public service obligations can only be imposed with regard to a route to fulfil transport needs which cannot be adequately met by an existing air route or by other means of transport" (see Point 70). State aid in the form of public service compensation is exempt from the notification requirement of Article 108(3) of the Treaty if the requirements set

---

28 The Commission Communication regarding the application of European Union regulations on State aid to the compensations received for the provisions of services of general economic interest (SGEI) and the Commission Regulation, of 25 April 2012, regarding the application of Articles 107 and 108 of the TFUE to *de minimis* aid awarded to companies that provide services of general economic interest offer indications of the conditions under which public financing of SGEI constitutes State aid as established in Article 107, section 1, of the TFEU.

In this regard, CJEU Judgment of 24 July 2003, *ltmark Trans and Regierungspräsidium Magdeburg*, matter C-280/00, begins by mentioning that interventions of any kind that favor (directly or indirectly) companies or economic agents, or those that provide an economic advantage that would not have been obtained under normal market conditions, must be considered aid. It rules that public service compensations do not constitute State aid as established in Article 87 of the Treaty of Rome when the following criteria are fulfilled:

i) the beneficiary company must be charged with carrying out public service obligations and the obligations must be clearly defined;
ii) the parameters for the basis of calculation must be previously established in a clear, objective manner;
iii) the compensation may not surpass the amount needed to totally or partially cover the expenses arising from carrying out the public service obligations;
iv) if the company is selected outside of the framework of a public bidding processing, the compensation must be calculated based on a cost analysis that could have been borne by an average transportation company.

In this regard, see Merola, M.; Medina, C., "De l'arrêt Ferring à l'arrêt Altmark: continuité ou revirement dans l'approche du financement des services publics", *Cahiers de Droit Européen* 34 (2003), p. 3-4, and in relation to compensations for public service obligations and the decision in the *Altmarkt* case, Dony, M.; Smits, C., "Les compensations d'obligations de service public", in *Aides d'Etat*. Bruxelles: Institut d'Études Europeénnes, 2005, pp. 109-152.

out in Decision 2012/21/EU are met: i) airports in which average traffic does not surpass 200,000 passengers during the lifetime of the service provision agreement; ii) the companies (regarding connecting flights to the islands) in which annual average traffic does not surpass 300,000 passengers (Point 75 of the 2014 Guidelines).

Regarding public financing of airport infrastructure, State aid is considered to be both financing from any public power not acting as a private investor or not receiving adequate economic compensation, and the awarding of subsidies aimed at financing said infrastructure. The evaluation of its compatibility with the common market (Articles 106 and 107 of the TFEU) requires the European Commission to take into account whether it contributes to the achievement of a clearly-defined objective of common interest, such as regional development or accessibility[29] (Point 84 of the 2014 Guidelines), its need and proportionality to the set objective, its prospects for use in the middle term, its accessibility under equal conditions and non-discrimination, and its negative effect on trade (Point 79 of the 2014 Guidelines). The 2005 Guidelines distinguished between small and large airports, believing that aid to airports with less than one million passengers could barely alter competition, but this approach has been qualified as artificial. Therefore, the 2014 Guidelines (Point 79), following this trend of making a distinction based on the size of the airport, define the maximum intensity of aid allowed based on the size of the airport and establish that to consider the aid to be compatible with the inner market, the following cumulative criteria must be fulfilled:

1) Contribution to a well-defined objective of common interest that the market cannot achieve;[30]

---

29 The 2014 Guidelines indicate that investment aid awarded to airports will be considered to contribute to the achievement of an objective of common interest if it:

1) increases the mobility of Union citizens and the connectivity of the regions by establishing access points for intra-Union flights; or
2) combats air traffic congestion at major Union hub airports; or
3) facilitates regional development.

30 The following airport categories and their financial viability (Point 89 of the 2014 Guidelines):

1) airports with up to 200,000 passengers per annum may not be able to cover their capital and operating costs to a large extent;
2) airports with annual passenger traffic of between 200,000 and 1 million are usually not able to cover their capital costs to a large extent, but generally are able to partially cover their operating costs;
3) airports with annual passenger traffic of 1-3 million should, on average, be able to cover the majority of their operating costs and their capital costs to a greater extent;

2) Suitability of state aid as a policy instrument (that is, that there is no other better instrument) (Point 87 of the 2014 Guidelines);
3) Existence of incentive effect (Points 93 and following 2014 Guidelines);
4) Eligible costs or maximum aid intensity. Initial investments in infrastructure (Points 97 and following 2014 Guidelines);
5) Proportionality: aid limited to the minimum necessary and maximum eligible aid intensity;
6) Negative effects (Points 106 and following 2014 Guidelines);
7) Airport access;
8) Notification requirements of the aid schemes and individual aid measures.

The 2014 Guidelines attempt to ensure that there is an adequate correlation between public and private investment.

Finally, the 2005 Guidelines (Points 71 to 81)[31] and the 2014 Guidelines (Points 138 and following) pay special attention to start-up aid being justified, due to the numerous claims filed on this specific aspect in recent years. From this perspective, start-up aid for new routes is possible, but limited in time, and only available when the cumulative conditions set out in Point 79 are fulfilled. The compatibility of aid has been configured keeping in mind the most recent Commission decisions. Specifically, it states that:

1) Start-up aid to airlines will be considered to be compatible with the common market if it contributes to the achievement of an objective of common interest, which will not be the case if there is a comparative, alternative form of transport[32] in the same catchment

---

4) airports with annual passenger traffic of above 3 and up to 5 million should, in principle, be able to cover, to a large extent, all their costs (including operating costs and capital costs) but, under certain case-specific circumstances, public support might be necessary to finance some of their capital costs;
5) airports with annual passenger traffic above 5 million are usually profitable and are able to cover all of their costs.

31 The Guidelines incorporate the criteria set in the Decisions adopted in the Ryanair and Intermed cases as well as the principles set out by the Committee of the Regions in the Opinion of 22 December 2004 (Opinion of the Committee of the Regions, *Low cost airlines and territorial development* (2004/C318/02, DO No. 318, of 22 December 2004, p. 7) regarding the Guidelines' requirements on state aid (observations 20 and following).

32 Meaning a high-speed rail service or another airport in the same catchment area, Point 151 of the 2014 Guidelines.

B. Sánchez Pavón believes that the search for maximum complementarity between rail and air transportation through the prohibition of awarding public start-up aid for new

area. However, this will be the case if it increases the mobility of Union citizens and the connectivity of the regions by opening new routes, or if it facilitates the regional development of remote regions (Points 139 and 140 of the 2014 Guidelines);

2) The confirmation that companies require incentives to assume the risk of operating from unknown airports or of opening new routes led the 2005 Guidelines to state that this risk can be compensated by the temporary granting of aid (for a maximum period of 3 or 5 years) under certain conditions, with the aim of providing an incentive to open new routes or frequencies solely at regional airports (basically those in category C or D; exceptionally, at national airports in category B) which would allow them to reach the "profitability threshold" in a limited time frame, ensuring their "future viability" and their "decreasing nature".[33] The 2014 Guidelines (Point 142) establish, conversely, that aid will only be provided for routes that connect an airport with fewer than 3 million annual passengers (except for those located in the outermost regions), provided that there is no other connection with the same conditions. On routes with annual passenger traffic of between 3 and 5 million which are not located in remote regions, aid will only be compatible in exceptional circumstances. When traffic exceeds 5 million passengers, no aid will be allowed under any circumstances;

3) The revised Guidelines require an *ex ante* business plan that demonstrates the long-term viability for the route receiving aid, showing that it will become profitable for the airline without public financing after 3 years (Point 147 of the 2014 Guidelines);

air routes implies the recognition of the fact that, "except for very specific cases, (large hubs that require intermodal connections to guarantee their area of influence) high-speed trains compete for demand with air transport and, if we are trying to guarantee just one efficient access to a territory, both means of transport are, more than complementary, alternatives." This, in his opinion, contradicts the principle of intermodality which, in accordance with the Guidelines, yields to the principle of optimizing the use of infrastructures (see Sánchez Pavón, B., "Public aid and its effect on competition between European airports. Analysis based on Community regulations and case law", *European Union Journal*, 12 (2007), cit., pp. 15-16).

33 There is no objective figure that determines the profitability threshold. The Committee of the Regions in its Opinion of 2 July 2003 (on the "*Capacities of regional airports*") indicates that according to the calculations made with the *Airport Business Model* (RAND Europe, 2003), an airport needs approximately 1.5 million passengers a year to be profitable. The previously cited study done at the University of Cranfield states that the figure can vary among countries and depending on how the airports are organized (5.33 and 6.11), and therefore sometimes a figure of 500,000 passengers a year is enough, while other times that figure must reach 1 million.

4) The aid may cover 50% of the start-up costs for a new route or a new schedule with more frequent service for a maximum period of 3 years (Point 150 of the 2014 Guidelines). If there were no business plan for that route, the airline must commit to operating the route for a period equivalent to at least the period during which it received aid;
5) The awarding of aid should not be discriminatory; therefore, the project must be made public in good time and with adequate publicity (Points 37, 148-149 and 152 of the 2014 Guidelines);
6) Start-up aid may not be combined with other types of aid provided for the operating of a route (Points 158-159 2014 Guidelines) and may cover up to 50% of airport fees applicable to a route during a maximum period of 3 years.

With these conditions, the European Commission intends to reconcile the development of regional airports with the principle of free competition, prohibiting those public interventions in airport and airline financing that give rise to a distortion in competition.

It will have to be seen whether these Guidelines fulfil the objectives set. For now, the recent Report published by the European Court of Auditors (Report of 16 December 2014) is especially revealing.[34] It shows, after the financing of 20 airports located in 5 Member States was completed (Spain, Estonia, Greece, Italy, and Poland), that the investments financed by the EU in airports between 2000 and 2013 (a total of €666 million) did not produce the expected results and were hardly profitable. In fact, a real need for the investments made by the European Union can only be shown for half of the airports; in the others, on the contrary, the infrastructures are under-utilized and in some, they are not used at all. Only in half of these airports reviewed by the European auditors was there a real increase in air traffic; in general, the increase in traffic predicted was over-estimated. These were not the only problems detected by the European auditors. On the contrary, they found delays in the construction and finalization of infrastructures, cost overruns in nearly half of the airports, an absence of strategic airport development plans for the long term, and a lack of coordination in planning investments on the national level. More specifically, of the 20 airports studied, 7 were unsustainable financially speaking (and therefore would either close or require constant aid). This problem is a constant in those airports with fewer than 100,000 passengers per year. Added to this is the problem of excessive proximity between some of the airports that have received public financing, and over-sized infrastructures.

---

[34] http://www.eca.europa.eu/fr/Pages/ecadefault.aspx.

It can be seen that European financing is not adequately coordinated by the Member States. Additionally, in order to correct the situation and prevent the use and abuse of public financing, improvements should be introduced in the Commission's supervision scheme, as it generally is unaware of which airports receive financing and how much they receive. In short, the Commission lacks a complete vision of all of the investments made, which limits its ability to improve the correct application of aid and prevents it from applying an appropriate infrastructure financing policy. Therefore, the Court of Auditors recommends, firstly, that in the period 2014-2020 Member States only grant aid to financially viable airports and for investments whose need has been proven, meaning that they must be studied and confirmed by the European Commission. Secondly, the Court of Auditors recommends that Member States prepare consistent airport development plans in order to prevent over-sizing, duplications, and uncoordinated investments in airport infrastructures.

3. A note on new commercial techniques for financing

Currently, we have seen the instalment of a wide range of commercial practices implemented among airports and airlines that falsifies air transport markets (advertising contracts, payments by airports or by authorities of incentives, aid for the commercialization of companies, etc.). Those practices are often seen with suspicion by European Union Institutions, as they believe that it breaks the rules on competition.

Indeed, in recent years there has been a proliferation of public intervention instruments aimed at increasing the amount of travellers to certain airport destinations which are being combined with traditional aid schemes.[35] These are mechanisms of a cooperative nature aimed at increasing passenger traffic to a certain area as well as mechanisms of a commercial nature that link the provision of advertising services by the airline to its permanence in a certain airport or to the opening of new routes.[36] Thus,

[35] From this perspective we cannot forget the paradigm shift that the sector has undergone in recent years. Before, it was understood that airports were managed to guarantee accessibility and territorial cohesion. However, in recent years, an increasing number of airports also have commercial objectives and they compete amongst one another to attract traffic. Therefore, the evolution of the market has led to a large variety of commercial practices being developed by airport managers with the aim of attracting more people to use their infrastructure, as the 2014 Guidelines (Point 7) themselves show.

[36] Commission Decision of 23 July 2008 regarding measures granted by Germany to DHL and the Leipzig/Halle airport. C 48/06 (ex N 227/06), points 168 to 172 indicate that "until recently, airport development followed a purely territorial logic or, in some cases, responded to military needs. Their operation was organized as part of the public administration and not as a business incentive. Also, competition between airports and operators was scarce. Under these circumstances, it was believed that the financing of

the airline grants the airport management company the rights to advertise in the spaces it has available (in-flight magazine, promotional material, website, promotional tickets for tourism purposes, etc.) and the public entity pays for the services provided.[37] Whatever the instruments used, the airline commits to maintaining its presence in an airport or to opening routes. These cooperation mechanisms worry National Competition Authorities given that they cause distortions in the efficient operation of airport management and, therefore, in the market. To date, Spain has not notified the Commission about any of these instruments in compliance with the provisions of Articles 107 and 108 of the TFEU and with the 2014 Guidelines. On the contrary, there are many analogies between these instruments and traditional public support measures[38] that justify the concern of National Authorities. On the European level, several formal

---

airports and airport infrastructures was the responsibility of the public authorities and, therefore, in principle, there were no issues regarding state aid. However, the situation has changed in recent years. While certain aspects of territorial management and administrative structures are still important, it is also true that in many cases the State has transferred control of airport management to the regions and their operation has been entrusted in part to public companies or even to the private sector. In general, the transfer process to the private sector has taken the shape of privatization or of a progressive opening of capital. In recent years, private equity firms and investment and pension funds have expressed great interest in acquiring airports. As a result, the European airport sector has undergone fundamental organizational changes, which demonstrate not only the lively interest of private investors in this sector, but also the change in attitudes of public authorities regarding private participation in airport development. This evolution has led to greater diversification and complexity of the functions that airports serve. The recent changes have also led to an evolution in commercial relationships among airports."

37 Collaboration can be carried out either through a "collaboration agreement" (cooperation for a common goal) or through a contract (with reciprocity of benefits). For a contract, the price of benefits is determined by the budget set when awarding the contract – similar to the tender budget – and is also subject to the principles of disclosure and competition. On the other hand, agreements are not subject to said principles. The price is set based on the agreement, with fees and average costs established by airlines for this type of advertising by unit, plane, and time.

38 The Court of Justice has always adopted a flexible interpretation of the term company given the differences regarding said concept in the different European legal systems. Thus, the CJEU Judgment of 23 April 1991, in the matter *Höfner v Macrotron GmbH*, point 21, establishes that "[...] in the context of competition law [...], the notion of company comprises all entities that exercise an economic activity, regardless of the legal status of said entity and its method of financing."

According to consolidated European case law, the management and operating activities of airports constitute economic activities subject to the regulations on state aid, Court of First Instance Judgment of 12 December 2000, matter T-128/98 *Aéroports de Paris v the European Commission.*

investigation proceedings have been opened regarding certain aid to the sector through advertising agreements.[39]

The importance of those instruments should not be dismissed, especially if we look at the data provided by the Spanish National Authority (National Commission for Markets and Competition, CNMC).[40] Indeed, their data show approximately 124 advertising agreements between regional public entities and airlines in the 2007-2011 period (April), which translate into €250 million of public funds invested by regional public entities. However, their data also show that:

- There is not a positive correlation between funds invested and air traffic;
- The advertising contracts seem to have the objective that the airline operate with origin and destination in certain airports in the sphere of influence of the corresponding public entity, which means that they do not really have a promotional purpose;
- The advertising agreements constitute a type of public intervention through which routes or airports that do not serve a real present or future demand are maintained through hidden subsidies. It is logical to believe, therefore, that the effect of these funds is not the creation of a market, but rather the diversion or substitution of air traffic towards low cost airlines. This leads to an inefficient allocation of resources that, without a doubt, affects the development of effective competition between airports, leading to a type of race for subsidies;
- Additionally, the funds awarded through the aforementioned instruments have prolonged the life of some airlines that in spite of everything have resulted unfeasible;
- Indeed, these tourism advertising agreements may have an effect on the degree of efficiency of airport infrastructures and the transport market and on the development of effective competition

[39] Marseilles (France) airport dated 13.07.2011, the Commission ruled that the Agreement between the Chamber of Commerce (operator) and Airport Marketing Services (a Ryanair subsidiary) on compensations for advertising agreements constituted illegal aid. Timisoara (Romania) airport, commercial agreement signed in 2008 between the airport and the Hungarian company Wizz Air (22.07.2011). They are not the only ones; in Germany the agreements between Frankfurt-Hans and Ryanair have been investigated (opening of formal proceedings on 13.07.2011, on the awarding of guarantees and soft loans to the company), as has the Leipzig Halle airport (formal investigation proceedings opened 15.06.2011, on injection of public capital to compensate infrastructure costs).

[40] 3rd Report on public aid in 2010, available at:
http://www.cncompetencia.es/Inicio/AyudasPublicas/Informes/tabid/218/Default.aspx (See especially p. 51).

Bibliography

Dony, M., *Commentaire J. Mégret: contrôle des aides d'Etat – Droit communautaire de la concurrence.* 3rd ed. Bruxelles: Eds. de l'Université de Bruxelles, 2007, Vol. 3, Book No. 2.

Dony, M.; Smits, C., "Les compensations d'obligations de service public", in *Aides d'état*. Bruxelles: Institut d'Etudes Europeénnes, 2005.

Estoa Pérez, A., *El control de las ayudas de Estado.* 1st ed. Madrid: Iustel, 2006.

Fernández Torres, I., "Aeropuertos regionales y libre competencia. En busca de un ansiado equilibrio mediante la aplicación de las directrices de 2005. (Análisis de las decisiones y jurisprudencia comunitarias)", *RCD* 4 (2009).

Kristoferitsch, H.; Signes de Mesa, J., "El futuro de las aerolíneas de bajo coste (A propósito de la decisión Charleroi y las Directrices sobre la financiación de aeropuertos y puestas en marcha de nuevas rutas"), *REDE* 20 (2006).

Merola, M.; Medina, C., "De l'arrêt Ferring à l'arrêt Altmark: continuité ou revirement dans l'approche du financement des services publics", *Cahiers de Droit Européen* 34 (2003).

Mönter, R., "The Commission's state aid policy and airline restructuring: a "one last time" opportunity or never-ending story?", *European Business Law Review*, February 1997.

Pérez Rivarés, J. A., *Régimen jurídico de las ayudas públicas al transporte aéreo en la Unión Europea.* Barcelona: Bosch, 2011.

Petit Lavall, M. V., "Las Directrices 2005 de la Comisión Europea sobre ayudas públicas al sector aéreo tras las Decisiones Ryanair e Intermed", *Derecho de los Negocios* 182 (2005).

The Portuguese Development Financial Institution and State aids

The postponement of the development bank

Nuno Castro MARQUES[1]

Introduction

The creation of a development bank was first publicly discussed when the Portuguese Government announced its intention to review the strategy of the public bank Caixa Geral de Depósitos (CGD).[2] The Portuguese Government's intention was to significantly shift CGD's traditional credit operations structure into tradable goods and services and into supporting exports and the internationalization of Portuguese companies.[3] This intent walked side-by-side with the reorientation of the strategy for future use of EU structural and cohesion funds, as reached by agreement between the European Commission (EC) and the Portuguese Government. The newly agreed strategy has defined new investment priorities which intend to contribute to: the development of Portugal's new economic policy; the use of structural and cohesion funds to improve the process of resource reallocation in the economy, with the involvement of credit institutions; the establishment of new mechanisms for venture capital co-investment; and to engage CGD's in the development of solutions aiming a timely absorption of structural funds and a better use of public resources.[4]

After a period of public discussion, the focus shifted to whether the above mentioned types of economic development functions should instead be assigned to a specific to-be created institution. Also in the context

1 Assistant Director, Portuguese Health Regulation Authority; Invited Professor at the Faculty of Economics, University of Porto.

2 CGD is Portugal's largest national commercial bank.

3 This purpose was formally assumed in the Government Programme submitted and approved by the Parliament – see Portugal, G. d., "Programa do XIX Governo Constitucional", *Diário da Assembleia da República*, II, série A, No. 4/ XII/1, 2011.06.28.

4 *Ibid.*

of preparation of the new EU structural and investment funds package for 2014–2020 (ESIF), the Government determined that a new institutional model for governance of EU funds should be put in place, so as to attain better policy coordination and to enhance concentration of programming, coordination, certification and payment functions. Within that framework, it determined that technical studies should be conducted to support the creation of a Development Financial Institution (IFD) for the managing of financial instruments funded by the European Investment Bank and other financial institutions. This IFD would also manage the repayment of cohesion funds associated with different programming periods.[5] Council of Ministers' Resolution No. 73/2013, of 19 November 2013,[6] determined the formal commencement of the process leading to the creation of a credit institution named Development Financial Institution (IFD), owned by the Portuguese State, and to whom the following general objectives have been set:

a) Contributing to the implementation of public policies promoting growth and employment, aiming the creation of a smart, sustainable and inclusive development;
b) "Wholesale" managing public financial instruments, aiming the business investment into tradable goods and services;
c) Improving Portugal's financing conditions by:
    i) Reducing costs and increasing maturity of companies' financing;
    ii) Increasing liquidity in the economy, including a counter-cyclical perspective;
    iii) Establishing new instruments for companies' financing and capitalization;
d) Improving the institutional architecture of financial instruments, by increasing the efficiency of the economy's financing instruments and promoting the principles of good governance; and
e) Providing, in addition, technical support on public funding models for competitiveness and internationalization promotion.

Moreover, it was determined that the IFD should also be responsible for:

a) Managing financial instruments using financing from EU structural and investment funds;
b) Managing financial instruments using funding from the European Investment Bank and other foreign financial institutions; and

[5] See the Council of Ministers' Resolution No. 39/2013, in *DR*, 1.ª série – No. 113 – 14.06.2013.

[6] In *DR*, 1.ª série – No. 224 – 19.11.2013.

c) Managing the reimbursements associated with different programming periods of European funds.

Following that Resolution, the Bank of Portugal authorised, in September 2014, the creation and activity of the IFD as a financial institution. The IFD was dully completed with the publication of Decree Law No. 155/2014,[7] which also approved its by-laws.[8]

The EC was notified, under Article 108(3) of the Treaty on the Functioning of the European Union (TFEU), of the creation of IFD. Following Article 107(3)(c) TFEU the EC concluded that: (i) "the proposed measure providing an initial capital injection of €100 million for the setting up of the IFD is compatible with the internal market on the basis of Article 107(3)(c) TFEU"; (ii) "all plans to modify the measure, including but not limited to further funding or modifications to the remit and duration of the IFD, must be notified to the Commission, in compliance with Article 108(3) TFEU"; and (iii) the "approval does not extend to any potential aid to undertakings and/or co-investors resulting from the IFD's interventions".[9] With this ruling, the EC narrowed the scope of its authorisation decision, as several "limitations" are found in its decision and may raise doubts on what the authorised activities of the IFD are,[10] as well as what its purpose is. Our article aims to shed light on this aspect.

The scope of the Commission decision

The EC makes clear, in paragraphs 24 to 29 of the decision, that the authorised activities are comprised under the IFD's "First Phase", and "consisting of the establishment of the IFD and the definition of part of its remit", thus enabling "the Portuguese authorities to have the

[7] In *DR*, 1.ª série – No. 203 – 21.10.2014.

[8] Decree Law No. 155/2014 and IFD by-laws retain *lato sensu* the objectives of IFD activities that were already determined in the Council of Ministers' Resolution No. 73/2013.

[9] See Commission decision of 28.10.2014 in case "State aid SA.37824 (2014/N) – Portugal – Portuguese Development Financial Institution", hereinafter "decision", paragraphs 71 to 73.

[10] E.g. paragraphs 17 and 18 of the decision refer that legal base does not determine a concrete duration for the IFD but the approval for the IFD's First Phase activities is granted until 31 December 2020. Also in paragraphs 22 and 23 the Commission considers that the exact details and parameters of all the planned activities of the IFD in the long run are not yet defined and then the subject of the decision "is only the First Phase of the IFD's activities, consisting of the establishment of the IFD and the definition of part of its remit, i.e. the activities that are already clearly defined by the Portuguese authorities and which relate to the implementation of ESIF in the 2014-2020 period."

institutional structure in place when the implementation of the current ESIF programmes starts".

It is therefore clearly stated that in its "First Phase", the IFD "will manage and channel ESIF funds allocated to Portugal for the 2014–2020 financing period [acting] as a beneficiary entity in the context of the European rules for the management of financial instruments under the 2014–2020 framework and acting strictly in accordance with those rules [...] It will manage holding funds or specialised funds with co-investment from private investors to address market failures related to SMEs' access to debt, equity and quasi-equity funding. [...] The Portuguese government will also mandate the IFD to manage the funds resulting from the reimbursements of ESIF programmes, including, but not limited to the current 2014–2020 period. The IFD will strictly follow the Partnership Agreement between Portugal and the Commission, the relevant operational programmes and the terms defined by the Portuguese managing authorities as regards the activities, funds allocated, duration, scope and terms of the programmes, eligibility criteria for the final beneficiaries, and the eligibility and selection criteria for the participating financial intermediaries. [...] The IFD will not take deposits or other repayable funds from the public and will not invest in debt issued or guaranteed by the public sector [and] will be strictly prohibited from conducting business with the Portuguese public sector in general [...]. The IFD will act as a wholesale entity, always in coordination with and via commercial banks, private investors and other private financial intermediaries. Those banks and other financial intermediaries will act as the IFD's partners in the promotion, distribution, placement and co-financing of the programmes managed by the IFD."[11]

This cautious approach of the Commission is even more evident on paragraph 30, where it is stated that "Eventually, in a second phase, the activities of the IFD may be extended, in particular to so-called on-lending activities. It is planned that the additional on-lending activities of the IFD will be funded by multilateral financial institutions and national promotional[12] banks. The exact details of such programmes and partners are still under negotiation and the Portuguese authorities have committed to notify any such extension to the Commission and not to commence any additional activities before they obtain approval from the Commission."

---

11 See the referred paragraphs 24 to 29 of the decision.

12 The English version of the decision uses this expression, but the Portuguese version uses the correct expression of "national development banks", which is the only compatible with Article 4 c) of IFD's by-laws.

Considering the above, it is the Commission's decision, with all its "caveats",[13] what needs to be evaluated under the criteria established for the EU State Aids assessment.

The EU State aids criteria

The TFEU does not define the concept of State aid and Article 107 (1) only states that "any aid granted by a Member State or through State resources in any form whatsoever which distorts or threatens to distort competition by favouring certain undertakings or the production of certain goods shall, in so far as it affects trade between Member States, be incompatible with the internal market."

The EC and the European Court of Justice (ECJ) are responsible for the creation of a legally sound framework for the application of the rules concerning the control of State aids. The same is true for other competition related frameworks under the TFEU,[14] resulting in several cumulative criteria established to a greater transparency and legal certainty of the EU State aid investigations and decisions.[15] As a consequence, it is now established that for a measure to be considered as a State aid, it has to (i) involve the use of

---

13 Although an usual practice, several authors criticize an "EU policy [that] continues to be over extensive addressing cases where the distortions of competition are minimal. This is particularly the case for restructuring aid, where the effects of the aid on competition are hardly analysed in the Commission decisions. [...] However the Commission, while often authorizing the aid, tries to overcome moral hazard by attaching a number of very intrusive conditions to its authorization decisions" – Heimler, A., *European State Aid Policy in Search of a Standard – What is the Role of Economic Analysis*? (2009). Retrieved from: http://ssrn.com/abstract=1492585, p. 1.

14 E.g. Articles 101 and 102 of the TFEU.

15 Winter, J. A., "Re(de)fining the notion of state aid in article 87(1) of the EC Treaty", *Common Market Law Review* 41 (2004), pp. 475-476. See also Fauré, V., *L'Apport du Tribunal de Première Instance des Communautés Européennes au Droit Communautaire de la Concurrence*. Paris: Dalloz, 2005, and for a detailed analysis of the State aid control procedure and criteria see Almeida, J. J. N. d., *A Restituição das Ajudas de Estado Concedidas em Violação do Direito Comunitário*. Coimbra: Coimbra Editora, 1997; Biondi, A.; Righini, E., "An Evolutionary Theory of EU State Aid Control", in Chalmers, A. A. D. (ed.), *The Oxford Handbook of European Law*. Oxford: Oxford University Press, 2014; Jurcys, P., "General Principles of EC Law and Rights of Private Parties in State Aid Proceedings", in Goldammer, Y. (ed.), *The Long Road of Smaller Countries into the Enlarged European Union*. Vilnius: Eugrimas, 2006; Monopolkommission, *The "More Economic Approach" in European State Aid Control*. Bonn: Monopolkommission, 2008. Retrieved from http://ssrn.com/abstract=1332765; Rodriguez-Miguez, J. A., "El control europeo de las ayudas públicas: Visión general y la prohibición general de las ayudas (la noción de ayuda de Estado)", in Coordina, J. M. B. P. (ed.), *Tratado de Derecho de la Competencia: Union Europea y España*. 2nd ed. Barcelona: Bosch, 2014; Santos, A. C. d., *Auxílios de Estado e Fiscalidade*. Coimbra: Almedina, 2003; Sauter, W., Schepel, H., "'State' and

State resources; (ii) confer an advantage on undertakings; (iii) be selective in and limited to certain undertakings; and (iv) be likely to distort competition and affect trade between Member States.[16] The State aid criteria have been clarified over the time, mainly to cope with the diversity of situations that should be subject to State aid rules, and we follow Manuel Martins when defining State aid under EU rules as: 1) an advantage; 2) granted by a Member State or otherwise using State resources; 3) that favours certain undertakings, productions or services; 4) and distorts or menaces to distort competition; 5) as well as affects trade between Member States; and 6) irrespectively of the form assumed by the aid.[17]

As for the concept of *advantage*, it has been established, for a long time now, that it is to be interpreted in a *lato sensu*, as the ECJ has always considered that the "concept of aid is nevertheless wider than that of a subsidy because it embraces not only positive benefits, such as subsidies themselves, but also interventions which, in various forms, mitigate the charges which are normally included in the budget of an undertaking and which, without, therefore, being subsidies in the strict meaning of the word, are similar in character and have the same effect".[18] But this advantage has to be gratuitous,[19] considering that a separation between a State aid and a State "measure that has the appearance of a support measure [but that] may aim to compensate the recipient for some economic disadvantage [and f]or that reason [...] under certain circumstances, a financial benefit will have to be regarded as a quid pro quo for the economic value of goods supplied or services rendered [and] then ought not to be categorized as aid".[20]

'Market' in the Competition and Free Movement Case Law of the EU Courts", *TILEC Discussion Paper*, 2007. Retrieved from: http://ssrn.com/abstract=1010075.

16 The EC analysed the criteria in paragraphs 33 to 38.

17 Martins, M., *Auxílios de Estado no Direito Comunitário*. Cascais: Princípia, 2002, p. 52. Lane, R., *EC Competition Law*. Essex: Longman – Pearson Education Limited, 2000, p. 334, also underlines the fact that a State aid is an aid granted by a Member State or through State resources *in any form whatsoever* which distorts or threatens to distort competition.

18 See Judgment of the ECJ of 23.02.1961, *De Gezamenlijke Steenkolenmijnen in Limburg v High Authority of the European Coal and Steel Community*, Case 30-59, p. 19. For a more recent case and relating a Portuguese company, see Judgment of the Court of First Instance of 13.06.2000, *EPAC – Empresa para a Agroalimentação e Cereais, SA v Commission of the European Communities*, joined Cases T-204/97 and T-270/97, § 64-65.

19 See Judgment of the Court of 22.03.1977, *Steinike & Weinlig v Federal Republic of Germany*, Case 78-76, § 19 to 21.

20 Winter, J. A., "Re(de)fining the notion of state aid in article 87(1) of the EC Treaty", *Common Market Law Review*, 41, 2004, p. 488. See also Sauter, W., "The Criterion of

Also bearing in mind that an aid is *granted by a Member State or* using *State resources*, an all-embracing understanding favouring the imputation to the State whenever the aid derives from, or affects, public resources is used. In this regard, the definition of State is taken in a wide perspective as the Treaty rules "[...] refer to aid granted by the States or through State resources 'in any form whatsoever'. Consequently, those provisions must be interpreted not on the basis of formal criteria but rather by reference to their purpose, which [...] is to ensure that competition is not distorted. It follows that all subsidies from the public sector threatening the play of competition are caught by the abovementioned provisions, it being unnecessary for those subsidies to be granted by the government or by a central administrative authority of a Member State [...]".[21][22]

The main question to be asked is therefore one which aims to find a secure and clear criterion for when to stop defining as State aids the public measures with impact on the competitive behaviour of undertakings. Advocate General Jacobs, in the Opinion delivered in *PreussenElektra AG v Schleswag AG*, stated that "[...] the more extensive interpretation would oblige the Member States, affected undertakings, the Commission, the national courts and ultimately the Community Courts to decide in respect of all legislation regulating the relationship between enterprises whether it does confer selective advantages on certain undertakings within the meaning of Article 92(1). Since such an assessment is a difficult exercise with an uncertain outcome, it seems preferable that legislation regulating the relationship between private actors is as a matter of principle excluded from the scope of the State aid rules".[23][24]

Advantage in State Aid: Altmark and Services of General Economic Interest", *TILEC Discussion Paper*, 2014. Retrieved from: http://ssrn.com/abstract=2426230.

21 See Judgment of the Court of First Instance, 12.12.1996, *Compagnie Nationale Air France v Commission of the European Communities*, Case T-358/94, § 56.

22 As for the lending activity, it is also settled that "public intervention through banking institutions is 'equivalent to State aid' when granted by an entity designated by the State" – Sansonetti, V.; Rossi-Maccanico, P., *State Aid in the Lending Sector*, 10 (2007), pp. 5-6. Retrieved from: http://ssrn.com/abstract=962050.

23 Opinion of Advocate General Jacobs delivered on 26.10.2000, *PreussenElektra AG v Schleswag AG*, Case C-379/98, § 157. Alongside another complex question equally arises and relates to the limits of competition law where, as Prosser, T., *The Limits of Competition Law – Markets and Public Services*. New York: Oxford University Press, 2005. correctly points out, "much of the confusion has been due to a failure to separate two distinct issues; whether an activity is economic and so falls within the scope of Community competence, and whether there are nevertheless good reasons, such as the role of social solidarity, for modifying the application of the competition rules" (p. 130).

24 See also Von Danwitz, T., "The Concept of State Aid in Liberalised Sectors", *EUI Working Paper*, 2008. Retrieved from: http://ssrn.com/abstract=1330933, p. 12.

As for the criterion of the *selectivity* of a measure, essential to be considered as an aid *that favours certain undertakings, productions or services*, it allows for a necessary distinction between general economic measures and those which effectively benefit one or several undertakings or productions. Without measure selectivity, a State cannot be held responsible for the adulteration of the relation between the different market forces, acting in a way which is beneficial to one(s) and detrimental to other(s), a disruption which is caused by a direct or indirect advantage of (positive or negative) usage of public resources. Finally, without the *selectivity criterion*, it would be impossible to state that a public measure *distorts or menaces to distort competition*, considering that all market forces would be equally affected by the measure.[25]

It was stated above that one of the criteria for the classification of an aid as a State aid is that the aid *affects trade between Member States*. This is a common rule of European competition law because it helps distinguishing between competences held by the EU and national legislative bodies. It also helps classifying a measure as a State aid, by actually or potentially, directly or indirectly, affecting the pattern of trade between Member States.[26] If more than one Member State is affected, the EU has exclusive competence to intervene.[27]

The author considers that the "discussion of the issue of imputability has shown that Community Courts will have to live up to the basic standards established in PreußenElektra and in Stardust Marine. Quite evidently, these judgments have not provided us with a standard of review which is so easy to handle that most proceedings before the Commission and the Community Courts have or will become superfluous. […] The standards of review in state aid control need to be designed in a way which takes two aspects into account. A certain degree of flexibility is necessary to ensure a reasonable application in the Commission's practice and in particular in order to cover future evolutions. But a solid concept with a visible profile is indispensable to give Member States and public undertakings the orientation which they clearly need."

25 The necessary result of these criteria (selectivity and distortion of competition) is the recognition of *locus standi* to actual or potential competitors that are directly and individually affected to challenge positive or negative Commission decisions under Article 263 of TFEU. See Giannakopoulos, T., "The Right to Bring an Action before the European Courts against the Various Decisions of the Commission in State Aid Cases", *World Competition* 23 (3), 2000, pp. 81-102.

26 See Alves, J. M. C., *Lições de Direito Comunitário da Concorrência*. Coimbra: Coimbra Editora, 1989, pp. 151-155; Campos, J. L. M. d., *Manual de Direito Europeu*. 6.ª ed. Coimbra: Wolters Luwer Portugal – Coimbra Editora, 2010, pp. 610-612; Gorjão-Henriques, M., *Direito da União: História, Direito, Cidadania, Mercado Interno e Concorrência*. 6.ª ed. Coimbra: Almedina, 2010, pp. 662-668.

27 Under Article 3(1)(b), the EU has exclusive competence in the establishing of the competition rules necessary for the functioning of the internal market. See Craig, P.; De Búrca, G., *EC Law – Texts, Cases, and Materials*. Oxford: Clarendon Press, 1995,

Finally, a measure may and shall be considered as a State aid *irrespectively of its form*, as long as the other criteria (selective advantage granted by a Member State or otherwise using State resources that distort competition and affect trade between Member States) are fulfilled. *In rigore* it shall not be considered as a criterion for the aid appreciation, and only highlights that the analysis of a measure will go beyond any *a priori* limitation and will verify if an undertaking is benefiting, in any form, from an advantage directly or indirectly based in present, past or future public resources.[28]

Revisiting the scope of the Commission's decision and its caveats under the light of EU State aids criteria

As mentioned above, the EC tried to narrow the scope of its decision, and the "limitations" found in the decision's text must be confronted with the State aids criteria in order to understand if they indeed produce an effect of restricting IFD's future activities. In other words, if several aspects of the decision are to determine a *de iure* or even a *de facto*, restrain the IFD's legal and statutory competences, that would undermine the decision itself for two reasons: firstly, its arguments would be contradictory; and secondly, because the measure, as configured, could not be defined as a State aid.

It is necessary to note that the basis for the EC analysis is IFD's by-laws. The Commission refers to it as the "legal base of the measure",[29] while considering that it is jointly composed by the Council of Ministers' Resolution No. 73/2013, which regulates the creation of the IFD; the Decree Law determining the IFD's incorporation; as well as the IFD's by-laws. This means that the "measure takes the form of an initial capital injection into IFD"[30] with the legal purpose of complying with the share capital requirement for the IFD's establishment.

The aid is therefore inextricably linked to the IFD creation. The IFD's activities, to be pursued after incorporation, do not create an artificial separation between the capital injection for its incorporation and the activities that are determined as the object of the undertaking.[31] Hence

---

pp. 113-115; Louis, J.-V., *L'Ordre Juridique Communautaire*. Luxemburg: OPOCE, 1993.

28 For various examples of different forms that a State aid may take, see Schapira, J.; Le Tallec, G.; Blaise, J.-B.; Idot, L., *Droit Européen des Affaires*. 5.ª ed. Paris: PUF, 1999, pp. 354-355.

29 See paragraph 5 of the decision.

30 See paragraph 3 of the decision.

31 In paragraphs 19 and 20 of the decision it is stated that "total budget of the measure is €100 million, which corresponds to the starting capital of the IFD, fully subscribed and

the analysis of the measure should have considered the completeness of IFD's corporate object and competences established in the Decree Law determining its incorporation in its by-laws.

The difficulty arises when the Commission explicitly acknowledges IFD's complete activities by making reference to Article 5[32] of its by-laws in paragraph 21 of the decision and, on paragraph 23, considers that the "subject of this decision is only the First Phase of the IFD's activities, consisting of the establishment of the IFD and the definition of part of its remit, i.e. the activities that are already clearly defined by the Portuguese authorities and which relate to the implementation of ESIF in the 2014–2020 period. The approval of the First Phase is necessary to enable the Portuguese authorities to have the institutional structure in place when the implementation of the current ESIF programmes starts". After explaining what is included in the "First Phase" of IFD's activities,[33] the EC sets out what is defined as a "Second Phase", subject to new notification to the EC and creating a standstill obligation prior approval: the extension of the activities of the IFD to "additional on-lending activities of the IFD [...] funded by multilateral financial institutions and national [development] banks" and the integration of the "existing and ongoing financial instrument programmes within the IFD [...] expected to bring about further efficiencies and effectiveness."[34]

That brings us to the initial question, which we may now reformulate in a more accurate manner: has the Commission only approved the functioning of IFD as an institutional structure dedicated to activities

paid in cash by the Portuguese government" and that "Investments made by the IFD will be done from separate programmes with dedicated budgets, not from the initial capital injection". But without the initial capital injection, IFD would not have been created and incorporated, nor would it be possible to access other funds necessary to create those "separate programmes with dedicated budgets".

32 In the final version of IFD by-laws, approved by Decree Law No. 155/2014, there was a renumbering, corresponding in fact to Article 4.

33 See paragraphs 25 to 29 of the decision.

34 See paragraphs 30 and 31 of the decision. We emphasize the use of the expression "additional", clearly establishing a distinction between on-lending activities of the IFD within the context of ESIF funds, that must be considered as included in the approved "First Phase", and the eventual on-lending activities of the IFD having no relation with ESIF, being only the latter that shall be considered to belong to a "Second Phase" not covered by the decision.

Also relating to the integration of the "existing and ongoing financial instrument programmes within the IFD", and taking into account the existing institutional panorama where several financial instrument programmes are developed by mutual guarantee societies, it cannot be excluded that it could configure a merger operation rather than an State aid subject.

connected with the implementation of ESIF in the 2014–2020 period? In our opinion the answer must be negative.

The EC deals with this delicate matter in paragraph (35) of the decision, by assuming that it "has examined whether it is necessary to adopt this decision or whether the IFD could start its operations without an approval of the Commission, seen that its activities in First Phase will be principally to implement financial instrument programmes financed from the ESIF, which have to be compliant with State aid law", and within that context, the EC has considered that "there are several factors which necessitate the Commission's approval by this decision", and specifically that:

- "The Decree Law and the by-laws of the IFD [...] define the IFD's corporate objective more broadly than the First Phase activities" and that "Portuguese authorities themselves intend to define the remit of the activities of the IFD in a progressive manner, leaving many possibilities open at this stage, including intervening on the market to provide financial support to SMEs in Portugal in a manner similar to market operators in the banking sector. Even if the aim underlying the creation of the IFD is to remedy a market failure in the financing of those SMEs, that activity may qualify as economic, thereby conferring on the IFD the status of 'undertaking' for State aid purposes. Therefore, it is necessary that the Commission assesses step-by-step the parameters of the IFD2s remit";
- "The measure involves the initial capitalisation by €100 million of the IFD by the Portuguese State, including for the setting up of the IFD, which is not made on market terms and does not require a return in line with those which would be required by a market operator";
- "The IFD will manage programmes financed by ESIF. The exclusive management of ESIF is not considered to involve State aid to the management entity, as that entity is acting on behalf of the State in the implementation of State aid programmes. The mere management of ESIF-funded State aid programmes, including when that service is remunerated (and that remuneration does not involve overcompensation), does not constitute economic activity. However, the initial capitalisation of IFD is not explicitly for the budget of the measures that the IFD will implement"; and
- "The IFD will manage refunds from Union fund programmes, including from earlier periods than the 2014–2020 period. Such refunds constitute State resources. The Portuguese authorities do not yet know how such reimbursements will be utilized by the IFD. Therefore, the Commission cannot at this stage take a position on

> whether the utilization and management of those refunds will provide an advantage to the IFD making it a beneficiary of aid, or not, and cannot exclude that there might be State aid involved in that respect."[35]

Based on the above mentioned arguments, the EC considers that the measure constitutes State aid.[36]

Nevertheless, they are, in our opinion, only partially acceptable, as they do not draw a clear division between a situation where the incorporation of IFD would not constitute an aid and that where it would. Neither a division between a positive decision would be necessary for its present activities *vis-à-vis* the need for future State aid positive(s) decision(s). Indeed, as stated by the EC, the fact that programmes financed by ESIF are managed by the IFD does not signify that a State aid was used. The same reasoning applies to refunds from EU fund programmes, including from periods before 2014–2020, as IFD is still acting on behalf of the State.[37]

Building on what it was said before, it may be argued that the creation of the IFD would not differ, in any way, from an internal, strictly national and sovereign decision of (re)structuring the institutional framework for management of European funds and its reimbursements. It is not possible to discuss the existence of an economic activity and forcibly of a competition restraint because EU fund management is exercised by the Member States regardless of the decision to perform through a central or direct administration bodies, indirect administration or public institutes, or even (as IFD) through a fully owned State financial institution. Therefore, the injection of the capital required for the IDF's incorporation could never be regarded neither as an advantage nor as distorting competition – as the latter is non-existent. Furthermore, all other criteria (selectivity and impact on the trade between Member States) are entirely absent.

As a result, a preliminary remark is that if the EC wanted to limit its analysis to a "First Phase" of the IFD's activities, according to which it would only perform EU fund management activities, then the decision

---

35 See the referred paragraph 35 of the decision.

36 See paragraph 36 of the decision.

37 For a detailed analysis of the broad concept of public bodies used in European law, embracing any "body, whatever its legal form, which has been made responsible, pursuant to a measure adopted by the State, for providing a public service under the control of the State and has for that purpose special powers", see Sauter, W.; Schepel, H., "'State' and 'Market' in the Competition and Free Movement Case Law of the EU Courts", *TILEC Discussion Paper*, 2007. Retrieved from: http://ssrn.com/abstract=1010075, p. 34.

must be classified as unnecessary, as none of the elements leading to the application of EU State aids rules is found.

Notwithstanding the above, the content of the decision may be regarded as useful, considering that it accepts that the IFD's activities may produce an anti-competitive effect, even if outweighed by the positive impact created by its creation and fulfilment of its purposes. In addition, the decision is limited to the capital injection for the incorporation of the IFD, which means that the granting of ESIF funds to target SMEs must be authorised by specific positive decisions when involving State aid for the final beneficiary.[38] Finally, it is necessary to accept that the scope of the decision may allow the IFD to perform economic tasks which may hinder the competition.

This conclusion is reinforced by the decision's argument connected with the criteria of *distorting of competition and affection of trade between Member States*, where the Commission has declared that "Financial services are global markets and by their nature affect trade between Member States. The provision of capital on terms which are more favourable than those available on the market is capable of distorting competition."[39] Firstly, if the "provision of capital" is to be defined as the sole purpose of the creation of an institution, this would limit IFD to the management of European funds and its reimbursement, and it would not constitute an advantage as it would strictly deal with the public allocation of funds for the development of public policies. We must also bear in mind that the decision acknowledges the ability of the IFD to use the "provision of capital" (or the deriving advantages) for other activities. And mainly because in the decision the "gratuity" of the advantage is not assessed,[40] while being accepted by the EC that the "integrated management of financial instruments is indeed likely to bring about efficiencies".[41] If efficiency gains were to be channelled or used in the benefit of the State, then they should

[38] The Commission makes reference to this aspect in paragraph 41, making clear that "IFD will manage and channel indirectly via other financial intermediaries ESIF funds to target SMEs. Those investments may involve State aid, for the purposes of Article 107(1) TFEU, to final beneficiary undertakings, in particular where the investments are not in line with market conduct or do not comply with the *de minimis* aid rules. However, the existence and compatibility of investments at that level are outside the scope of this decision. It is planned that where necessary, the Portuguese authorities will notify separately the aid schemes to be managed by the IFD, in line with State aid rules".

[39] See paragraph 38 of the decision.

[40] For a detailed analysis of the "gratuity" of an aid, see Winter, J. A., "Re(de)fining the notion of state aid in article 87(1) of the EC Treaty", *Common Market Law Review* 41 (2004), pp. 487-501.

[41] See paragraph 52 of the decision.

have been assessed to ascertain whether the initial "capital provision" would be repaid to the State (e.g. by economies of scale or risk reduction in the management of EU funds). In other words, the absence of an analysis of the eventual gratuity of the measure confirms that the IFD may use the aid and the subsequent advantages in economic activities.

Conclusion

As a conclusion, the EC decision must be interpreted as comprising a broader scope than the mere assessment of the IFD's activities while managing ESIF's funds and its reimbursements. This means that the IFD may also act as a proper financial institution in the context of the ESIF funds, within the limits of its by-laws. In fact, Article 3(4) of its by-laws declares that in order "to guarantee a prudent and sustainable" activity and "not to generate any fiscal risks" deriving from the IFD's activities, a limitation on the lending activity through intermediated instruments ("on-lending") is imposed to the IFD, limiting it to intermediated instruments with other credit institutions and financial companies operating in the market. Thus it is solely the extension of those on-lending activities to situations where there is no link whatsoever with the ESIF programs that may require a new EC appreciation.

Notwithstanding the above, it would be preferable to have a clearer decision, which may only be obtained by a future submission to the Commission, where a more detailed explanation of the IFD's future full activities is submitted.

Bibliography

Almeida, J. J. N. d., *A Restituição das Ajudas de Estado Concedidas em Violação do Direito Comunitário*. Coimbra: Coimbra Editora, 1997.

Alves, J. M. C., *Lições de Direito Comunitário da Concorrência*. Coimbra: Coimbra Editora, 1989.

Biondi, A.; Righini, E., "An Evolutionary Theory of EU State Aid Control", in Chalmers, A. A. D. (ed.), *The Oxford Handbook of European Law*. Oxford: Oxford University Press, 2014.

Campos, J. L. M. d., *Manual de Direito Europeu*. 6.ª ed. Coimbra: Wolters Luwer Portugal – Coimbra Editora, 2010.

Craig, P.; De Búrca, G., *EC Law – Texts, Cases, and Materials*. Oxford: Clarendon Press, 1995.

Fauré, V., *L'Apport du Tribunal de Première Instance des Communautés Européennes au Droit Communautaire de la Concurrence*. Paris: Dalloz, 2005.

Giannakopoulos, T., "The Right to Bring an Action before the European Courts against the Various Decisions of the Commission in State Aid Cases", *World Competition* 23 (3), 2000.

Gorjão-Henriques, M., *Direito da União: História, Direito, Cidadania, Mercado Interno e Concorrência.* 6.ª ed. Coimbra: Almedina, 2010.

Jurcys, P., "General Principles of EC Law and Rights of Private Parties in State Aid Proceedings", in Goldammer, Y. (ed.), *The Long Road of Smaller Countries into the Enlarged European Union.* Vilnius: Eugrimas, 2006.

Lane, R., *EC Competition Law.* Essex: Longman – Pearson Education Limited, 2000.

Louis, J.-V., *L'Ordre Juridique Communautaire.* Luxemburg: OPOCE, 1993.

Martins, M., *Auxílios de Estado no Direito Comunitário.* Cascais: Princípia, 2002.

Rodriguez-Miguez, J. A., "El control europeo de las ayudas públicas: Visión general y la prohibición general de las ayudas (la noción de ayuda de Estado)", in Coordina, J. M. B. P. (ed.), *Tratado de Derecho de la Competencia: Union Europea y España.* 2nd ed. Barcelona: Bosch, 2014.

Sansonetti, V.; Rossi-Maccanico, P., *State Aid in the Lending Sector*, 10 (2007).

Santos, A. C. d., *Auxílios de Estado e Fiscalidade.* Coimbra: Almedina, 2003; Sauter, W., Schepel, H., "'State' and 'Market' in the Competition and Free Movement Case Law of the EU Courts", *TILEC Discussion Paper*, 2007.

Sauter, W., "The Criterion of Advantage in State Aid: Altmark and Services of General Economic Interest", *TILEC Discussion Paper*, 2014.

Sauter, W.; Schepel, H., "'State' and 'Market' in the Competition and Free Movement Case Law of the EU Courts", *TILEC Discussion Paper*, 2007.

Schapira, J.; Le Tallec, G.; Blaise, J.-B.; Idot, L., *Droit Européen des Affaires.* 5.ª ed. Paris: PUF, 1999.

Von Danwitz, T., "The Concept of State Aid in Liberalised Sectors". *EUI Working Paper*, 2008.

Winter, J. A., "Re(de)fining the notion of state aid in article 87(1) of the EC Treaty", *Common Market Law Review* 41 (2004).

EUROCLIO – Published Books

N° 92 – *Que dire à l'Espagne ? De l'isolement franquiste à la démocratie européiste, la France au défi, 1957-1979*, Pablo MARTIN-PAÑEDA, 2015

N° 91 – *Francis Delaisi, du dreyfusisme à « l'Europe nouvelle »*, Éric BUSSIÈRE, Olivier DARD, Geneviève DUCHENNE (dir.), 2015.

N° 90 – *European Parties and the European Integration Process, 1945-1992*, Lucia BONFRESCHI, Giovanni ORSINA, Antonio VARSORI (eds.), 2015

N° 89 – *Européanisation et démocratisation des États baltes dans la période de préadhésion à l'UE. Le rôle de la conditionnalité politique des organisations européennes*, Anne-Sylvie PIGEONNIER, 2015.

N° 88 – *Le Continent basket. L'Europe et le basket-ball au XXe siècle*, Fabien ARCHAMBAULT, Loïc ARTIAGA, Gérard BOSC (dir.), 2015.

N° 87 – *The Convention on the Future of Europe. How States Behave in a New Institutional Context of Negotiation*. Francesco MARCHI, 2015.

N° 86 – *Christian Democrat Internationalism. Its Action in Europe and Worldwide from post World War II until the 1990s. Volume III. The European People's Party Continental and Social Cooperation*. Jean-Dominique DURAND (ed.), 2014.

N° 85 – *Pela Paz! For Peace! Pour la paix ! (1849-1939)*. Maria Manuela Tavares RIBEIRO, Maria Fernanda ROLLO, Isabel Maria FREITAS VALENTE, Alice CUNHA (eds.), 2014.

N° 84 – *Economic Crisis and New Nationalisms. German Political Economy as Perceived by European Partners*. Antonio VARSORI, Monika POETTINGER (eds.), 2014.

N° 83 – *European Constitutionalism. Historical and Contemporary Perspectives*. Alexandre DUPEYRIX, Gérard RAULET (eds.), 2014.

N° 82 – *Cross-Border Cooperation Structures in Europe. Learning from the Past, Looking to the Future*. Luis DOMÍNGUEZ, Iva PIRES (eds.), 2014.

N° 81 – *The European Community and the World. A Historical Perspective*. Giuliana LASCHI (ed.), 2014.

N° 80 – *Christian Democrat Internationalism. Its Action in Europe and Worldwide from Post World War II until the 1990s. Volume II: The Development (1945-1979). The Role of Parties, Movements, People*. Jean-Dominique DURAND (ed.), 2013.

N° 79 – *Christian Democrat Internationalism. Its Action in Europe and Worldwide from Post World War II until the 1990s. Volume I: The Origins*. Jean-Dominique DURAND (ed.), 2013.

N° 78 – *Investment Banking History. National and Comparative Issues (19th-21st centuries)*. Hubert BONIN & Carlo BRAMBILLA (eds.), 2013.

N° 77 – *Citizenship and Solidarity in the European Union. From the Charter of Fundamental Rights to the Crisis, the State of the Art*. Mariana CANOTILHO, Pedro MADEIRA FROUFE & Alessandra SILVEIRA (eds.), 2013.

N° 76– *The OSCE: Soft Security for a Hard World. Competing Theories for Understanding the OSCE*. Roberto DOMINGUEZ (ed.), 2013.

N° 75 – *Euroscepticism, Europhobia and Eurocriticism. The Radical Parties of the Right and Left* vis-à-vis *the European Union*. Cesáreo RODRÍGUEZ-AGUILERA DE PRAT, 2013.

N° 74 – *Fermer les mines en construisant l'Europe. Une histoire sociale de l'intégration européenne*. Nicolas VERSCHUEREN, 2012

N° 73 – *Reflets de la construction européenne. Réflexions, références et refus du débat sur l'Europe*. Bertrand VAYSSIÈRE (dir.), 2012.

N° 72 – *The International Relations of Local Authorities. From Institutional Twinning to the Committee of the Regions: Fifty Years of European Integration History*. Fabio ZUCCA, 2012.

N° 71 – *Histoire du Conseil de l'Europe (1949-2009)*. Birte WASSENBERG, 2012.

N° 70 – *The EU, Security and Transatlantic Relations*. Finn LAURSEN (ed.), 2012.

N° 69 – *Européanisation au XXe siècle. Un regard historique / Europeanisation in the 20th Century. The Historical Lens*. Matthieu OSMONT, Émilia ROBIN-HIVERT, Katja SEIDEL, Mark SPOERER & Christian WENKEL (dir./eds.), 2012.

N° 68 – *Consensus and European Integration. An Historical Perspective / Consensus et intégration européenne. Une perspective historique*. Daniela PREDA & Daniele PASQUINUCCI (eds./dir.), 2012.

N° 67 – *Générations de fédéralistes européens depuis le XIXe siècle. Individus, groupes, espaces et réseaux*. Geneviève DUCHENNE et Michel DUMOULIN (dir.), 2012.

N° 66 – *Raymond Aron, penseur de l'Europe et de la nation*. Giulio DE LIGIO (dir.), 2012.

N° 65 – *Europe Twenty Years after the End of the Cold War. The New Europe, New Europes? / L'Europe vingt ans après la fin de la guerre froide. Nouvelle Europe, nouvelles Europes?* Bruno ARCIDIACONO, Katrin MILZOW, Axel MARION & Pierre-Étienne BOURNEUF (eds./dir.), 2012.

N° 64 – *Aux origines de la diplomatie européenne. Les Neuf et la Coopération politique européenne de 1973 à 1980*. Maria Gainar, 2012.

N° 63 – *Europe and the Middle East. The hour of the East?* Birte WASSENBERG & Giovanni FALEG (eds.), 2012.

N° 62 – *Quelle architecture pour un code européen de droit international privé ?* Marc FALLON, Paul LAGARDE, Sylvaine POILLOT-PERUZZETTO (dir.), 2011.

Euroclio European Network

together with the SEGEI Network

Coordination : Chaire Jean Monnet d'histoire de l'Europe contemporaine (Cehec)
Collège Erasme, 1, place Blaise-Pascal, B-1348 Louvain-la-Neuve

Germany
- Jürgen Elvert
- Wilfried Loth

Belgium
- Julie Cailleau
- Jocelyne Collonval
- Yves Conrad
- Gaëlle Courtois
- Pascal Deloge
- Geneviève Duchenne
- Vincent Dujardin
- Michel Dumoulin
- Roch Hannecart
- Pierre-Yves Plasman
- Béatrice Roeh
- Corine Schröder
- Caroline Suzor
- Pierre Tilly
- Arthe Van Laer
- Jérôme Wilson
- Natacha Wittorski

Spain
- Enrique Moradiellos
- Mercedes Samaniego Boneu

France
- Françoise Berger
- Marie-Thérèse Bitsch
- Gérard Bossuat
- Éric Bussière
- Jean-François Eck
- Catherine Horel
- Philippe Mioche
- Marine Moguen-Toursel
- Sylvain Schirmann
- Matthieu Trouvé
- Laurent Warlouzet
- Emilie Willaert

Hungary
- Gergely Fejérdy

Italy
- David Burigana
- Elena Calandri
- Eleonora Guasconi
- Luciano Segreto
- Antonio Varsori

Luxemburg
- Charles Barthel
- Etienne Deschamps
- Jean-Marie Kreins
- René Leboutte
- Robert Philippart
- Corine Schröder
- Gilbert Trausch

The Netherlands
- Anjo Harryvan
- Jan W. Brouwer
- Jan van der Herst

Poland
- Józef Laptos
- Zdzisiaw Mach

Switzerland
- Antoine Fleury
- Lubor Jilek